A Feminist Philosophy of Religion

I go on a quest through an indefinite number of bodies, through nature, through God, for the body that once served as place for me, where I (male/female) was able to stay contained, enveloped. Given that, as far as man is concerned, the issue is to separate the first and the last place. Which can lead to a double downshift: both of the relation to the unique mother and of the relation to the unique God. Can these two downshifts come together? . . .

As for woman she is place. Does she have to locate herself in bigger and bigger places? But also to find, situate, in herself the place that she is. If she is unable to constitute, within herself, the place that she is, she passes ceaselessly through the child in order to return to herself.

. . . A place of place. Where bodies embrace? Both in and not in the same place; with the one being in the other that contains.

Luce Irigaray*

* The epigraph is taken from Luce Irigaray (1993a, 34–5, 55), and might be read as a response to the reproduction of *The Lovers* (1913) by Käthe Kollwitz (1867–1945) on the front cover of this book. In her diary entry of November 1913 Kollwitz also refers to her sculpture, *The Lovers*, as *The Mother and Child*; see Kollwitz 1989, 134.

A Feminist Philosophy of Religion

The Rationality and Myths of Religious Belief

Pamela Sue Anderson

First published 1998

2 4 6 8 10 9 7 5 3 1

Blackwell Publishers Ltd
108 Cowley Road
Oxford OX4 1JF, UK

Blackwell Publishers Inc.
350 Main Street
Malden, Massachusetts 02148
USA

British Library Cataloguing in Publication Data

A CIP catalogue record for this book is available from the British Library.

Library of Congress Cataloging-in-Publication Data

Anderson, Pamela Sue.
A feminist philosophy of religion : the rationality and myths of religious belief / Pamela Sue Anderson.
p. cm.
Includes bibliographical references and index.
ISBN 0-631-19382-0 (hardback : alk. paper). — ISBN 0-631-19383-9 (pbk. : alk. paper)
1. Religion – Philosophy. 2. Women and religion. 3. Feminist theory. I. Title.
BL51.A562 1997
210'.82 – dc21 97-10145
CIP

Commissioning Editor: Martin Davies
Desk Editor: Jane Hammond Foster
Production Controller: Rhonda Pearce

Typeset in Bembo on 10.5/12 pt
by SetSystems Ltd, Saffron Walden, Essex
Printed in Great Britain by Hartnolls Ltd, Victoria Square, Bodmin, Cornwall

This book is printed on acid-free paper.

Contents

Preface

In 1994 a special issue of *Hypatia* raised the question: Where are all the feminist philosophers of religion? In response, several feminist theologians, as well as some feminist philosophers, wrote articles. In this book, I offer another philosopher's response. My argument is addressed especially to philosophers who have been trained at or are working in institutions which limit philosophy of religion to empirical realist forms of theism, yet who are open to new perspectives from Anglo-American feminist epistemologies and Continental philosophy.

Without engaging directly in arguments for and against the central claims of the classical form of western theism, I intend to get behind debates about a personal deity which has ideal attributes such as perfect goodness and bodilessness. I will raise fundamental questions concerning the philosophical presuppositions underlying arguments for divine power and knowledge. In particular, I will investigate what has been assumed about religious belief in terms of reason, objectivity, and desire; assumptions about sex/gender feature in these investigations.

I question the picture of reality which is both assumed by empirical realist accounts of theistic belief and debated according to strictly formal, adversarial methods of reasoning. The concomitant lack of attention to substantive issues concerning objectivity and myth in philosophy of religion has resulted in a failure to recognize the ways in which formal accounts of our world, ourselves, our desires and passions have been biased against women; and this means variable biases against women who themselves differ by creed, class, race, and ethnicity. To fill this lack, I confront substantive issues while retaining a form of realism which still makes possible nonrelativist claims about truth and justice.

I find it unfortunate that the dominance of a naive empirical realist approach to questions of theistic belief has left little room for the valuable contributions of Continental philosophy, and virtually no room for the increasingly significant issues of feminist epistemologies. The currently dominant form of classical theism seems to me too narrow on a variety of philosophical questions. Admittedly cumulative arguments are being used more frequently by philosophers of religion to justify theistic beliefs, with the intention of broadening the sorts of experience which can count as evidence for religious knowledge. However, the assumed standpoint of justification and the accepted form of this theism continue to prohibit a fuller picture of relevant issues in epistemology, ethics, metaphysics, and women's studies.

At the same time, I do not adopt the recently popular nonrealist approach to religious belief, even if it rejects empirical realist forms of theism and proposes alternative presuppositions for its philosophical framework.[1] The decisive problem for me with a nonrealist philosophy of religion is not being able to take a stand against real injustices or against biased and pernicious beliefs. By contrast, as a feminist I feel compelled to seek a means by which philosophers can legitimately recognize and acknowledge the falsehoods about women propagated by specific forms of theism, as well as injustices committed against marginalized men and women by powerful men and women (including myself) on the grounds of mistaken beliefs.

To avoid both the possible narrowmindedness of naive realist forms of theism and the potential dogmatism of nonrealist forms of theism, I would like to propose the framework for a feminist philosophy of religion. The focus of my proposal is the rationality of religious belief. A feminist approach to this issue of rationality involves more than justifying belief on the grounds of experience tested for its coherence, simplicity, unity, or design. It is my conviction that a feminist approach to the rationality of religious belief would offer the tools for thinking which is critically alert to fanaticisms, illusions, and patriarchal biases of all sorts.

Summarizing overall, I intend to supplement contemporary approaches to the philosophy of religion. My approach is reformist, reaching back to rebuild philosophy at the level of fundamental presuppositions. To cite a well-known statement by Willard van Orman Quine (1908-) about rebuilding philosophy,

> We can change [the conceptual scheme that we grew up in] bit by bit, plank by plank, though meanwhile there is nothing to carry us along but the evolving conceptual scheme itself. The philosopher's task was well compared by Neurath to that of a mariner who must rebuild his ship on the open sea.

> We can improve our conceptual scheme, our philosophy, bit by bit while continuing to depend on it for support; but we cannot detach ourselves from it and compare it objectively with an unconceptualized reality. Hence it is meaningless, I suggest, to inquire into the absolute correctness of a conceptual scheme as a mirror of reality. (Quine 1953, 78–9)

I agree with the above point that philosophers cannot detach themselves completely from their conceptual scheme to achieve an absolutely correct representation of reality. But this does not imply that philosophers have to give up the search for objectivity or for true belief. In the picture of philosophy created by Otto Neurath (1882–1945), the planks of the ship include the mistaken beliefs which are necessarily part of our conceptual scheme; the point is that philosophers must rely upon both true beliefs and falsehoods when changing the planks of mistaken beliefs in order to stay afloat. For Neurath, to be without the ship is to be in the sea without any beliefs. But to qualify Quine's references to 'a mariner' and 'his ship on the open sea,' if these are taken to mean that the rebuilding of a philosophical framework is done by a lone man then they will also have to be supplemented with additional images from the feminist philosopher – for whom the subject of knowledge is not a discrete, simple self with its very own set of beliefs.

Modern, philosophical texts have frequently used images of the sea as outside the territory of rationality, in relation to the (rational) secure ground of an island. In particular, Immanuel Kant (1724–1804) employs the stormy sea to represent the illusions which threaten and surround the land of truth.[2] In the Kantian picture, the definite line separating the philosopher or seafarer from the sea represents the limits of ordered rationality and pure understanding. But if this line is drawn by men alone and represents the limits to their reasoning, can and should it be pushed back? According to certain feminists, human rationality should seek to grasp the contents of the marine waters whose turbulence evoke images of desire, birth, and love. By emphasizing these additional images, feminists offer a more comprehensive, however complex, account of reality. And this means that at times I will deviate from Neurath's picture of philosophy in order to rethink pervasive Kantian imagery.

So, unlike Neurath, Kant uses the sea to represent the danger of false belief and illusion as contrasted with the true beliefs and secure reality of the island. The feminist objection to the latter contrast is that desire and disorder associated with water and fluidity are feared, while reason and order linked with stability and solidity are highly valued. The question is whether unexplored possibilities are contained in the formerly devalued imagery of the open sea lying beyond the seafarer's pure understanding. The contents of these unknown waters are yet to be adequately acknowledged and articulated by male and, specifically, female philosophers as material potentially transformative of their rebuilding task. Ultimately Kant's possibly less prominent imagery of practical reason constructing an edifice or building may prove more compatible with the rebuilding of a philosophical framework.

Leaving aside for the moment the question of the correct imagery, I have divided my general argument into four parts in order to build the framework for, while also negotiating the content of, a feminist philosophy of religion. Part I on Background Matters begins a detailed discussion of the definition and symbolization of reason, with a focus upon the role of reason in the justification of religious belief. I move on to criticize a modern feminist attempt to degender reason, as well as to criticize an empirical realist attempt to justify theistic belief on the basis of formal reasoning alone. The last two sections of part I anticipate my presentation of feminist epistemological frameworks of belief, as well as the refigurations of those beliefs which have been configured by dominant, patriarchal myths.

Part II contains three chapters, addressing the question of the rationality of religious belief according to three possible, epistemological frameworks. Outlining these frameworks helps to introduce the valuable insights of recent feminist epistemologies. I am concerned with the epistemology of belief, especially substantive issues having to do with reason, objectivity, and desire. I leave the actual construction of particular doctrines about God or goddesses to theologians. Instead I consider the 'whose?' and the 'for whom?' of belief.

Part III consists of two chapters on the refigurations of belief. In these chapters, I use a combination of two feminist frameworks to illustrate the possibility of transforming the practice of philosophy of religion; this involves supplementing a formal justification of religious beliefs with a rational refiguration of beliefs which would include the significant material content of desire and sexual difference. I illustrate my refigurations of belief by taking two distinctive figures from patriarchal configurations: one from a nonwestern form of theistic belief, the other from a western form of civil belief. Both figures are women who dissent from privileged female roles, finding support for their actions in broadly construed religious beliefs. Ironically the memory of these female acts of dissent and the sexually specific content of their beliefs have been consistently reconstrued to support the philosophical limits of western patriarchy.

Part IV on Final Critical Matters picks up some of the critical issues initially raised in part I and variously addressed in parts II and III. The aim of part IV is to come to a general account of the philosophical imaginary, exposing the role of women, desire, and belief in modern philosophers' configurations of rationality. I touch on critical issues concerning the symbolic, Enlightenment reason and patriarchy. Here a special focus upon the images of death found in a philosophical text illustrates the destructive and creative significance of miming the figure of woman's living death.

The Summary reviews briefly the salient points about the rationality of belief explored in the preceding chapters for a feminist philosophy of religion. Amongst other points, it is imperative to see that the concept of reason sharply contrasted with desire is too formal or 'thin' to deal adequately with beliefs of embodied persons; that desire cannot be sufficiently understood as long as its content remains excluded by reason; and that philosophical analysis of and feminist concern with a combination of reason and desire, as found in expressions of yearning for truth, need to supplement contemporary approaches to philosophy of religion.

I would like to dedicate this book to the solitary woman who has been forced to struggle with pure thinking, at the expense of her own full embodiment as a female philosopher, in order to succeed in an academic discipline which insists upon the denial of desire, love, and any inordinate passion for true justice. But equally I hope that many other philosophers who seek institutional access to doing philosophy may be persuaded by the alternative proposed here. I propose that initially feminist philosophers may seek to gain coherence, unity, harmony for their lives and beliefs; but ultimately they will be persuaded to assess the very construction of rational beliefs, and even to refigure them.

Notes

1. Basically these nonrealist philosophers of religion reject the propositional claims of empirical realist forms of theism; for them, God is not an object 'out there.' But depending upon the nonrealist point of view, the religious philosopher may still assume and analyze the same general forms of belief as the classical theist, while seeing no need to justify rationally the beliefs as objectively true. For example, one sort of nonrealist analyzes religious practices such as prayer and belief in the afterlife which are traditionally associated with the God of theism; these practices are analyzed as meaningful forms of life, and not defended as true or false. But the danger with the potentially indefensible relativism of a nonrealist philosophy of religion would be dogmatism.
2. The origin of this imagery in Kant will be discussed in part I.

Acknowledgments

I originally conceived the project for a book on feminist philosophy of religion in the spring of 1991, when I was a Visiting Assistant Professor in the Philosophy Department at the University of Delaware. At Delaware I had the absolute good fortune to work briefly with Professor Sandra Harding. I cannot forget that my initial inspiration to work on feminist philosophy came from Sandra who immediately gained my respect as a woman philosopher and a feminist. Now I only hope to have done justice to Sandra's brilliant work in feminist epistemology.

In Oxford in Trinity Term 1993, I was next given encouragement by Dr Graham Ward to pursue publication of *A Feminist Philosophy of Religion* – and Alison Mudditt of Blackwell Publishers took on my project. However, starting a new job in Philosophy at the University of Sunderland in the fall of 1993 meant that work on my book was delayed. Yet I was greatly impressed, when I met Michèle Le Doeuff in the spring of 1994. Although I had written to Michèle to invite her to give a Royal Institute of Philosophy lecture at the Universities of Durham and Sunderland, she inspired me on the occasions when we met to talk about her lecture. She clearly increased my incentive to produce a piece of feminist philosophy of my own.

Then in 1995, Dr Grace Jantzen gave both encouraging words and critical comments on an early draft of the book. Grace, along with an anonymous Blackwell's reader, moved my thinking forward with some honest and helpful reports.

So over the years of work on this project, I have gained guidance from various sectors. And here I add acknowledgment to David Leopold for his longstanding friendship, his astuteness and support as a political philosopher. In the same breath, I want to thank Lucinda Rumsey and her brother Paul for their excellent suggestions of works by women artists for the cover design – even if David's suggestion of Käthe Kollwitz's woodcuts led me in the end to choose one of Kollwitz's marvelous sculptures.

Others who should be given special mention include Dr Alison Jasper, who in the very early stages urged my work on Julia Kristeva, and Dr Bridget Nichols, who responded to my philosophical ideas with her characteristic patience and sensitivity, offering careful comments for my nonphilosophical readers.

In addition, during the past few years I had the good fortune of particular expertise from Dr Pamela Clemit and her impeccable editorial knowledge (as well as her thoughts on myth) and from Dr Adrian Moore and his philosophical acumen, especially with his analytic insights on Kant and on objectivity (despite first appearances, we found more ground for philosophical agreement than expected). Of course all the remaining lapses in style or form and philosophical precision are my own.

I would like to thank my ideal reader, Hanneke Canters, who read the whole manuscript bit by bit – and sometimes more than once – to give me the response I needed from a woman postgraduate who had already studied philosophy of religion and is currently engaging with feminist epistemology as part of her doctorate in philosophy. Hanneke's genuine enthusiasm, in fact her remarkable excitement, about *A Feminist Philosophy of Religion* convinced me in the last stage of trying to complete this book that I could imagine my audience: the lived experiences of certain women philosophers would make them especially eager to read what I have to say.

Thanks to all the other people who in one way or another believed in me, allowing me to express both determination and conviction in what has been written here.

Finally, chapter 4 is adapted from my 'Myth, Mimesis and Multiple Identities: Feminist Tools for Transforming Theology', *Literature and Theology: An International Journal of Theory, Criticism and Culture*, 10:2 (June 1996), 112–30. Acknowledgment goes to Oxford University Press.

I
Introduction

Background Matters

He defends his privilege of being the sole safeguard of speech, truth, intelligence, reason – the fairest of all possessions – though at the same time he raves a little wildly in his relations with the gods and with women.

Irigaray 1985a, 219

1 Reason, Belief, and What is Excluded

Western philosophers since the fourth century BCE[1] have made the definition of reason central to philosophy's own definition. In general, tackling the definition and function of reason is central to doing philosophy, but it is also central to the rational construction and justification of religious belief. My aim in the present book is more specific than to define reason in philosophy. I intend to question the current functioning of reason in philosophical justifications of largely theistic belief: with my focus upon the rationality of religious belief, I am asking philosophers of religion to begin by scrutinizing the construction of belief prior to its justification.

Here in part I, I offer some groundwork for the critical rethinking of certain clusters of central concepts including reason, philosophy, and objectivity; belief, religion, and theistic beliefs; sex/gender, sexual difference, and desire; symbol, myth, and mimesis. But my ultimate goal is to conceive the possibility of supplementing philosophy of religion with feminist tools for achieving less partial and less biased beliefs than those beliefs rationally justified by the dominant forms of classical theism.

By the concept of belief I mean thoughts taken up – whether in being handed down or, in some sense, being discovered – and held as true.[2] Religious beliefs are distinctive in forming binding truth-claims often about empirically unknowable aspects of reality. Theistic beliefs form more distinctive but also highly various truth-claims about the existence of a personal deity. For instance, theistic beliefs include binding claims about the one personal, creator God of Christianity, the one transcendent, creator God of Judaism, and the one God of Islam; there can also be theistic devotion to a god(dess) in Hinduism and possibly Buddhism. So theistic claims can be made to support different accounts of belief in some goddess(es) or god(s). These accounts include anything from atheism (the belief in no personal deity), through monotheism (the belief in one personal transcendent-creator God who demands a total commitment), pantheism (the belief that the god or goddess is all or identical with all of nature), and polytheism (the belief in a multitude of existing personal deities, female and male), to henotheism (the belief in one god or goddess out of many existing deities, notably in a Hindu's devotion to Krishna).

In making up a particular religion, very general theistic beliefs also bring together both the actions endorsed by and the emotions evoked by more specific beliefs. The implication is that specific religious beliefs can become binding truth-claims expressible in rites and forms of worship. The adjective 'religious' often describes some communally binding action. But it could also describe an individually binding devotion to a personal deity. For example, religious truth-claims are expressed in monotheistic rites of purification of defiled persons and in monotheistic forms of worship of the undefiled deity. This is notably the case in certain forms of ancient Greek religion, as well as in the ancient form of Hebrew religion. But taking an even more specific example, religious belief can be expressed in *bhakti*, a specific form of Hindu devotion to a personal deity. In brief, believing in the context of a religion is an activity which can be variously configured in actions of submission and humiliation, in images of domination and subordination, or even in figures of dissent and marginality. Later I will discuss two female figures of religious dissent and marginality, the ancient Greek figure Antigone and the medieval Indian figure Mirabai.

Since the time of the earliest Greeks, philosophers of religion have brought myth and mimesis into the assessment of the truth-claims comprising religious beliefs. Myth can be defined as a story configuring into a narrative unity the actions endorsed by and the emotions evoked by men's and women's theistic or nontheistic beliefs. And mimesis, in its capacity to imitate or re-enact, can refigure the dominant configurations of religious beliefs. In this book, the capacity of mimetic refiguring will offer feminists the possibility of imitating myths disruptively, as in mimicry or miming. Most importantly the philosophical significance of sex, gender, class, ethnic, and race differences is allowed to emerge in myth and mimesis.

My accounts of traditional philosophical terms and concepts, symbols of reason and desire, myths of ritual action and bodily life, will lead into critical issues of sex, gender, race, ethnicity, and class. I intend to gradually raise crucial questions about accounts of religion other than the dominant realist form of western monotheism; these other accounts condition the subjectivities of and constitute the structures of nonwestern societies. Legitimate questions for a feminist philosopher of religion would be: Does the principle of self-projection, which has come to seem implicit in Christian realist forms of monotheism, function in religions without an anthropomorphic deity?[3] And are women in other religions imagined as divine?[4]

From the outset of this book, I maintain that sexual difference remains latent in the unconscious conditions and the unacknowledged excess of male gendered identity in patriarchal religions. My task, then, is to expose the sexual difference conditioning religious belief; yet this is not to force either the other (e.g. the otherness of desire) or the outsider (e.g. the marginalized other of religious defilement) into roles defined by contrast with dominant self-sameness or the self-same privileged subject.[5]

Following other contemporary feminist philosophers, I would like to question in some detail even at this early stage the significant modern distinction between gender and sex. This distinction has become a cultural variable. Initially modern feminists introduced sex/gender into their arguments, as a nature/culture distinction, aiming to combat inequalities between men and women by 'degendering.' More recent accounts have challenged the distinction, arguing that gender and sex are constructed and not opposed as culture to nature. So these two terms are no longer neatly opposed or separable as natural/cultural categories.[6]

The implication of this sex/gender question for those feminist philosophers who claim that reason has been constructed as masculine is that the degendering of reason would still leave certain injustices unchanged. The elimination of gender as a cultural construction no longer seems – if possible – acceptable as an adequate solution to inequalities between men and women, since it would leave sexual difference excluded from the content of rationally justified belief. In particular, I will contend that changing or eliminating gender, if a viable task, as the cultural side of the sex/gender opposition does not solve problems related to the exclusion of sexual difference in the rational justification of theistic belief. Precisely what makes men and women different inhibits making formal equality the marker for justice.[7] Certain feminists today even contend that gender is in trouble.[8] So allow me to give some background to this contention.

2 Sex/Gender and Reason

Only in recent times has the technical term 'gender,' defined as a cultural construction, been sharply opposed to sex as a natural or biological characteristic. In 1929 and again in 1938, Virginia Woolf does not have gender on hand as a technical term. Yet Woolf discusses the social, institutional and cultural differences between women and men.[9] Contemporary theorists would most likely identify Woolf's discussions, first on women, education, and writing, and next on women, education, and war, as accounts of gender. But considered more closely, accounts of gender such as Woolf's suggest that the natural and cultural meanings of sex/gender have probably always varied to a greater or lesser degree.

Currently there are feminist philosophers who recognize not only the variable cultural constructions of gender, but also the various criticisms of 'gender' as a technical term. The straightforward opposition of sex to gender is being undermined in a number of ways. For feminist philosophers such as Moira Gatens, the sex/gender distinction has become a problematical variable.[10] In particular, drawing a distinction between sex and gender does not tackle the problem with traditional symbolizations of reason as male and masculine; degendering reason does not confront reason's supposed maleness. As I will contend, the limits of reason need to be constantly sought and possibly reconceived in order to value rather than to exclude significant content such as female desire[11] from philosophical accounts of rationality and reality.

In addition, instead of degendering, Continental feminists such as Rosi Braidotti insist upon recognizing an ontological difference.[12] And if the ontological status of sexual difference can be established, given value, and no longer eclipsed by male self-sameness, then the term 'gender' will become redundant. In any case, Italian-speaking and French-speaking feminists simply lack a term for gender.[13] Increasingly a simple degendering appears both contrived and counter-productive for feminists concerned with the global rights of women and minorities and with various injustices of sex/gender, race, class or caste, and ethnicity.[14] If Anglo-American feminists insist first of all on defining gender and then on eliminating it altogether, the consequence is that actual differences are ignored. The dangers with the degendering 'solution' can be indicated with a variety of concrete examples on a large or small scale. So why not move directly to an account of sexual difference?

Another argument concerning the sex/gender distinction is that, under patriarchy and according to patriarchal forms of reason, gender has been constructed as white, male, and heterosexual, while sex is repressed as female; and hence, as patriarchy has been increasingly challenged and undermined, gender is rendered questionable.[15] Sex and gender, in comprising dominant heterosexual characteristics, are both questioned since they are made up of cultural variables. In this scenario nothing seems to be left unquestioned: even primary and secondary sex characteristics are debatable – whether the debate be about facial hair, short hair, or bald heads being only male, about sexual defilement being naturally female due to women's anatomy, or about sex-changes for those whose bodies do not match their desires. There are also those who argue for a third sex, finding evidence for their argument amongst certain native American Indian tribes and amongst other religious norms.

The consequence of these various challenges to the sex/gender distinction is that sex and sexual difference, as opposed to male sameness, cannot be defined simply with reference to universally agreed natural, biological, or anatomical characteristics. But when I look more closely at discussions of sex in western philosophy, it appears that sex has never been defined merely by specific anatomical references. What, precisely, constitutes sex has been contentious for centuries. For instance, Aristotle's (384–322 BCE) value-laden account of female anatomy as that of a defective male eventually led to Augustine's (354–430 CE) contentious claims about the defilement of sex and the natural inferiority of female anatomy; such claims remain latent in philosophical history and theology. Aristotle and Augustine paved the way for the sexual morality of medieval theologians such as Thomas Aquinas (1225–74) who privileged men over women, and male over female anatomy.[16]

Clearly definitions of sex in western philosophy and theology have always involved more than specific anatomical references. Similarly on a global scale, differences concerning sex/gender – as a nature/culture distinction – can be expected within all major world religions, while western philosophers' pretense of gender neutrality often conceals their male-sex bias.[17]

Notwithstanding the various debates about sex and gender, the central problem for a feminist philosopher of religion remains clear: the largely unacknowledged exclusion of sexual difference, by the unfair privileging of dominant figures of male self-sameness and by the exclusive use of reason. Some feminists have made apparent the privileging of male identity in philosophical representations of God's ideally male attributes and in western philosophers' ideal of pure rationality.[18] But the erasure of female identity and sexual difference by male ideals of rationality and divinity will continue as long as the sex/gender symbolization of philosophical reason remains unacknowledged and unchanged.

It is of great concern to women, and at least to some men, seeking recognition as philosophers of religion, that reason has been defined by the symbolic if not the actual exclusion of femaleness. To do philosophy, at least in the west, women have had to deny their femaleness in order to achieve recognition as rational subjects; or they have had to fail as the female other to be acknowledged as philosophers.[19] Genevieve Lloyd states a claim which has been repeated frequently in recent years. That is, from the beginning of western philosophy in ancient Greece, 'femaleness [is] symbolically associated with what Reason supposedly left behind – the dark powers of the earth goddesses, immersion in unknown forces associated with mysterious female powers' (Lloyd 1993 [1984], 2).[20] According to this account of the symbolism of reason, the history of philosophy begins by imagining female powers as what had to be excluded by thinkers seeking to be rational. In Lloyd's terms, the mysterious powers of goddesses were left behind by reason in western philosophy.

The term 'philosophy' itself derives from the ancient Greek for love of wisdom. In practice, this remains a love of questioning, modeled after the activity of a sage, traditionally an old man, who has sought truth about goodness, beauty, and God by constant investigations. Rationality is, in this tradition, recognized in the achievement of a life and of beliefs thoroughly integrated according to formal principles of order, of coherence, of logical simplicity. But let me consider, instead, another contemporary historical sketch of philosophical accounts of rationality.

In ancient Greece, Aristotle defined reason by stipulating what distinguished humans from animals. Humans are defined as animals, but with a difference: their difference is the capacity to use reason in the context of a community (*polis*); so animals other than reasoning political animals, i.e. other than men, could not be rational. Moreover the origin of this capacity to reason is conceived to be both divine and male.[21] But even before Aristotle, the Pythagoreans (570 BCE), as well as Aristotle's archetypal predecessor, Socrates (469–399 BCE) and Aristotle's mentor, Plato (428–347 BCE), all made reason the central focus of western philosophy. Contemporary philosophers continue to turn to Aristotle's comprehensive corpus of writings for accounts of reason's functioning in logic, physics, ethics, and metaphysics. Yet Aristotle himself learns from Socrates and Plato that reason in the just man is ideally the ruling part of the soul over its other two parts, i.e. emotion and appetite. Interestingly, although Aristotle conceives women as defective males, he neither follows Plato in simply rejecting emotions as 'womanish' nor fears 'female' emotions.[22]

The classic list of opposites used to define reason in western philosophy is first developed by the Pythagoreans in fourth-century BCE Greece and is restated by philosophers from Aristotle to Georg Wilhelm Friedrich Hegel (1770–1831). The Pythagorean list of opposites contains a series of contrasting terms in which reason above all is represented with images (terms) of that which limits, unifies, enlightens, orders, rests, straightens. This list has been criticized recently by contemporary feminist philosophers such as Michèle Le Doeuff (1948-) and Luce Irigaray (1930-), as well as Margaret Whitford in her discussion of Irigaray and Genevieve Lloyd in her popular work on the history of reason in western philosophy.

As pointed out by Le Doeuff, Hegel restates the Pythagorean list of opposites as limit and infinity, unity and multiplicity, masculine and feminine, light and dark, good and evil.[23] Lloyd presents this same list as ten contrasts: limit/unlimited, odd/even, one/many, right/left, male/female, rest/motion, straight/curved, light/dark, good/bad, square/oblong.[24] Whitford claims that Irigaray's psychoanalytic refiguring of the still-dominant male imaginary in its repression of the female imaginary picks up (and mimes) Aristotle's use of the Pythagorean contrasts.[25]

It is Le Doeuff, however, who suggests the crucial line of questioning for my present assessment of the rationality and myths of belief. The very nature of the philosophical imaginary must be queried in its employment of imagery which, in turn, constitutes the unity of reason and so of philosophy itself.[26] Hence the crucial question: Is reason something that can be defined only if images indirectly represent rationality by portraying the exclusion of the irrational? This question implies that the irrational, imagined as female and symbolized variously as the feminine, the disorderly, the incoherent, and so on, has something to do with the nature of reason and hence philosophy – not necessarily with the nature of being female.

In contrast, it is not until the Preface to the second edition (1993) of her highly popular *The Man of Reason: 'Male' and 'Female' in Western Philosophy*, that Lloyd acknowledges the need to work out the precise role of symbols and images in the self-justification of philosophy as an enterprise guided by the man of reason. In other words, the philosophical nature of symbols and of the imaginary are not at the source of Lloyd's history of the man of reason. But following Le Doeuff's perceptive argument, I recognize the philosophical urgency of seriously assessing the necessity and function of the philosophical imaginary as fundamental to doing philosophy: even images of the female demand philosophy's scrutiny. Otherwise there is dogmatism which would be unphilosophical.

Le Doeuff elucidates various images in philosophical texts. In her provocative essay, 'Long Hair, Short Ideas,' Le Doeuff uncovers images employed to represent the female as nonthinker, since short on ideas. She assembles the imaginary portrait of woman in western philosophy: woman is portrayed as a power of disorder, a being of night, a twilight of beauty, a dark continent, a sphinx of dissolution, an abyss of the unintelligible, a voice of underworld gods, an inner enemy who alters and perverts without visible sign of combat, a place where all forms dissolve.[27]

In order for philosophy to define its own function, it seems to need to contain, restrict, confine, or unify reason by excluding its opposite. And in contrast to philosophical thinking (confined as a unity), what is excluded can only be imagined or symbolized with opposite images. So it is possibly a contingent matter that the philosophical imaginary uses the feminine and 'woman' (*la femme*) to symbolize the irrational. In other words, to define reason and to delineate the domain of philosophy, the female other serves as the source for images of the outside, as what lies beyond the limit of philosophical unity; hence she is conceptualized as that which lacks rationality, while it is the male subject who reasons. In the images of the Enlightenment, reason is transcendent and male, while irrationality is immanent and female as 'the other of reason,' as the mystical, the maternal, the mythical. But this still does not mean that irrationality is endemic to being female.[28]

An important, ancient distinction – again originally in Pythagorean thought – between form and matter also runs through the history of western philosophy. This distinction, in turn, can illustrate the way in which reason has been defined in contrast to unreason, i.e. form in contrast to matter.[29] However, caution must be exercised before generalizations are made which are too sweeping. In particular, it should be stressed that differences exist amongst philosophers concerning reason's definition and function. For instance, concerning reason there are great differences between the ancients and René Descartes (1596–1650), and between Descartes and Francis Bacon (1561–1626), and between Bacon and Immanuel Kant (1724–1804).[30] More specifically, what about the coherence of reason? Would all of the aforementioned philosophers agree upon a single, unambiguous statement on what is rationally coherent?

I might speculate about the different possible answers to the question: Does the rationality of belief, of arguments and persons, only seem to be coherent, or does rationality have to be (if it can be) coherent? Think of informal reasoning: it does not always seem coherent, but may be so. Could I then say of reasoning by a woman who is called irrational that her reasoning process should be probed for its coherence? But if a coherent unity is what defines reason and what justifies a philosophical argument, then should the question be asked: Whose coherence is this? Who set that particular limit which makes possible (that particular) coherence? Talk of a coherent unity could be simply a claim for partiality, excluding that which does not help to contain or maintain unity or identity. This issue of the instability of coherence, unity, or identity has great consequences for the myths of religious belief. For instance, I will be assessing the argument for the coherence of empirical realist forms of theism. Does this argument succeed only by the exclusion in myths (or often unnoticed imagery) of significant material content concerning bodily life and other aspects of human reality?

Carefully reading Kant, for example, I find that he recognizes a problem with attempts to make rationality and reality correspond on the grounds of divinely inscribed principles of reason. Roughly stated, already in the eighteenth century Kant demonstrates the instability of the embodied rational subject and so the instability of coherence. Kant also exposes the lack of correspondence between rationality and reality for any individual embodiment of reason and, hence, the limitations of human reason alone. Yet Kant employs imagery to achieve the closure or unity of his own philosophical reasoning. Le Doeuff illustrates this point by recalling Kant's use of an island to represent the pure understanding of philosophy.[31] In Kant's words,

> the territory of pure understanding . . . is an island, enclosed by nature itself within unalterable limits. It is the land of truth – enchanting name! – surrounded by a wide and stormy ocean, the native home of illusion, where many a fog bank and many a swiftly melting iceberg give the deceptive appearance of farther shores, deluding the adventurous seafarer ever anew with empty hopes, and engaging him [*sic*] in enterprises which he can never abandon and yet is unable to carry to completion. Before we venture on this sea, to explore it in all directions and to obtain assurance whether there be any ground for such hopes, it will be well to begin by casting a glance upon the map of the land which we are about to leave, and to enquire, first, whether we cannot in any case be satisfied with what it contains – are not, indeed, under compulsion to be satisfied, inasmuch as there may be no other territory upon which we can settle; and, secondly, by what title we possess even this domain, and can consider ourselves as secured against all opposing claims. (Kant 1950, 257, B294–5/A236)

Perhaps some would read the sea – 'the native home of illusion' – as indicating another set of images for the female, representing what is beyond philosophical unity and security; the pure understanding would, then, be man's territory. In the Preface, I considered Quine's use of Neurath's picture of the philosopher as a mariner rebuilding his ship on the open sea.[32] Now does the mariner have any affinity with Kant's seafarer? At first glance, the subjects in both pictures appear to be men who venture out on the open and stormy sea. But Neurath's philosophers do not begin on the secure land of truth; his picture contains no island. So women philosophers should take care to confront the imagery of Kant and Neurath separately.

To offer some rough guidelines, I would ask, first, do women philosophers following Kant stand in a different relation to the sea from past male philosophers who begin by viewing the sea when securely placed upon the land of truth? Perhaps contemporary women philosophers would be more like Neurath's mariners and find themselves already on the open sea. But, second, would women philosophers be aboard 'his ship,' which Quine identifies as the evolving conceptual scheme of Neurath's mariner? To be without a ship would mean being without beliefs, apparently, in the sea. So in this picture, to have any beliefs, to have a conceptual scheme, women would have to be carried along in a ship; but once recognized as philosophers, women could seek to rebuild the ship's planks of mistaken beliefs. The question is: If philosophers who are self-conscious about their sex/gender, race, class, and ethnicity join in the rebuilding task, how would their involvement transform the shape of the mariners' ship? As already suggested, feminist epistemologists would insist at least that the rebuilding task could not be done by a lone philosopher, whether privileged male or female. Yet before asserting anything about the new beliefs which might supplement Kant's philosophy and transform Neurath's ship, it would be necessary to do more sustained studies of Kant and of Neurath, especially to explore questions related to the sex/gender of the seafarers and of the mariners' beliefs, respectively. To support such studies, I will be exploring the new subjects of feminist epistemologies and the construction of their beliefs in part II.

For the moment, suffice it to say that whatever the possible sexed/gendered overtones of their philosophical imagery, I find support for a feminist philosophy of religion both from Kant's critical philosophy and from Quine's critique of the dogmas of empiricism.[33] On the one hand, Kant's limitation of the functioning of theoretical reason will support my criticism of the empiricist truth-claims concerning a nonempirical territory of metaphysics. In particular, I am critical of theistic claims about a transcendent yet personal deity made exclusively on empiricist grounds with use of the rational principles of coherence, probability, simplicity, and credulity of cumulative evidence (which must also be logically consistent). On the other hand, Quine's claim concerning philosophers in their task, that we must be carried along by an evolving conceptual scheme,[34] will also hold in check any of my proposals concerning a new principle of objectivity. In particular, no a priori principles can come to the aid of epistemology if it follows Quine.[35]

3 Contemporary Philosophy of Religion

In the second half of the twentieth century, Anglo-American philosophers of religion have worked to revive empirical realist forms of theism. The increasingly sophisticated debates in philosophy of religion have given new significance to the meanings of empiricism and theism, at the same time as rendering problematic the use of experience as a foundation for religious knowledge. In this book, I am unable to do justice to the various nuanced positions generated by these theistic debates.[36] I can sketch only those features of empirical realist forms of theism which raise critical issues for a feminist philosophy of religion.

One common feature of the variations in empirical realist forms of theism is the fundamental role of their conceptions of experience. In the most general terms, empiricism ties knowledge to experience thought of as whatever is expressed in some designated class of statements that can be observed to be true by use of the senses; and empirical realism affirms the independent existence of those phenomenal objects to which the empiricist statements refer. No matter what its different conceptions, experience remains the measure of all theories and claims to knowledge of God for the empirical realist. The issue for a feminist philosopher is that the traditional theists' uses of experience have implied radically privileged, formally male-neutral ideas, impressions, perceptions, sensations, sense-data, evidences, or noninferential beliefs. By male-neutral I mean that whatever the primary stuff of the phenomenal world, broadly construed as experience, when gathered by philosophers it has been male but under the pretence of sex/gender neutrality. So whether Augustinian, Anselmian, Thomist, Lockean, Humean, or even Calvinist, contemporary philosophers of religion continue to be concerned with (their conceptions of) experience as the gauge of knowledge and belief; and for many empirical realists, experience still serves as the foundation for the justification of true belief.

Foundationalism essentially names the modern view that knowledge is proven true, i.e. justified, as part of a certain bedrock or as derived from a solid basis. For the empiricist, this basis is in experience, provided by evidence, by arguments from design of the universe, or by a cumulative case including various inductive arguments. In its strict sense, foundationalism assumes that a properly justified set of beliefs is formed only when beliefs are either grasped as self-evident or known indirectly in the sense of being justified by their relationship to self-evident beliefs.

Admittedly certain prominent philosophers of religion have advocated either a nonfoundationalism or a proper basicality as warrant for true belief. The nonfoundationalist claims that no justification is possible, while the claim to properly basic beliefs assumes that no justification needs to be inferred from evidence or certain premises. Yet in either case, experience is, arguably, still at issue as the guarantee of true belief. The nonfoundationalist philosopher of religion often finds support from a particular interpretation of Wittgenstein's forms of life,[37] while the idea of proper basicality as the ground of justified beliefs derives uniquely from the Calvinist epistemology of Alvin Plantinga. Another name for Plantinga's position is an anti-evidentialism which remains experiential; the point is that although Plantinga rejects strict foundationalism, his properly basic beliefs remain in some sense foundational, based on unmediated experience.[38] This alternative formulation of the latter position could then include, besides Plantinga, quite different, religious epistemologists. For example, despite their differences, William Alston, like Plantinga, would reject the use of evidence and probability in inferential arguments for the existence of God while still maintaining the importance of reason, experience (in Alston's case, perceptual experience), and noninferential grounds for an epistemology of religious belief.[39]

To give slightly more background to the increasingly significant and distinctive position of Plantinga, an intricate picture emerges in his account of how beliefs can be warranted when they function as God-designed. Plantinga appeals to the Reformed theologian John Calvin (1509–64) who asserts that a person can possess a sense of God which allows perception of God in the world.[40] In this way, Plantinga places the issue of warrant within metaphysics and combines it with an epistemic case for the rationality of religious belief. Plantinga and others, like Nicholas Wolterstorff, who also appeal to Calvin, contend that one can correctly – rationally – hold theism as a basic tenet that is foundational without being justified in terms of any deeper set of beliefs.[41] Plantinga's ongoing, impressive work on warrant has tried to demonstrate that belief in God may be properly basic and fully sanctioned without having to be justified with the traditional arguments for the existence of God from design, miracles, or cumulative evidence. That God exists can be a fundamental belief that is often involuntary, as fixed and stable as any other basic beliefs about oneself and the world. Thus Plantinga offers an original argument for turning the epistemological critique of modern foundationalism into an advantage for empirical realist forms of theism: he asserts the epistemic autonomy and self-warranting nature of theistic belief.

From the preceding examples of how experience functions as a fundamental feature of theistic debates, it may have been obvious that the other common feature of Anglo-American philosophy of religion generally is its arguments concerning, or warrants for, a privileged model of God: traditional theism. By this I mean that twentieth-century philosophers of religion have revived debates about the doctrine of God, a matter which, at least since medieval times and possibly since the early Church Fathers, has exercised western theologians and philosophers including Augustine, Anselm (1033/4–1109), Aquinas, Descartes, and Kant; this theistic doctrine has also been assumed by Protestant theologians, not typically called philosophers, such as Calvin, Martin Luther (1483–1546), and Karl Barth (1886–1968). Today the prominent philosopher Richard Swinburne, amongst others, is exemplary in continuing this long tradition.

Swinburne's writings offer a sustained, formally rational defense of traditional theism. At the outset of his cumulative case for the existence of God, Swinburne makes the following statement: 'I take the proposition "God exists" (and the equivalent proposition "There is a God") to be logically equivalent to "there exists a person without a body (i.e. a spirit) who is eternal, is perfectly free, omnipotent, omniscient, perfectly good, and the creator of all things"' (Swinburne 1991 [1979], 8; cf. 1977, 2).[42] This conception of God represents the heart of traditional theism as it has been revived and debated by Anglo-American philosophers of religion. I will return to give more attention to Swinburne in the next chapter.

My contention at this stage is that a feminist philosopher of religion would confront, at least, the two problematic features found in the empirical realist forms of theism held by contemporary philosophers of religion: their reliance upon an unstable notion of experience,[43] especially but not only in the form of evidential foundationalism, and their formally rational arguments concerning the existence of the God of traditional theism.

Prominent philosophers of religion including Plantinga, Swinburne, and Norman Kretzmann have all had enthusiastic twentieth-century disciples.[44] Roughly summarized, those philosophers who follow Plantinga accept that properly basic beliefs are warranted according to a Reformed epistemology; those who follow Swinburne debate logical and evidential proofs for the existence of God, bringing in probability to support a cumulative-case argument; and those following Kretzmann maintain the compatibility of faith and reason so important to Augustine, Anselm, and Aquinas in all their rational defenses and analyses of traditional theism. In short, for all of these disciples, philosophy of religion within the Anglo-American tradition of philosophy offers formally rational statements for or against theistic belief, calling upon experience, however differently construed, to support justifications or guarantees of truth and falsehoods.[45]

In contrast, I submit that a feminist philosopher will feel compelled to ask: Whose beliefs are these that are given warrant, rational proof or justification? For whom have these beliefs been constructed? The beliefs in question generally constitute the dominant Christian realist form of monotheism; and the experiences of theists or atheists support their respective arguments for or against the existence of this God. In addition, I find it philosophically necessary to raise further questions about the functioning of the rational principles of coherence, of simplicity, of credulity, as well as questions about other formal principles of basic beliefs which immediately justify certain forms of theism.[46] Finally, I will argue that the danger in restricting philosophy of religion to formal arguments presented by empirical realist forms of theism is at least twofold.

First, these theistic arguments are likely to be inadequate, since they are built upon exclusion of the potentially significant, material content of bodily life, desire, and sexual difference. An unasked and indeed unresolved question exists concerning the significance of desire for religious beliefs.[47] But the larger, decisive problem is that the empiricist efforts to develop rational defenses of theistic beliefs on the basis of evidences or self-warranting experiential claims, build a privileged view of ultimate reality which actually excludes or devalues material issues of desire, need, ethical truth, and justice.

Second, these theistic arguments are more than likely to be male-neutral, if not immoral, since they assume the status quo of patriarchal beliefs. By patriarchal, I mean beliefs or truth-claims which have been covertly constructed according to a male gender-differentiation between men and women, and a sexed/gendered hierarchy of privileged men over marginalized others. The decisive problem here with patriarchal forms of theistic belief is the privilege given to the attributes and actions of a male God. Such privileging is unselfconsciously biased against women and partial toward men.

Thus my contention is that the popular empiricist (which, as should be obvious by now, I use broadly to include the evidentialist as well as the anti-evidential experientialist) methods of defending or attacking theistic beliefs confirm the status quo of patriarchy in the history of western philosophy. A defense in favour of this status quo not only privileges fathers and so all male figures of authority, but it sets up a hierarchically ordered set of personal and political relations. This can be illustrated especially in the ramified beliefs of traditional theism. Generally conceived, the ramified beliefs in, for example, sin and redemption necessarily entail the less ramified – i.e. more restricted – belief in an omnipotent, supremely good, creator God which is at the heart of empirical realist forms of theism.[48] The rigid, patriarchal, and androcentric account of sin must rely upon particular defenses of God's justice in allowing gratuitous evil. These theodicies are, generally speaking, callous toward the inordinate and innocent suffering of women throughout western history, due to unacknowledged material and mental conditions of inequality and injustice – particularly those generated by western philosophy and theology – for them as young women (virgins), daughters, mothers, wives, and widows.[49] But the less ramified theistic beliefs also uncritically assume the hierarchy of gendered, vertical relations between man and his transcendent God and horizontal relations between man and woman; hence these are biased toward the privileged male form of Christianity in following from the highly ramified beliefs of traditional theism.

A first major philosophical problem, to be confronted in part II and the first chapter of part III of this book, is that in assuming specific beliefs in order to justify them, a dangerous circularity has gone unchecked in the justificatory arguments of dominant forms of theism. The contemporary philosopher who debates empirical realist forms of theism and atheism assumes and so privileges what is supposed to be concluded: belief or unbelief in a creator God who is supremely good, omnipotent, omniscient, eternal, yet personal. In one significant case at least, the claim is even made and rationally defended that this theistic God has morally and rationally sufficient reasons for allowing incalculably large amounts of evil.[50]

The alternative offered here aims to develop a feminist philosophy which builds into its epistemology tools to avoid both circular reasoning and oppressive, often pernicious, beliefs. Epistemological tools are used to scrutinize critically and dialectically the construction of rational beliefs, as well as the principles of rationality which perhaps unwittingly exclude the desires and needs of women and nonprivileged men. The most questionable form of religious belief depends upon truth-claims about an ultimate reality, formulated from allegedly unmediated experience of the world and reached by inductive reasoning from a supposedly neutral point of view. The implied objectivity, with its naive standpoint on the empirical world, can be easily challenged; but the standpoints of less naive empiricists might wisely be scrutinized as well.

I will argue in part II that a *de facto* privileged point of view on the world reveals itself as such once the subject of knowledge attempts to reinvent himself or herself as other. As will be demonstrated, as soon as subjects begin to think from the lives and the beliefs of differently formed theists, from other religious standpoints, the formerly objective standpoint begins to appear biased and partial.[51] The challenge is simply not to think strictly from one's own beliefs alone.

Statedly succinctly, I criticize the rationality and objectivity which contemporary theists have used for the justification of binding beliefs. The timeliness of this critical feminist assessment of beliefs should be without question. In the light of ever-increasing conflicts and wars over entrenched and exclusive religious and political positions in our contemporary, global world, it becomes more and more necessary that students of the philosophy of religion learn to think carefully, critically, and concretely about others' beliefs in order to rethink their own. The phenomenal popularity of reactionary religious beliefs amongst powerful persons of all ages should be reason enough to transform philosophy of religion into a tool for refiguring biased beliefs. Without a doubt, there is the constantly growing danger of religious fanaticism and with it the resurgence of sexisms, ethnocentrisms, classisms, and racisms of all sorts.

4 Thinking from the Lives and Beliefs of Others

A second major philosophical problem, to be addressed in chapters 1–3 of part II, but variously recalled in chapters 4 and 5 of part III, concerns objectivity. The problem rests with the notion of objectivity supporting the rationality of religious belief as advocated by empirical realist forms of theism. A critical account of this objectivity questions the neutrality and impartiality of its philosophical notions of objective belief and objective reason. Arguably the dominant empiricist form of Enlightenment objectivity has been too 'weak', since blind to its own biases. The focus of a major feminist epistemological critique is largely this empiricist notion of objectivity.

In chapter 2, I consider two significant ideas in discussion of feminist attempts to render objectivity 'strong'. Significant for revising the dominant epistemology are the two ideas of (1) reinventing ourselves as other and (2) thinking from the lives of others. In chapter 5, these ideas, derived from feminist epistemology, become imperatives in figuring the rationality of religious belief. I also give the idea of (1) reinventing ourselves as other a double source for its material: (i) the repressed other of female desire; (ii) the outsider on the margins of patriarchy. The other, understood in this double sense as a source for more objective thinking, will be imagined as 'the outsider within' the identity of a group determined by its religious beliefs.

One of my central aims in proposing a feminist philosophy of religion is to study both feminist objectivity and female desire as essential concepts for achieving less partial and less biased beliefs than presently found in dominant forms of theism. I use feminist (so-called 'strong') objectivity to unite theoretical and practical reason[52] in figuring myth and mimesis as forms of transformative praxis. Here mimesis is meant ultimately to imitate disruptively, in order to unearth female desire.

I approach a third major philosophical problem in chapters 3 and 4, when querying the relationship of desire to both reason and religious belief. I confront the problematic role of sexual difference in the configuring and refiguring of female desire in religious devotion. By assessing two mythical configurations of dissent and religious devotion, I indirectly answer the two questions: Does the principle of male self-projection, implicit in Christian realist forms of theism, function in religions without a unique, ideal, and anthropomorphic deity? And, how are women in other religions imagined as divine? In this way, I endeavor to analyze the nature and function of specific religious beliefs in constituting qualitative personal identities for religious women and men; but I also critically assess the mythical configurations of the specific actions and emotions that are evoked by these beliefs.

The argument that theistic belief is strictly a matter of narcissistic projection of sexual desires is rejected. I offer a defense of the complex nature and meanings of the existence of a personal deity; empirical existence is not the only or the most significant meaning of a deity's existence. In contrast to a view of the deity as a self-projection, as in a mere phantasy, theistic devotion can be rationally grounded in a desire or active passion for more equal, free, and just relationships. Such rational desire is mimed in religious myths of female dissent.

In addition to the three major problems of circular and narrowly coherent reasoning, of weak and strong objectivity, of the exclusion of female desires by reason and belief, I seek to uncover new philosophical tools in recent accounts of myth and mimesis. Here a debt to Paul Ricoeur (1913–), whose threefold account of mimesis is critically employed in chapters 4 and 5, must be acknowledged. Ricoeur's hermeneutical account of symbolism is important for my assessment of issues concerning gender or sexual difference in narratives of religious identity.[53] Ricoeur's notion of narrative identity informs my discussion of myth and religious identity. Yet I admit that his own notion becomes an object of feminist critique insofar as it supports a dominant sexual identity.[54]

Unlike a feminist theology, my proposal for a feminist philosophy of religion is not to develop or defend any specific doctrine of belief in one particular religion, one God, or some particular goddess(es). Instead I contend that a feminist philosopher should be concerned with tools for critically assessing epistemological frameworks of belief, including tools for critically refiguring reason. To reinstate one crucial aspect of my ultimate goal, I intend to develop a philosophical framework which can generate less biased, less partial, and so less false beliefs. But specific formulations of doctrinal beliefs are left to feminist theologians.

So the present book does not offer any proposal for new anthropomorphic, androcentric, or gynocentric accounts of the divine.[55] There is no proposal for fixing myths of a personal deity in female form. Yet there is a proposal for constructing and assessing beliefs in terms of their objective and inclusive content. This content would include all relevant material and formal aspects of reason and desire, without privileging the perspectives of one sex, race, ethnicity, class over another.

5 Anticipating Configurations and Refigurations

My central theme in this book is equally a central and important topic for traditional philosophy of religion: the rationality of religious belief.[56] In the words of Robert Audi, 'There is no question that belief is of the first importance in the philosophy of religion, and that if religious belief (of a suitably rich kind) can be shown to be rational, then the problem of reconciling faith and reason is at least largely solved' (Audi 1993, 74). However, Audi's comment only raises issues for me. An implicit issue for a feminist philosopher of religion is: Whose rationality is demonstrated in the reconciliations of faith and reason? Moreover why assume that 'the problem' is to reconcile faith, especially if this is a patriarchal form of theistic faith, and reason? More important in this context are the problems of defining reason and constructing frameworks for rational beliefs.

In particular, I supplement the traditional approach to this topic by confronting the question of the rationality of belief in female dissent from a privileged and dominant perspective of reality. To defend the rationality of female dissenting belief in chapter 5, I employ the tools and frameworks presented in chapters 1–4. I refigure the rationality of belief from the perspective of lives at the margins. The marginalized lives of special interest are those of particular female figures in their devotion and their religious actions of dissent. Mimetically refiguring these female figures, from the perspectives of lives at the margins, should give expression to individual and communal yearning as indicative of repressed desire and sexual difference. For example, a feminist account of Indian myths explains:

> Since myth does not exist in a pure form . . . it is clear that mythological traditions about female deities will not only have a bearing on perceptions of their human counterparts – a largely unconscious feature of mythology – but also have often been quite consciously designed or remodelled to reflect particular ideas on sexual polarity as a metaphor in talking about the divine. Thus the changing emphasis on each partner in the relationship, for instance, of S[h]iva and Parvati/Kali/the Goddess, is partly an unconscious reflection of deeply held views on the relationship of the sexes, but it is also the result of conscious thought on the nature of the divine. Of course, the metaphorical terms in which that thought is mythically expressed reflect perceptions of gender norms (by their negation as often as by their affirmation), but in order to approach the myths it is necessary to understand something of the various theoretical frameworks. (Kearns 1992, 199)

In the above passage, Shiva is the male deity and Parvati, his wife, is the female deity who takes on constantly changing forms as different aspects of one reality; these forms include Kali (meaning 'black') as goddess of anger and aggression which emanate from Parvati. In subsequent chapters, I will show that myths can be refigured exactly on points of unconscious reflection, in order to mime the multiple identities of female desire and the nature of the divine. Besides configuring anthropomorphic deities, myths expressed in new forms of mimesis can help to refigure in the present life of the reader the distinctive rationality, devotion, and action of females who dissent as outsiders within the group identity of particular religions.

There is not scope in this book to elucidate the central male and female deities in dominant mythical configurations. But again, accounting for the nature of dominant deities would be a theologian's task. Instead philosophical effort is made to suggest a comprehensive framework – epistemological, linguistic, historical, social, and political – for reading and assessing female figures of belief. And one of two main examples used to elaborate such a framework is the Indian *bhakti*-saint Mirabai. This legendary female saint is to be considered in the light of the changing configurations which emerge from both her devotion to the Hindu god, Krishna, and her belief in a people's morality. Mirabai's defiance of male prerogative and dishonoring of the ruling clan in refusing to marry a prince are endorsed by her specifically female religious devotion and form of theistic belief: 'conflictual and differing cultural configurations . . . formed around the figure of Mira, and the changing faces of Mira over the different historical periods . . . [are] bound up with and permeated by the prevailing concerns and contemporary anxieties of the *bhajniks* [as the people who sing Mira's devotional songs]' (Mukta 1994, 4).[57]

Notwithstanding the significance of nonwestern figures and beliefs in enabling our thinking from the lives of others, it may still be that I tend to privilege western myths. In particular, the dominant western configuration of Antigone, the Greek heroine who defies the king's edict by burying her brother, serves as my other pivotal example for the mimetic refigurations of patriarchal myths in this book. But as a central female figure of religious dissent and marginality in western political philosophy, Antigone helps me to explore certain possibilities in disruptive imitations of dominant patriarchal myths.

Thus, on the one hand, insight is taken from an Indian legend of female religious devotion which has suffered (amongst other things) the impact upon it of dominant configurations of belief in the misconstrual of its religious meanings. From this critical insight, I seek a new utopian vision for female and male expressions of religious belief freed of the fixed-gender hierarchy of patriarchal appropriations of myth. On the other hand, historically changing configurations of western myths provide an opening through which to critically challenge the male-neutral assumptions of empirical realist forms of theistic belief.

My focus in both configurations – in the figuring of Mirabai as Indian *bhakti*-saint and in Antigone as Greek tragic heroine – is upon the steadfastness, or the sustained religious devotion, of the dissenting woman's reason and belief. It becomes significant that patriarchal configurations have construed these female lives in such ways that their actions manage to support male prerogatives. This misconstrual occurs despite indications of distinctive female dissent in rationally chosen acts of religious devotion by marginalized women with beliefs especially unpopular to the powerful.

In the end, I support an account of female desire, in the form of a rational passion named 'yearning', as a vital reality of religion. This account builds upon the imperative, from chapter 2, to think from the lives of others, especially to think from the lives of outsiders within the dominant cultural framework. A reading of bell hooks in particular enables me to begin to learn to think from the lives of African-Americans:

> [Imagine] the time black folks (especially the underclass) spend just fantasizing about what our lives would be like if there were no racism, no white supremacy. Surely our desire for radical social change is

> intimately linked with desire to experience pleasure, erotic fulfillment, and a host of other passions. Then, on the flip side, there are many individuals with race, gender, and class privilege who are longing to see the kind of revolutionary change that will end domination and oppression even though their lives would be completely and utterly transformed. (hooks 1990, 12–13)

According to hooks, yearning constitutes this shared space of desire, as a rational passion for justice. I suggest that such sexual and transformative desire can disrupt dominant myths of religious belief. But even more than disruption, rational construction of belief is a crucial issue for a feminist philosophy of religion. The rationality at issue in a feminist construction of belief would not be disembodied. Instead the content of belief and of reason's relation to the corporeal would be found configured in myth. Moreover belief and reason could be further refigured in miming the transformative desire of the outsider and the other.

Notes

1. BCE stands for 'before the common era' and will be used instead of BC.
2. Cf. Anscombe 1979.
3. For brief comments on incarnate male figures of the divine in Buddhism and Hinduism, see Kearns 1992, 191, 199–203, 211; Armstrong 1993, 100–3; cf. Feuerbach 1989, 12–33.
4. This raises the further question of the need for divine women; see Irigaray 1993c, 61–72.
5. See chapter 5, section 1, below.
6. Concerning the emergence of twentieth-century definitions of gender and the subsequent, contemporary challenges to the very distinction of sex/gender, see Beauvoir 1989 (1949); Stoller 1968, vol. I, vi–vii, 72–4; Harding 1983, 311–24; Flax 1983, 246ff, 269–71; Gatens 1991a, 139–57; 1996, 3–20; Braidotti 1991, 16–24, 122–3; Irigaray 1993b 17–36; 1993c, 107–23; Schüssler Fiorenza 1995, 34–43, 57–63.
7. Ibid.; Braidotti 1994a, 146–72, 173f, 258–80; 1994b, 49–70; Chanter 1995, 1–9, 23–6; Cornell 1995a, 5–7.
8. Butler 1987b, 128–42; 1990, 6–34 especially.
9. Woolf 1981 (1929); 1991 (1938).
10. Gatens 1991a, 139–57; 1996, 3–20; cf. Harding 1983, 311–24.
11. In the context of a book on feminist philosophy of religion, I have chosen to study the exclusion of 'female' desire from the rationality of belief. Other feminist philosophers have begun to study notions such as intuition or emotion which have been devalued as female in philosophical accounts of rationality. For example, Fricker asks, 'Why "female" intuition?,' arguing that intuition

has had a significant, often implicit role in human reasoning broadly construed; yet naming intuition female has suggested the inferiority of women's rational powers. Why? See Fricker 1996 (1995), 36–44.

I do not stipulate any precise definition of female desire. I leave the meaning of this notion especially vague at the outset of my argument, with the intention of demonstrating that the discovery of the content of sexually specific desire has to be made gradually. The search itself for this content becomes a highly significant task. But to clarify one initial ambiguity, desire will have a different relation to men from that which it has to women. Minimally from the standpoint of men, female desire remains that which has to do with embodiment and so tends to be excluded, in order to achieve a pure rationality and a disembodied identity. In contrast for women, female desire is that which can render them sexually specific subjects as mothers and daughters, and as subjects in love. The latter points to a major obstacle in giving an adequate definition of desire: what makes women's desire sexually specific – something called sexual difference – has been repressed. In order to discover the full meaning of female desire as a generic term, as well as the specificities of female desires of particular women, the sexual difference between two subjects must be allowed to emerge freely.

12. Braidotti 1989, 89–105.
13. Braidotti 1994b, 52–70.
14. For more on the global debate concerning women, gender, and justice, see the essays in Nussbaum and Sen (eds) 1993; Nussbaum and Glover (eds) 1995. For an incisive argument concerning gender-identification, see Korsgaard 1995, 401–4.
15. Cornell 1995a, 5–17.
16. Aristotle 1984 (1912–52), I, 731b20–732a24, 765b; Augustine 1959; 1961, 343–5; Aquinas 1981; cf. Ranke-Heinemann 1991, 75–6, 183–200. For a contemporary argument on Christian morality which, although unaware of the sex/gender hierarchy, assumes the superior role of man's mind over animal nature on the basis of Aquinas's writings, see Kretzmann 1988, 172–95.
17. Aristotle 1984, II, 729a; Bynum et al. (eds) 1986, 1–20; Ranke-Heinemann 1991, 9–21, 324f; Kearns 1992, 199, 203–19; King (ed.) 1995, 1–38; Schüssler Fiorenza 1995, 163f, 170–7.
18. Daly 1986 (1973); Lloyd 1993 (1984).
19. Le Doeuff 1989; Beauvoir 1989.
20. For specific details on ancient Greek goddesses, see Harrison 1980 (1903); Furlong 1992, 3–22; and on ancient Near East goddesses, see Smith 1992, 65–101. For the philosophical exclusion of mythical images of mysterious female powers, see Frankfort and Frankfort 1949, 237–63; Flax 1983, 255–70; Irigaray 1985a, 243–311; Le Doeuff 1989, 113–17.
21. Aristotle 1984, II, 1245b4–6, 12–16; 1254b24–26; 1255a2–5.
22. For studies supporting a more nuanced reading (than given by many feminists) of Aristotle on reason and emotion, which distinguishes him from Plato, see

Green 1995, 4–6, 24; Nussbaum 1986, 307–17, 378–94; 1992, 261–90; 1995, 360–95. In addition to a cognitive view of emotions in Aristotle, Nussbaum (1995) offers important references to both a fear of 'female' emotions and a defense of emotions, which are distributed along gender lines only for contingent social reasons, in western philosophy and literature as well as in Indian and Chinese literature; this includes consideration of the various possible relations between emotions and beliefs. Important for my arguments in chapters 5 and 6 is Nussbaum's reference to beliefs being constituent of passions in classical Indian tradition, as well as in ancient Greek philosophy; see Nussbaum 1995, 374n39–376. Nussbaum herself defends a cognitive view of emotions as residing at the core of one's being and making sense of the world.

23. Le Doeuff 1989, 113.
24. Lloyd 1993, 3. For further discussion of the gendered terms of reason, see Rooney 1991, 77–103.
25. Whitford 1991b, 59ff; cf. Aristotle 1984, II, 986a.
26. The imaginary in Le Doeuff's philosophy is not a psychological term. Instead it refers to the necessary but often unrecognized use of figures and imagery in philosophical texts; see Le Doeuff 1989, 1–2, 4–20. And for a more recent definition of the imaginary which distinguishes the sexual and social imaginaries, see Gatens 1996 (note Gatens' refusal to interpret the social imaginary in an Irigarayan sense, which renders it similar to ideology and opposed to reality).
27. Le Doeuff 1989, 113; also see Beauvoir 1989, 139–98.
28. See Le Doeuff 1990, 1–13; cf. Beauvoir 1989, 139ff; Green 1995, 11–13.
29. For additional feminist comments on the contrast between form and matter, see Lloyd 1993, 3; Hein 1996, 437–53. Cf. Aristotle 1984, II; Aquinas 1981.
30. Descartes 1986 (1641); Bacon 1974 (1660); Kant 1950 (1781; 1787); cf. O'Neill 1989, 3–27.
31. Le Doeuff 1989, 8–19.
32. See my Preface; cf. Quine 1963, 79; 1969, 126–7.
33. Quine 1963, 20–46.
34. Quine 1963, 79.
35. Quine 1969, 126–7.
36. For impressive collections of recent essays on theism, faith, and reason by prominent philosophers of religion, see Stump (ed.) 1993; Senor (ed.) 1995; for a contemporary guide to the major theistic concepts, debates, and arguments, see Quinn and Taliaferro (eds) 1996; and for a comprehensive introduction to contemporary debates in mainstream philosophy of religion, see Taliaferro 1997.
37. In my Preface, I refer to this nonfoundationalist position as nonrealism, indicating that I do not explore it in any detail in this book. For defenses of nonfoundationalism, see Malcolm 1977; Phillips 1970; 1986; 1988; 1993; Tilghman 1993. For some criticisms of nonfoundationalism, see Frankenberry 1987, 11–13; and for other criticisms of nonrealism as self-contradictory, see Trigg 1992; 1993.

38. For brief clarification of anti-evidentialism, with additional references, see Audi 1993, 70–89.
39. For these two, quite different examples of experiential approaches to religious epistemology, see Plantinga 1979; 1981; 1993; Alston 1987; 1991; 1993. Alston's epistemology of religious belief introduces the significant notion of *doxastic* practice. Alston defines '*doxastic*' as belief-forming, but use of 'practice' here is not to imply the voluntary nature of belief formation (Alston 1993, 7–8, 14, 124–33). Instead this notion implies that theistic faith embodies belief of certain propositions. In other words, *doxastic* practices reflect what a person noninferentially believes about God in relation to the world. There is not space to go into Alston's religious epistemology here, but I would strongly encourage a feminist philosopher of religion to explore the role of *doxastic* practice in determining the value of perceptual experience according to sex, gender, race, and class. For example, it might be asked: Wouldn't the justification of religious belief as *doxastic* practice simply reinforce the male bias in the rationality of traditional theistic belief? This question is especially relevant in confronting biased constructions of the beliefs of, for example, female mystics: it could accompany feminist work on the social constructions of mysticism, such as Jantzen 1995, 1–25, 328–46.
40. Plantinga 1981; 1983; 1992; 1993; cf. Tomberlin and Van Inwagen (eds) 1985.
41. Wolterstorff 1983, 135–86; 1986, 38–81.
42. For examples of agreements and disagreements with this conception of God, see Abraham and Holtzer (eds) 1987, 22, 44–51, 66, 171–3, 177–9, 189; Stump (ed.) 1993, 3–11, 223–33.
43. For more on the instability of this notion of experience, see part II, chapter 1, section 2 below. Roughly speaking, the notion is unstable because it assumes at the same time intensely subjective experiences and completely general experience frequently described as 'the view from nowhere'; the latter description of an objective view on experience will also be critically assessed here in chapters 1 and 2.
44. Tomberlin and Van Inwagen (eds) 1985; Padgett (ed.) 1994; Stump (ed.) 1993.
45. Swinburne 1991 (1979); Plantinga 1992. For a Thomistic approach to theism, see Davies 1993 (1982); also, see Kretzmann 1988, 172–95; Stump 1988, 61–91; (ed.) 1993, 10–11, 328–57. For a relatively new development in theistic debates, the experiential approach, see Alston 1991. For an earlier, critical study of the Anglo-American preoccupation with the justification of theism, see Frankenberry 1987, 1–35; in this work, Frankenberry's alternative to naive empiricist justifications of belief is a more radical form of empiricism; however, in a more recent essay, Frankenberry also strongly supports a feminist philosophy of religion; see Frankenberry 1994, 1–14.
46. For an example of a philosopher who assumes the same form of theism and the same selective use of certain rational principles as Swinburne yet comes up with a case for atheism, see Mackie 1982.
47. For examples of the exclusion of bodily life from rational analysis of suffering,

loving devotion, or moral action, see, respectively, Swinburne 1981, 33–71; 1987, 165–7; Adams 1986, 169–94; Kretzmann 1988, 173ff.

48. On ramified and unramified beliefs, see Franks Davis 1989, 24–5, 124–6, 171–6, 239–43, 248–50; cf. Swinburne 1991, 219; Prevost 1990, 21–31; Jantzen 1994, 197–9. But on the possible reversal of this entailment, see chapter 1, section 5, below.
49. Interestingly McCord Adams does not identify a specifically male form of reason as the source of the callousness exhibited toward suffering undergone by women due to their sex or gender, but she does recognize the callousness of theodicies of two men who exclude feelings as irrelevant to 'rational considerations'; see McCord Adams 1993, 326–7; cf. Swinburne 1987, 167; Craig 1989, 186–7. For her earlier essay on suffering, see McCord Adams 1986, 248–67.
50. See Swinburne 1991, 200–24; 1987; 141–67; 1996, 95–113. I will return to Swinburne's theodicy in part II, chapter 1, section 3, below.
51. Chapter 2, below, presents and assesses a new standpoint on objectivity for feminist epistemologies.
52. The distinction between theoretical and practical reason derives from Kant. In the *Critique of Pure Reason* Kant demonstrates that theoretical reason is unable to answer the questions of speculative metaphysics: of God's existence, the immortality of the soul, and the freedom of the will. Nevertheless theoretical reason constantly seeks for the unconditioned, asking whether God, the soul, and freedom are real; human reason is thus compelled by its nature to ask questions it cannot answer; cf. Kant 1950, 299–300, 319–20, 325n*a*, 327–8. Moreover this demonstration of the limits of theoretical reason sets out the concerns of practical reason; bringing reason to the world and directing all human beings as free and autonomous, practical reason becomes the enterprise of morality, the work and hope of humanity in politics and religion. For a clear exposition of this Kantian distinction between theoretical and practical reason, see Korsgaard 1996, 3, 9–12, 241–3.

    Moreover according to Kant, the union of theoretical and practical reason is achievable in a rationally intelligible world, in a system of purposes organized around free rational beings, i.e. a Kingdom of Ends. Cf. Kant 1951 (1785), 95–6; 1956 (1788), 43, 47–8, 111–20, 139–47; Anderson 1993c, 44–5, 52.
53. Ricoeur 1967. For studies on the sex/gender of Ricoeur's symbolism, see Bynum et al. (eds) 1986; White 1995.
54. Ricoeur 1988; 1992; cf. Warner 1995; Anderson 1996a, 1997.
55. For more on gynocentrism, see Young 1985, 173–83.
56. There are numerous significant collections of recent essays on the rationality of religious belief in contemporary philosophy of religion; in particular, see Delaney (ed.) 1979; Plantinga and Wolterstorff (eds) 1983; Audi and Wainwright (eds) 1986; Hester (ed.) 1992; Stump (ed.) 1993; Senor (ed.) 1995.
57. For the specific gendered imagery and the motifs of sex reversal in the religious poetry of *bhakti*, see Hawley 1986, 231–56; Knott 1987, 111–26.

II

Epistemological Frameworks of Belief

1

The Rationality of Religious Belief: Reason in 'Crisis'

the alternative between a hegemonic reason and a revolt of unreason can be seen as mythical, a connivance or complicity between forms which present themselves as opposites.

Le Doeuff 1989, 118

In one sense, this chapter aims to be introductory. Continuing the purpose of part I, it presents, yet with increased focus, the central topic of the book: the rationality of religious belief. It moves ahead by introducing more specific, critical aspects of this topic. But in another sense, the chapter also presents the impetus of the whole book. The heart of its argument is that philosophy of religion should continue to be concerned with the rationality of religious belief, but that the approach to this topic must be supplemented, in order to address both contemporary debates concerning philosophical reason and feminist debates on women and reason. The latter debates in particular can help to expose the inadequacy and weaknesses of rational justifications of religious belief, especially those of the dominant empirical realist forms of theism.

1 The So-called Crisis of Rationality

A so-called crisis has raised the question of reason's adequacy to its own principles. This includes questioning its adequacy to rational principles of coherence and simplicity, as well as to objectivity and impartiality. Rationality has come to seem inadequate insofar as it has been equated with masculinity and the male subject, while excluding femininity as its opposite. This exclusion means that femininity, in turn, has been equated with irrationality while the configurations of the female other in symbol and myth reflect the unconscious condition of masculine embodiment and so of the rational subject's very own materiality.

But can irrationality be figured as the material condition of the subject's rationality? Here 'material' includes biological, cultural, economic, and social conditions. Interestingly the possible consequence of this paradox for women is to suggest that the female other is now in a place of potential intellectual privilege. Although the female other has been symbolically excluded from the male conception of rationality, women have something to offer the rational subject in being the projection of his own materially conditioned status. Moreover recognition of this material content as having been excluded and repressed renders questionable the male preoccupation with justification of belief.

'Epistemology' means theory of knowledge, but the dominant form of modern epistemology has equated knowledge with justified true belief and so the overriding epistemological task has been the justification of belief. In fact 'modern' in philosophy means from the seventeenth century when Descartes shifted the focus of his philosophy from metaphysics, ethics, or politics to epistemology, to questions of knowledge and certainty. In doing this, Descartes also helped to move the central focus of western philosophy from questions about divine truth to questions of human truths and rationality. Descartes' *Meditations on First Philosophy* (1641) decisively influenced the epistemological foundationalism of subsequent philosophy, including the view of knowledge as justified true belief.[1] Yet by following other feminist epistemologists in questioning the adequacy of reason, I intend to suggest that the construction of belief has taken on significance as an epistemological task which should precede the justification of belief.

As one feminist argument goes, in order to achieve his authority and autonomy as rational, the male subject has projected fundamental aspects of his materiality or physicality onto the female other.[2] In symbols and myths, the female other configures the material content of affections, desires, biological needs, of life from natality to mortality; this material is precisely what the rational subject lacks but needs. In the end it is to the subject's detriment that, while belief has been tested rationally and justified rigorously according to formal principles of logic, the material content of life has been symbolically and literally excluded from and devalued in the construction of religious belief. For instance, the formal side of belief construction might include the a priori and empirical principles of coherence, of credulity, and of simplicity while the material side of belief, including the believer's own bodily life, would be excluded and then devalued as female, defiled, or abject.[3]

Contemporary assertions concerning a so-called death of the rational subject will be considered later on. Before that, epistemological questions about rationality and its supposed crisis need to be raised as part of the search for proper rational tools to broach a definition of feminist philosophy of religion. The rethinking of rationality in its role of constructing religious belief might even begin with this questioning. It should become clear that the rational (re)construction of belief needs to be taken seriously as an urgent task existing prior to the justification of true belief. Both phenomenological accounts of women's lived experiences of desire, defilement, and death and psychoanalytic critiques of such accounts can offer content for the reconstruction of religious belief.[4]

The crux of the present argument is that the grid or, more accurately, the epistemological framework by which one's beliefs are constructed makes all the difference. One's epistemology is of decisive significance. In its empiricist form, modern epistemology has determined both the covert construction and overt justification of rational belief. My contention is that a feminist philosophy of religion has a crucial epistemological role to play in transforming the overall framework of belief in contemporary philosophy of religion. This is an epistemological framework biased according to sex/gender, race, ethnicity, and class. Hereafter the essential task is to supplement and reform philosophy of religion with less biased methods developed from certain feminist insights.

2 Religious Belief, Experience, and Epistemic Duty

As a preliminary step, I take up a philosophical line of questioning which, in one sense, assumes John Locke's notable claim concerning the philosopher's epistemic duty or responsibility in the realm of religious beliefs. But, in another sense, my questioning goes beyond this assumption to challenge the priority given, by empiricists after Locke, to justification over construction of belief in religious epistemology.

In the seventeenth century, Locke claimed that faith is an assent of the mind (e.g. to a proposition). So faith should always be reasonable. In his words,

> Faith is nothing but a firm assent of the mind: which if it be regulated, as is our *duty*, cannot be afforded to anything, but upon good reason; and so cannot be opposite to it. He [*sic*] that believes, without having any reason for believing, may be in love with his own fancies; but neither seeks truth as he ought, nor pays the obedience due his maker,

> who would have him use those discerning faculties he has given him, to keep him out of mistake and error. He that does not do this to the best of his power, however he sometimes lights on truth, is in the right but by chance; and I know not whether the luckiness of the accident will excuse the irregularity of his proceeding. This at least is certain, that he must be accountable for whatever mistakes he runs into: whereas he that makes use of the light and faculties God has given him, and seeks sincerely to discover truth, by those helps and abilities he has, may have this satisfaction in doing his duty as a rational creature, that though he should miss truth, he will not miss the reward of it. For he governs his assent right, and places it as he should, who in any case or matter whatsoever, believes or disbelieves, according as reason directs him. He that does otherwise, transgresses against his own light and misuses those faculties, which were given him . . . (Locke 1975, IV, 17, 24)[5]

For contemporary philosophers of religion, this passage from Locke reflects a key element in the modern, foundationalist tradition in epistemology. That is, the modern epistemologist finds herself or himself compelled by duty to give a proper, rational foundation in experience and proper reasoning to all claims of true belief. But notice that Locke's duty seems to be built upon the a priori assumption of God as creator and man as rational creature. Locke's implicit, even stronger claim is that there exists an epistemic duty (to his maker and to himself as a rational creature) not to accept – in this case – theistic belief unless it is certain with respect to what is probable in the light of empirical evidence and proper reasoning. Rational creatures have a duty not to believe anything which they have not proven by reason; even religious belief must be rationally justified as true.

Yet I might ask: What about Locke's own underlying belief in God himself as his maker? Can this belief be warranted by the rationality he uses to prove it? What could it mean if a rational creature's duty demanded a proof, with evidence and proper reasoning, of both his own maker and his own rationality? It seems that this is a problem of circularity or of begging the question: in order to prove a particular duty as rational, an assumption must be made already about rationality and the creator of that embodiment of rationality. Alternatively, in order to prove the existence of a creator of rationality, a particular embodiment of reason has been assumed. But what could ensure this move from an assumed contingent, particular duty to a necessary, general – indeed universal – form of reason? For me, the decisive difficulty in logical and evidential arguments for the existence of the theistic God is that a particular and specific embodiment of reason seeks to prove the existence of an independent form of universal reason. At one and the same time Locke aims to prove both his own rational duty and his own creator. (And note that this is the difficulty which Kant will subsequently confront.)

I should add that I do not consider whether or not revelation could ensure both God's existence as creator and man's nature as rational. In focusing strictly upon our epistemic duty, I give priority to reason over faith in revelation, leaving the latter concern to theologians. This is more or less consistent with Locke himself who warns against giving up reason for revelation; he associates the dangers of relying upon revelation with 'enthusiasm' and with what I would call fanaticism. Yet even if faith were confidently given priority over reason in revealing the rational duty of man to himself, this would still leave the theodicy question unanswered for women, who have been globally devalued. And here I have in mind theodicies which use faith not only to justify the theistic God's failure to eradicate gratuitous evil but to ratify the greater, innocent suffering of women on the grounds of their anatomy.

Returning to the question of reason's justification, Plantinga as a contemporary self-confessed nonfoundationalist philosopher of religion would insist that religious belief can be rationally warranted as true without evidential justification.[6] As explained in part I of this book, Plantinga introduces the notion of properly basic beliefs which can be rationally warranted without having to establish an evidential foundation for their truth. For example, Plantinga thinks that feeling forgiven could be a properly basic belief, if felt as a natural disposition and under certain circumstances; the belief is properly basic when I know of no positive reason for thinking that my experience of feeling forgiven might be delusive. According to Plantinga, it is on the basis of such properly basic beliefs as feeling forgiven that belief in God would be immediately justified.[7]

However, the question is: Who formulated this belief in feeling forgiven? The properly basic beliefs might merely be held as true due to their origin in the patriarchal social-symbolic order which constitutes our present culture and our western history. More generally stated, any supposed natural disposition could be determined by that same privileged male order, and so the example of feeling forgiven becomes questionable for women. In addition, it has been claimed by other philosophers of religion that Plantinga's nonfoundationalist justification of properly basic beliefs remains an argument on the basis of religious experience: that is, on the foundation of intense subjective perceptions.[8] From this I suggest that Plantinga does not avoid the unstable notion of experience to be discussed further on.

In the light of these specific examples of apparent circularity in empiricist claims to the rationality of religious belief, it seems appropriate to return to the question: Whose reason gives justification or warrant to Christian realist forms of theism?[9] More specifically, whose reason warrants Locke's account of God as creator of rational creatures? Here 'whose reason' means asking: Does the warrant for belief in a creator God come from a man's ideal of himself as rational creature projected onto his image of his own maker? One contemporary line of argument would assert that the white European man's reason simply justifies the belief (in his ideal self) which he in fact projects onto a transcendent father-figure.[10] Yet such an argument again forces my confrontation with the issues of circularity culminating in the question: Whose reason is in crisis? Is it only the reason of the 'man' who is preoccupied with formally rational justification?

It is important to recognize the critical implications for rationality and objectivity in this philosophical line of questioning. When asking further, for whom have the religious beliefs of empirical realist forms of theism been constructed, I am querying the supposed objectivity of the rational, individual, male-neutral subject of western philosophy and theology. After all, the rational subject who begins from the objective view-from-nowhere, understood in the sense of the God's-eye view, may promote ideas of omnipotence and omniscience which have dangerous consequences for religious beliefs and human values.[11] Justifying questions of religious belief from a God's-eye view can simply reinforce the power of the biased beliefs of privileged men and women.[12] The critical point becomes: the empirical realist forms of theistic beliefs are formulated exclusively for the subject as privileged, individual, rational, and male, or for the privileged woman who takes on this male-neutral stance. (This is a privileged stance with the pretense of classless, sex/gender neutrality.) Such idealizations of belief beg the questions of truth and justice, creating covert gendered ideals and excluding those who do not match the ideal as defective or inadequate.

The biases in justifying religious belief according to the supposed objectivity and rationality of empirical realism have been seen to affect women as well as men. For example, consider an Algerian woman's criticism of the empiricist bias in women's thinking, whether feminist or not: 'Academic women's work on Middle Eastern and North African women is dominated by the religious . . . paradigm and is characterized by a variant of . . . "abstracted empiricism". That is, the problems selected for study are limited by the method chosen to study them . . .' (Lazreg 1990, 329).[13] To develop this criticism, I would like to mention the important work done by philosophers of religion on the role of metaphor and models in the depiction of reality.[14] Although significant, this work has not moved philosophy of religion decisively beyond the weaknesses of an 'abstracted empiricism' which privileges western theism, despite efforts to include nonwestern accounts of religious experience.[15] To illustrate this, consider how the philosophical work on metaphor in religious language has enabled some theists to move beyond the naive realist position of theists who insist that all references to God must be stated in literal terms: the naive realist restricts description of religious truth to a particular model of God by maintaining that religious experience is only true to the degree that any metaphorical or ambiguous descriptions can be restated in the literal terms of traditional theism. In contrast, the critical realist has demonstrated that '"Critical realism" thus avoids both the naive realist's unsupportable claims about the primacy and incorrigibility of a particular model of God (together with the possible dangers of anthropomorphism) and the non-cognitivist's radical programme of demythologization, which reduces reports of religious experiences to poetically embellished statements about the human condition' (Franks Davis 1989, 14). So the critical realist account of religious experience can advance description beyond the naive realist's particular model of God by incorporating both literal and metaphorical statements of religious experience in its depiction of reality. Yet despite this significant advance, the critical realist descriptions of religious experience are still limited by the methods of abstracted empiricism which state and justify beliefs about a world already dependent upon the status quo of a very specific subject's perception. Hence an unstable tension exists between the dependence of empiricist knowledge upon the subject's own experiences and the independence of realist claims about the world from any single subject's experience. The abstracted method and idealized claims made by the empiricist subject about his or her experiences do not overcome this tension.[16] The resulting instability between the highly subjective and the general – indeed the universalized ideals – remains even if the subject's claims to individual religious experiences are stated metaphorically and confirmed by the linguistic continuity and shared associations of the subject's religious community.

Metaphorical statements about religious experiences are no more likely than literal assertions to change the empiricist's framework of individual and communal beliefs, their objects, their space and time framework – their world. The empiricist methods in the construction of beliefs are still determined by the privileged standpoint of the theist's values and norms.[17] Western theistic values color, while setting the norms for, the various empirical realist conceptions of religious experience. In turn, these conceptions maintain a privileged depiction of human and divine reality.

The problem is that a transformation of the dominant representations of reality cannot be achieved by mere comparison or redescription of empirical realist claims about the world in broader theistic terms. To confront this problem, I will suggest in the next chapter how a recent form of feminist epistemology aims to transform the standpoint of the empiricist subject in order to gain greater objectivity and less partial beliefs. And note that the unstable standpoint of the empiricist subject equally threatens certain feminist studies. Similar to the preceding criticisms of the theists who depend upon an abstracted empiricism in their depictions of reality, criticisms of an empiricist bias in feminist studies of world religions are articulated by Lazreg:

> the (particular) bias that suffuses most thinking about women in the Middle East and North Africa is expressed in a definite prejudice against Islam as a religion. Although U.S. feminists have attempted to accommodate Christianity and feminism, Judaism and feminism, Islam is inevitably presented as antifeminist. What is at work here is not merely a plausible rationalist bias against religion as an impediment to the progress and freedom of the mind but an acceptance of the idea that there is a hierarchy of religions. (Lazreg 1990, 329)

Fortunately there exist some serious proposals by various feminist epistemologists for collapsing the western hierarchy of belief. For this reason, I will follow the new proposals of certain feminist epistemologists in my endeavor to rethink the role of rationality in dominant forms of philosophy of religion. Thereby I strive to initiate the transformation of the overall framework of hierarchially biased, unconsciously partial, and ultimately pernicious religious beliefs.[18] Yet my proposed transformation does not necessarily aim to create a new or specifically female religion, even if this were to be for all women.

So, for instance, I avoid following Mary Daly in reversing the sexism of traditional Christian theology.[19] There may be temporary value in forms of separatism such as Daly's which is highly creative. But there seems to me little chance of any lasting virtue in merely changing the substance language of empirical realist forms of philosophy of religion in order to privilege the existential language of becoming woman.[20] In her early work, Daly puts across the valuable existential claim that every woman's action can be creative in transcending her condition and moving toward a new covenant of sisterhood. In her later work, she also offers important critical readings of religious myths as patriarchal paradigms.[21] Nevertheless Daly's overall project is open to the danger of instituting either new oppositions or new barriers between men and women. Daly herself tends to become a new female messianic or divine figure for women only.

My proposal is not to follow blindly either Daly or religious women who claim a revival of goddess worship and matriarchy. Instead, after having identified the contemporary crisis of rationality, I propose that religious knowledge be submitted to new epistemological scrutiny; and this includes religious knowledge in the modern philosophical sense of justified true belief according to the evidence and in the more recent philosophical sense of properly basic belief. My proposal relies upon recent work in feminist epistemologies. This work in epistemology enables vigilant ethical and political scrutiny of cognitive claims to the rationality or irrationality of religious belief.

3 The Empiricist Privileging of Formal Rationality

In this section, I would like to side-step momentarily any feminist issues concerning the sexed/gendered configurations of rational belief. This will allow me to develop a rough argument concerning our current everyday assumptions about rationality. Admittedly some readers may question the very possibility of this side-stepping.[22] The question is whether or not such rationality remains integral to the social-symbolic structure by which only male-gendered subjects have gained their autonomy and authority over the psychosexual. Does the social-symbolic order of rationality represent masculinity, while the place of desire and biological energies is repressed as femininity? If so, then even in this writing, as part of a patriarchal order, my language and reasoning would have to be at bottom male.

Notwithstanding any possible objection and despite any popular claims concerning a postmodern age of irrationality and relativism, I assume for the sake of this stage of my argument at least that western societies still tend to value a person, male or female, who appears to be rational – i.e. logical, consistent, coherent, credible, exhibiting a certain simplicity – with respect to her or his everyday beliefs, and regard it as a failing for a person to be irrational – i.e. illogical, inconsistent, incoherent, incredible, exhibiting a tendency to obfuscate in informal if not formal reasoning. Though it would be one thing for a belief to be rational and another thing for it to be true, again it could be assumed that most of us tend to think that rational beliefs are more likely to be true than either irrational beliefs or beliefs that are neither rational nor irrational. And, with certain qualifications, I might agree to retain many of the positive values that we normally – in the educated west – give to rationality. The next question to consider is whether or not religious beliefs are or are thought to be rational and, in this sense, true.

In their discussions concerning the rationality of the belief that God exists, contemporary Anglo-American philosophers of religion, especially those taking an empirical realist standpoint, have often debated the coherence[23] of the theistic concept of God as 'a person without a body who is eternal, is perfectly free, omnipotent, omniscient, perfectly good, and the creator of all things' (Swinburne 1991 [1979], 8–9).[24] One possible test for the rationality of this belief is the logical coherence or consistency of the theistic concept itself; but evidential consistency is also tested. Notably Swinburne uses a cumulative, causal argument to prove the coherence of a Christian realist form of theism on the grounds of the probability of the evidence for the existence of the traditional theist's God.

However, a critical and, for some, decisive issue of coherence arises for Swinburne's proof for the rationality of belief in the theistic God. That is, how is such belief compatible with the world created by this God, in which immeasurable amounts of moral and natural evil exist? Belief in the theistic God and the existence of evil creates both a logical and an evidential problem. As a logical problem, the intuitions about the pointlessness of evil events in the universe and the goodness of God form a set of prima facie incompatible propositions which must be made consistent; the classic argument that the existence of the theistic God is logically incompatible with the existence of evil in the world, generally attributed to David Hume (1711–76), is revived in this century, notably by J. L. Mackie.[25] As an evidential problem, there is a lack of fit between the existence of God and the reasons a good God might have for allowing evil; and this means a gap between evidence of the existence of a particular instance of evil and the postulated reason for God allowing it.

One contemporary critic, William Rowe, uses both a logical and an evidential argument concerning the problem of evil to demonstrate the inconsistency of theism. In Rowe's argument, the existence of evil is evidence against the existence of God: given what I know about the universe with the scale of evil it contains, belief in God is unreasonable. But Rowe admits that belief in God is not unreasonable because God's existence is logically incompatible with the existence of evil. Here he accepts – where others such as Mackie do not – that the existence of evil does not deductively entail the nonexistence of God. But then, in direct opposition to Swinburne in particular, Rowe maintains that the evil in the universe makes the existence of God improbable and so, in this sense, unreasonable.[26]

Similarly for feminists, the evidential problem of evil originates in the existence of pointless, gratuitous suffering of women in particular. If the evidence of suffering is decisive for women, the problem with traditional theism would be that the moral and natural evils suffered gratuitously by all nonprivileged living beings in the world would have greatly exceeded any reasonable limit for a supremely good, perfectly free, omnipotent God.

Swinburne's theodicy intends to counter the preceding position's logical and evidential problems by attempting to explain evil fully; he claims to give morally and rationally sufficient reasons for God's lack of intervention. Swinburne argues that the existence of creatures with free will warrants the existence of moral evil, and natural evil is warranted because it is a necessary condition for the exercise of that freedom. God's failure to prevent, for instance, Hitler's actions in order to save the Jews from innocent suffering is morally excusable because human free will would be of sufficient value, according to Swinburne, to warrant allowing the existence of the evils brought about by Hitler and the people associated with Hitler.[27]

Again in opposition to Swinburne, Rowe counters that even if God has a reason or purpose for his creatures in permitting some evil, this does not justify the extent of evil in this world for which there might be endless evidence. So Rowe's conclusion to the problem of evil is that the magnitude of evil in the universe is grossly disproportionate to any reason for allowing it, and so the existence of God in the light of the evidence of evil is improbable. More generally, for various critics of Christian realist forms of theism, the apparent logical incoherence of this concept of God, the improbability of his existence, and even his moral culpability have led to charges of inconsistency and immorality, ending in disbelief and atheism.[28]

In his theodicy, Plantinga maintains that whatever reasons God may have for allowing evil remain mysterious. And he builds a defense against Swinburne's probabilistic argument from evil, not by finding a morally sufficient reason for God, but rather by attacking the conceptions and uses of probability which undergird the cumulative evidence argument for traditional theism. Moreover Marilyn McCord Adams, who shares Plantinga's view that the reasons of God remain hidden from human minds, argues that the future experience of believers' union with Christ will atone for all evil suffered in this world; eternal union with Christ will make the evil which humans suffer in their lives minor by comparison. Hence she does not try to defend the justice of God in allowing evil, but argues that all suffering will be compensated.[29]

Briefly summarized, there are various contemporary defenses of God's justice which build upon the theodicies of ancient and modern philosophers, boldly developing their responses to atheistic critics such as Hume, Mackie, and Rowe. This history includes the theodicies of Swinburne, Plantinga, McCord Adams, and Stump, who continue rigorous defenses of traditional theism. And so theodicies continue to be standard topics for debates by contemporary, empirical realist philosophers of religion, theists and atheists alike.

Yet whether due to its lack of consistency or to its improbability, the theistic conception of God often does not satisfy contemporary philosophers. So the perceived failure to account for the amount and sorts of evil in the world can count decisively against the God of traditional theism; the logical and evidential problems of evil have led to the rejection of the Christian God by many contemporary men and women. In addition, finding no reason to believe that a patriarchal and anthropocentric God could be ethical or just in allowing the innocent and sex-specific suffering of women due to two thousand years of their unequal treatment, theologian Daphne Hampson underscores what is, for certain feminists, the immorality of the Christian God.[30] And Hampson's general claim only touches the surface of the unequal suffering of women. It can only encourage more in-depth studies of the particular, pernicious beliefs of traditional theists about female inferiority on the grounds of women's anatomy; these theistic beliefs have had highly specific and wide-ranging consequences for women.[31]

In this section, I began by presenting everyday assumptions concerning rationality and next sought to expose critical issues in the empiricist privileging of formally rational principles in their justifications of religious belief. Having confronted the logical and evidential problems of evil, I would like to encourage the reader to reflect upon questions concerning the material reality which has been excluded in biased constructions of theistic beliefs. These questions include the unequal and unjust treatment of women because of their social roles, their sex, desires, and bodily functions. The decisive question is: Has evil been ratified in the empiricists' rationally justified constructions of traditional theism?

4 Epistemological Frameworks of Belief

In focusing upon the rationality of religious belief, I do not intend to restrict myself to empirical realist arguments concerning God's justice in the face of the world's evil. Theodicy is not my primary concern. The more pressing aim is to raise prior questions about the very construction of the core belief of Jewish, Christian, and Muslim theisms. In particular, I question the construction of belief that God is a person, but without a body, eternal, perfectly free, omnipotent, omniscient, and perfectly good.[32]

As in preceding sections, a certain line of questions can be raised concerning empirical realist forms of theism. That is, whose reason warrants the core belief in the God of traditional theism, along with the other specific, highly ramified beliefs which accompany it? And from what content have theistic beliefs been constructed? Finally, for whom is the core belief of traditional theism formulated today?

To answer such questions, it is helpful to introduce new epistemological frameworks by which beliefs can be assessed, according to how they have been previously – covertly – formulated, structured, and conditioned. Generally speaking, this appears to be according to the method and goal of empirical realism. Three new epistemological frameworks delineated by feminists raise further questions concerning the material conditions for sexed/gendered configurations of rationality and religious belief.

First, there is feminist empiricism which, as a revised form of Enlightenment epistemology, accepts the empiricist method of justification and its goal in seeking objective knowledge. For instance, I noted that Locke's empiricist method bases belief upon evidence and proper reasoning. But as a feminist epistemology, feminist empiricism seeks to apply the empiricist method ever more rigorously and carefully to attain the justified true beliefs constituting knowledge and, ultimately, to eliminate any unacknowledged biases of androcentrism or sexism.

To illustrate briefly this form of epistemology, a feminist empiricist might attempt to purge the sexism and androcentrism from the empiricist examples in Swinburne's *The Existence of God* (1977). The task would not only be to render language inclusive (not the generic 'man', only language), but to expose biases in Swinburne's use of examples as evidence to support his arguments with infrequent references to women. This is a failure to apply rigorously enough his objective method. The feminist empiricist would undoubtedly find that, in his very few references to women, the women are never referred to as subjects of the examples. The subjects of Swinburne's examples are always only referred to as 'man,' as male with the pretence of sex/gender neutrality.[33] But more significantly the objects in these examples have to be women, since these involve explicit references to possessions of men or passive items for other men's seduction. Swinburne's mostly metaphorical references to women as objects in his examples are specifically to being married to beautiful women, to swallowing mother's pill, to inhibiting or cultivating affection for a woman (for a wife?), to married women who are in danger of being seduced by men who are not their husbands, to the mother of a man's children, especially the mother of the elder son, and to objects (women and children) which can be morally benefited or harmed, moulded or not.[34] To eliminate such sexism and androcentrism, the feminist empiricist would attempt to offer other more fair and objective examples in which women are not just passive objects to be controlled or harmed, desired or rejected, suffered or silenced.

Second, returning to the new epistemological frameworks, there is feminist standpoint epistemology. This second framework accepts neither the empiricist method nor its goal as sufficient grounds for objective knowledge or for rational justification of true belief. According to this standpoint, both the method and the goal of empiricism are affected – to a greater or lesser degree – by gender biases, including biases of sex, race, class, and ethnicity.[35] Essentially the contention of feminist standpoint epistemology is that a deep and pervasive sex/gender bias exists in modern science and modern epistemology. In particular, it is claimed that

> [These feminists] have criticized modern foundationalist epistemologies and moral and political theories, exposing the contingent, partial, and historically situated character of what has passed in the mainstream for necessary universal, and ahistorical truths. They have called into question the dominant philosophical project of seeking objectivity in the guise of a 'God's eye view' which transcends any situation or any perspective. (Nicholson and Fraser 1990, 26; cf. Harding 1983; 1993)

Originally informed by the philosophies of Hegel and Karl Marx (1818–85) amongst others, feminist standpoint epistemology aims both to acknowledge the social situatedness of the very best beliefs which any culture has arrived at or could in principle discover, and to use the knowledge of one's historicity and social situatedness as a resource for generating less partial and less false beliefs.[36] So the feminist standpoint epistemologist would not follow the attempts of the feminist empiricist merely to eliminate sexism and androcentrism by trying to apply the empiricist's own method more rigorously. But very importantly this position aims to propose a new, stronger conception of objectivity which nevertheless refuses to give up rationality or realism for relativism.

Third, there is feminist poststructuralism. Admittedly this position might be identifed as anti-epistemology, since the feminist poststructuralist clearly rejects the essential structure of male rationality, its objectivity and the patriarchal beliefs which go with it, as part of the dominant symbolic order. Yet the feminist poststructuralist is informed by post-Lacanian psycholinguistics which focuses upon language as the condition for all possible meaning and value; and the feminist poststructuralist studies language as a dynamic structure or process which has constituted (male) subjectivity and sexual identity. This distinctive focus means a critical advance on empiricist and standpoint epistemologies in not studying language merely as an object, and not studying language in the different uses given to particular words. One consequence of this is that the feminist poststructuralist aims to unearth the content of female desire and the expressions of sexual differences.[37] And it is this twofold aim which, in my view, is highly significant for feminist epistemologists.

Thus whether by feminist empiricism or by feminist standpoint epistemology, or even by the psycholinguistics of feminist poststructuralism, Enlightenment epistemology is shown to determine the gender-status given to rationality in logical, coherent, consistent sets of beliefs and actions.[38] Depending upon which of the three frameworks is used, a new epistemology might then be able (i) to purge rationality of sexism; (ii) to seek less partial standpoints on rationality according to concrete, material differences; or (iii) to subvert rationality as inherently male and patriarchal. Furthermore feminist epistemologies scrutinize the ethical truth and justice of logical, coherent, or simple (uncomplicated so more likely to be true) beliefs and actions for women in general, and for men and women of nondominant races, classes, and ethnicities, in particular. Why are uncomplicated beliefs more likely to be true? Arguably this use of simplicity conceals the greater and more complex reality of subjects and objects.

For instance, I might ask: Why has the specific hypothesis of a supremely good and all-powerful God been formulated, retained, and justified on the basis of such rational principles as those of coherence, of simplicity, of credulity, while seemingly ignoring or glossing over an inexplicable world of natural disasters, innocent suffering, human violence, over two thousand years of unequal treatment of women as half the human race, besides untold wars of ethnic and racial cleansing? This world includes evils and inequalities resulting directly from empirical and patriarchal frameworks of belief. Has the coherence of theism been achieved only by excluding just enough significant material content of desire, defilement, and death to ensure that moral evils, one's own biases, and anything which does not cohere do not threaten to undermine that very coherence of theism?

Why have various contemporary forms of monotheism, especially those appropriated from the Old Testament including fundamentalist forms of Judaism, Christianity, and Islam, been allowed to repress sexual, racial, and ethnic differences? It is practically incomprehensible yet actually the case that specific patriarchal beliefs have been retained even though marginalizing women and all nonprivileged beings. Yet it is indisputable that male figures of authority have dominated the various world religions, while marginalizing various female beliefs and the diversity of female emotions and actions, especially actions of female dissent.[39]

If, at the very least, the God of an empirical realist form of Christian theism is recognized as a male conception in the sense of a projection of ideal, masculine, and paternal attributes, then numerous questions arise concerning the relationship between this God and the necessarily oppressive conditions of life for women, believers and nonbelievers, and of all those who reject this form of theistic belief.[40] By oppression, I mean the specific relations of domination that are concealed and legitimized by the material, social, economic, cultural, and political conditions of patriarchy. So oppression should not be equated with depression or repression, as something wrong with an individual's psychology which can be altered by or cured in that individual. Instead due to the intricate nature of its interrelated conditions, oppression involves much more complexity than an individual consciousness can perceive; and so it is much more resistant to reform than either depression or repression. Essentially, oppressive conditions can only be structurally transformed.

Ironically, contemporary readings in philosophy of religion have far too frequently ruled out the significance of the nineteenth-century challenges posed to theism by Karl Marx, Friedrich Nietzsche (1844–1900) and Sigmund Freud (1856–1939) in particular.[41] Philosophers of religion of a certain empiricist persuasion have tended to call the challenges of these three thinkers reductive and, in so doing, have eclipsed their real significance for the construction of religious belief.[42] But in fact I might ask: Isn't it exactly the reverse? Hasn't the empirical realist reduced religion to a neat set of coherent beliefs only on the basis of either intense subjective perceptions (often of intellectually, culturally, ethnically, or racially privileged individuals) or a priori hypotheses about an eternal, perfectly good, omnipotent, omniscient, personal creator God? If so, should the popular alternative be to formulate a female concept in the sense of a feminine divine with another neat set of ideal attributes for women's sexual identity?

I again mention Mary Daly's affirmative answer to this question. This leads Daly to develop what can be described as a feminist reversal of Christian philosophy of religion – in which Daly herself becomes a Christ figure or ideal archetype – in a pilgrimage toward a post-Christian sisterhood of believers. But, as already intimated, it is necessary to recognize the potential problems with such feminist reversals of sexism. In addition to the dangers for truth and justice in any permanent form of female separatism, Daly presents what needs to be criticized as a nostalgia for religious normativity and unity; she claims to celebrate female becoming. But this exclusive emphasis on female becoming and sisterhood renders her position reactionary. Unfortunately in emerging out of a reaction to men, to patriarchal man, to Christianity, Daly's philosophy only changes the syntax of the male philosophy of religion. Her early work merely reverses the sexism with a new female form of methodological individualism.

The decisive problem is that the early Daly lacks the tools, despite her laudable efforts on behalf of all women, to transform social-symbolic structures or to achieve a dialogue which works to break down oppositions. Audre Lorde's 'Open Letter to Mary Daly' emphasizes the ultimate danger of racism and sexism resulting from Daly's reactionary point of view on religion.[43] However, before rushing to criticize Daly, my intention is to propose that for persons, whether male or female, to be rational with respect to their religious beliefs, it should be imperative both to probe the individual construction of their central beliefs and to examine the hypotheses which become the ground of justified true beliefs. Ideally such probing and examining would be aided by feminist epistemology. Whether the sex-bias of a Daly or a Swinburne is assessed, there remains an inevitable confrontation with the issue of whose beliefs these are. For whom have they been formulated?

5 Questioning the Neutrality of Rationality

In the context of the present book, I am asking: Whose rationality has formulated biased theistic beliefs? This is to challenge the supposed neutrality of rational belief in the light of concrete differences between embodied beings. Although Daly has every right to react to biased beliefs, such as the belief that a woman is inferior because of her anatomy, it is important to query even further whether new reactionary beliefs offer an adequate solution to sexism or racism.[44]

On one level of thinking, the rationality of religious belief is taken to be a feminist issue insofar as the supposed rational belief needs to be scrutinized for its fairness to women generally, to specific nonprivileged believers, and to nonbelievers in the underlying hypotheses or the dominant, core concept of the divine. On another level, sexual difference and desire remain resistant to scrutiny in terms of formal reasoning about fairness and equality; so I return to this other level of reflection at the end of the present section.

Concerning fairness, for instance, I might scrutinize the core concept of a personal deity as presented in Christian realist forms of theism. The basic assertion of the existence of this God is part of a restricted account in the sense of not including such ramified beliefs as belief in the atonement of Jesus Christ.[45] However, I might try reversing the argument: Does in fact the restricted theism necessarily entail the expanded theism, including various ramified beliefs which make false assumptions about women?[46] Was it first necessary to assume the core beliefs in the existence of the theistic God in order to articulate expanded theism? Perhaps the core belief in an eternal, perfectly good, perfectly free, omniscient, omnipotent, personal creator God has been presupposed before arriving at the redemptive purposes of this supremely good God in creating man as rational but morally free. But the decisive question is: Could the unramified belief have led to the justification of any other form of theism, except Christian realism? If not, then if the expanded theism is improbable (saying nothing about its immorality), would the restricted theism be less probable?

Certainly there are other forms of theism, such as other theistic forms of Christianity, theistic forms of both Judaism and Islam, and possibly even Buddhist or Hindu forms of theism including henotheism or polytheism.[47] Yet only a certain dominant, patriarchal form of theism appears to result necessarily from the restricted theism of empirical realists. The result is monotheism or monistic privilegings of the mind over the body, and man over woman. The consequence for women of this epistemological privileging is the consistent domination of mind over body, implying female inferiority and devaluing female anatomy, in creating and sustaining life from birth to death. The myth of female inferiority, configured according to anatomical differences, survives in various covert and overt ways, despite any evidence to the contrary.

A logical question to ask, if the highly ramified beliefs of Christian theism are presupposed as further explanation of the restricted form of theism, is whether the rationality of the expanded theism has already been assumed in assessing the unramified, core belief. Simply put, has the question of the rationality of belief been begged? The highly ramified beliefs of empirical realist forms of (Christian) theism include beliefs about the incarnation of God in Jesus Christ and in the doctrine of atonement which claims to reunite human sinners with God.[48] It follows that these beliefs also presuppose very specific but largely detrimental beliefs surrounding the Virgin Mother.[49]

I arrive at the conclusion that the dominant form of restricted theism (along with various expanded versions) must be scrutinized for what appear to be not only unwarranted, but unjust privilegings of men over women, certain men over other men, and men over nature.[50] And I wonder why such unjust and unwarranted beliefs have dominated and can still dominate two thousand years of western history. Unequal relations of power can be shown to have been one-sidedly consolidated in terms of sex/gender, race, ethnicity, and class, over periods of patriarchal history.[51] As the familiar patriarchal beliefs begin to look strange under scrutiny, it seems amazing that certain contemporary women philosophers of religion have accepted the rationally unwarranted and unjust privileging of men and their Father-God by willingly deferring to the authority of religious leaders, whether counsellors or confessors, Roman Catholic priests or Buddhists monks. But I feel compelled to do more than just wonder whether any relationship between an individual religious authority and an individual believer who is a female or a supposedly inferior male is ever neutral. It seems to be more ethical and just to acknowledge all such one-to-one, hierarchically structured relationships as potentially unfair, ranging from mildly exploitative to abusive.[52] There is an urgent need to find the means to disrupt and refigure religious configurations which sustain excessively unequal relations of power, especially on the basis of sex, race, ethnicity, or class.

Stated more directly, in this and future chapters I hope to expose a scandal of largely unacknowledged proportions in the circular reasoning of patriarchal forms of theism: despite its fallacious nature, this reasoning has been used to justify rationally a set of objective, coherent, credible, and simple or, simply, properly basic beliefs. The very hegemony of such a set of beliefs has prevented recognition of the unselfconsciously biased construction of beliefs which, in turn, has resulted in violent and oppressive consequences for women, other nonprivileged persons, and animals. Ironically, despite its circularity, this reasoning has been done in a highly sophisticated manner. This can be seen most clearly in contemporary analytic philosophers' defenses of the unramified beliefs at the heart of Christian realist forms of theism. As already noted, unramified means restricted to certain core theistic beliefs which, allegedly, are compatible with other forms of religious belief.[53]

For example, returning to the specific case of Swinburne and his philosophy students, a great amount of rigor has been applied by these Swinburnians to evaluating the evidence for the existence of God.[54] According to Swinburne himself, this includes evidence for the existence of a complex physical universe implying that

> It is very unlikely that this universe could exist uncaused, but rather more likely that God would exist uncaused. The existence of the universe is strange and puzzling. It can be made comprehensible if we suppose that it is brought about by God. This supposition postulates a simpler beginning for explanation than does the supposition of the existence of an uncaused universe, and that is grounds for believing the former supposition to be true. (Swinburne 1991, 131–2)

In the above passage, Swinburne makes his crucial appeal to the rational principle of simplicity in order to support his restricted belief in a core idea of God. On the basis of various evidence and in the light of the probability of this evidence, Swinburne claims restricted belief in a God who intentionally brings about the existence of the universe.[55] And initially Swinburne admits that one does not know from the evidence of a complex, physical universe what God's intentions were in acting to cause such phenomena. Yet both Swinburne and Franks Davis move from the evidence for their restricted beliefs to support the ramified beliefs of specifically Christian theism concerning atonement and God's purposes.[56]

This philosophical reasoning from restricted theistic belief to the highly ramified beliefs of Christianity becomes increasingly sophisticated as contemporary philosophers of religion assume and actively defend the existence of a personal creator God, especially in its empirical realist forms.[57] However, I do worry that these rational defenses are constructed, despite the injustices and inequalities being projected onto innocent and suffering nonprivileged others for whom evil is a daily reality and free will virtually meaningless.

In the end, empirical realist forms of theism appear reductive in reflecting only the present patriarchal privileging of father over son. The greater problem for women and marginalized men is that the father/son opposition also implies that the privileged male (philosopher) has power over the nonprivileged male or female student, and male mentor (or other student) over female student. Reflected in each of these relations is a hierarchy, whereby the first term is always given greater value and power. But why should such hierarchical relations go unchecked in our contemporary world? It may be inevitable that students of prominent philosophers, initially, act as supporters or as amanuenses to their mentors' (or partners') arguments.[58] But often, despite the integrity of individual academics, patriarchal structures reinforce and perpetuate a sexist privileging of philosophers (which typically implies male) with additional, longstanding inequalites and barriers for women philosophers of religion.

Faithfulness to the work of the philosophical (again, typically male) mentor might be assessed in terms of 'the Héloïse complex' which Michèle Le Doeuff so elegantly and provocatively describes.[59] Le Doeuff's contention is that there exists a specific danger for women here: a woman's admiration for her male mentor, which as a philosopher he genuinely needs, prevents her from seeing the value of her own thinking. This prevents the faithful woman from scrutinizing the rationality of her own beliefs, emotions or feelings, and desires.

In the classic case of Héloïse (1101–64) and Abelard (1079–1142), a female student of philosophy and her male mentor, there is the tragic and true story of a medieval couple's love and romance; and Héloïse's love seems to have endured, despite all its adverse consequences. In 1118, when Abelard is teaching philosophy in Paris, he has already (at the age 39) acquired an international reputation as a teacher and scholar of, especially, Aristotelian philosophy. At this time, Canon Fulbert asks Abelard to come to live with him and his highly intelligent niece, Héloïse, in order to give her private lessons in philosophy. A love affair quickly develops between teacher and student. The result is not only a pregnancy and the birth of a son, Astrolabe, but the wrath of Héloïse's uncle. Canon Fulbert insists upon a marriage between Abelard and Héloïse; the couple agree but insist upon keeping the marriage secret in order to save Abelard's reputation as a medieval philosopher. In twelfth-century Europe, a philosopher could not both do philosophy and be married; anyone who did marry descended from a superior to an inferior order. Yet Canon Fulbert becomes infuriated at the secrecy of the married couple who intend to maintain Abelard's reputation above his niece's; and so the uncle sends some men to castrate Abelard by night. The story continues with Abelard becoming an abbot in Brittany and Héloïse living out the rest of her life in a convent, eventually as an abbess. This true story is told in both Abelard's *Historia calamitatum mearum* and the letters of the two former lovers.[60]

As suggested already, the crucial aspect of the Héloïse complex is that the female student remains devoted to her mentor who, in turn, is in need of his student's admiration for his social and institutional status as a philosopher; a philosopher's reputation depends solely upon the successful dissemination of his ideas and arguments. In addition, the Héloïse complex means that at most the female student becomes a loving admirer who faithfully reproduces her teacher's philosophy as either a conscientious amanuensis or a faithful disciple; and this achievement also means that if, by chance, the woman succeeds at producing original philosophy herself, she does it unawares.[61]

Ironically in the face of claims to autonomous thinking in philosophy, the degree to which philosophical tradition has depended upon a few highly selective male figures or archetypes is remarkable. Admittedly within this tradition it is not only female students who remain faithful disciples of their mentors or partners in philosophy. There is also a long history of male philosophy students, from Platonists and Aristotelians to Plantingians or Swinburnians, becoming disciples, even preparing eulogies for their mentors.[62] But it remains a social and cultural fact that there have not yet been recorded in past or recent history the same numbers of women who, moving beyond faithfulness to their philosophical mentors, become renowned philosophers in their own right. Women in particular have too often in past philosophical history remained dependent supports *vis-à-vis* 'great,' male philosophers. As Le Doeuff explains, these women remain loyal to their philosophy mentors even when they have written philosophy without any recognition, since they have not generally had any other more direct access to doing philosophy or to institutions of philosophy.

The other example which Le Doeuff gives of a woman philosopher apparently suffering from an Héloïse-like complex is from twentieth-century French philosophy. This example is the now classic second-wave feminist Simone de Beauvoir (1908–86), who remained totally devoted to the French philosopher and her exact contemporary Jean-Paul Sartre (1905–80), despite her work on woman as the second sex. Again this identification is not meant to degrade the one who suffers from the Héloïse complex. To the contrary, in her more recent reflections on Beauvoir, Le Doeuff contends that certainly Beauvoir produced philosophy unawares.[63] So to suggest that any particular woman suffers from the Héloïse complex is not necessarily a personal criticism of that woman herself; rather it is a possible fact about her situation which should compel a more careful reading of her writings in order to discover if she, like other unrecognized women, produced unacknowledged or wrongly acknowledged philosophy – which has yet to become known.

Of course the problem of excluding certain individuals from being recognized as philosophers is wider than exclusion by sex. Philosophy today still tends to remain an institution for privileged men of a certain class and culture, or women and men who become privileged by being recognized within the philosophical tradition. The continuing, often blind privileging of male figures as mentors is a crucial source of the sex-biased, gender-biased, class-biased, and so partial nature of religious beliefs.

Le Doeuff offers this summation of the problem:

> Here we find a stereotype in philosophical liaisons. Since the days of Antiquity, women have been admitted into the field of philosophy chiefly when they took on the role of loving admirer: we can call this the 'Héloïse complex' . . . Worse (today), one is commonly asked whether one is a this man-ian or a that man-ian . . . I have long been doing my best to show that it is time for women to stop being the devoted followers . . . and that, once one becomes a whoeverian, that is the end of philosophy and of the desire for intellectual independence which should also be a characteristic of feminism. (Le Doeuff 1991, 59–60; cf. Le Doeuff 1989, 105, 117–20)[64]

Now on another level of reflection, the rationality of belief becomes a feminist issue in an even more problematic sense than the questions of fairness and the recognition of formal inequalities suggest. Feminist post-structuralists in particular have begun to address fundamental questions of sexual difference. Sexual difference and desire remain resistant to a formal level of rational scrutiny, since generally repressed or, in some sense, hidden. This further issue of rationality for feminists emerges once questions of the material conditions and content of religious belief are raised directly. I raise these questions here not to reject rationality, but to rethink its apparent neutrality.[65]

At this deeper level of thinking, it might be useful to consider rejecting one position on the neutrality of rationality in order to accept another. On the one hand, I might reject feminist positions which intend to preserve the scientific (cognitive-instrumental) rationality of empirical realism, even if possibly in a form purged of some surface gender-biases as manifested in unfairness and formal inequalities. On the other hand, I propose to follow an alternative feminist position which takes seriously Enlightenment versus postmodernist debates about epistemology and sexual difference. But this alternative still leaves a further choice between a radical and a reformist feminism.

In order to grapple with this further choice, it is worthwhile to tease out the ways in which feminism and postmodernism have an uncertain affinity, especially on the question of rationality. Many feminist positions, including those proposed in this book, ultimately choose to diverge from the extremes of postmodernism. This means that in chapter 2, for instance, I do not give up completely the modern, Enlightenment project of epistemology and its claims concerning the autonomous use of reason. Neither, in chapter 3, do I assume that an essential female desire exists which should be valued more highly than an essential male reason; nor do I use feminist poststructuralism to argue against epistemology.

6 Refiguring Rationality

Three deaths, metaphorically speaking, have been identified as marking the postmodern challenge to the specific forms of domination constituted by western philosophy.[66] The metaphorical deaths represent challenges to the dominance of (i) the rational subject, (ii) the single historical narrative of man's progress, and (iii) the metaphysics of presence or logocentrism. However, these postmodern challenges to philosophy in western societies do not converge perfectly with feminism and its goals, including the critique of philosophy, as they have been dominated by white western males.[67]

In particular, there is a problem for many feminists with the first 'death', that of the autonomous rational subject. Although the crisis of rationality proclaimed by advocates of postmodernism may initially converge with feminism, this convergence is not total. For instance, a feminist might criticize the dominant image of rationality as the man of reason, or criticize the equation of rationality with masculinity, but still not give up reason as a philosophical tool. Roughly speaking, reformist feminists[68] have made it a crucial aspect of their goal for women to enable female philosophers and others finally to achieve what they have long been denied: the autonomomy and integrity of action and belief which are paradigmatically represented in western ethical and intellectual circles by the rational subject. In fact the question of whether or not the rational subject of western philosophy should be rejected as male or reformed as a misrepresentation of rationality has produced a crisis internal to feminism.[69]

Essentially feminists disagree as to the significance of the metaphorical death of the man of reason, of the subject of male subjectivity, or simply, of the rational subject. On the one hand, certain feminists try to correct injustices by reforming accounts of the subject of rationality. These accounts have symbolized the subject as male, especially in relation to the God who represents ideal masculine and paternal attributes, in western philosophy and theology. But the reformist feminist remains cautious about a death of autonomous, rational agency, since such agency would be something women have never had, yet something they have sought from the inception of feminist movements for equal education, equal rights, and all sorts of more concrete freedoms.

On the other hand, there are feminists who might be called radical in celebrating the death of the rational subject as the death of the dominant male rule of western history. These radical feminists equate rationality with masculinity and so claim to repudiate it. Their equation is radical, not conservative, in asserting female difference as a site of marginality which, ironically, can become a site of epistemic privilege. Although conservative women have also endeavored to reclaim female difference, they do so without seeking to undermine patriarchal structures. To generalize: for the more radical feminist, male rationality, as well as the male hierarchy of beliefs, must be subverted. There must be no acquiescence by women to male divinity, authority, and rationality, and so no female submission to, or acceptance of, vulnerability.

However, it is not clear either how rationality can come to any decisive end or how the rational subject could be dead, unless rationality is assumed to be a particular cultural construct which could be given up. But it would seem that rationality is something more fundamental than a cultural construct, despite its different embodiments.

Yet how could feminists who intend to argue against specific injustices have the appropriate tools to do so without some criteria of rational argumentation which directly tackle the injustice? Or how could it make sense for feminists to seek the power to act for their own needs and interests if rational agency is given up? The feminist position, which seeks to embrace the death of the rational subject in order to achieve such goals as women's release from oppressive structures, appears self-defeating. Furthermore a rejection of rationality might play into the hands of misogynists who maintain the irrationality of women, or at least their lack of male rationality, as the grounds for women's marginalization and oppression.

Here is the view of a skeptical feminist:

> But traditional rationality has not justified the oppression of women. Men have claimed that it has, but that is a quite different matter; and it is not difficult to show that most of the arguments that have been doing the rounds for centuries are full of kindergarten mistakes in logic. If instead of exposing these, feminists demand new standards of rationality and logic, and make claims about feminist work that is [quoting Grosz] 'quite logical, rational, and true in terms of quite different criteria, perspectives, and values than those dominant now' they might just as well wrap them up in pretty paper and send them off to patriarchal man as a birthday present. (Radcliffe Richards 1991 [1980], 415)

Although an extremely strong statement, I will consider this criticism of more radical feminist views of a new sort of nondominant, nonpatriarchal rationality as valuable to a certain degree in advancing my present critical argument. If the standards of rationality, which function in our everyday world, were simply rejected, this could support the status quo of patriarchy. If the sort of rationality of belief which men and women tend to privilege in their thinking and living were simply given up by women, such action could end in ghettoizing women. This is especially likely if the rationality of belief were completely replaced by a new religion of Women, who separated on the grounds of their own logic, in a reactionary sisterhood.[70]

And yet the skeptical feminist quoted above does not understand fully the psychoanalytic account of rationality on which the poststructuralist feminists build their criticisms. What seems to be misunderstood is that rationality as an Enlightenment concept has been criticized by the feminist poststructuralists for being equated with masculinity.[71] This equation has been made by those who take the social-symbolic order to be male, while femininity constitutes the unconscious; femininity then underlies the discursive order of male rationality but emerges in symbols and myths. Taking this poststructuralist argument seriously, my later chapters explore the possibility of refiguring desire. However, this does not mean reason is to be given up.

Consider for a moment the argument that social-symbolic order constitutes rationality as masculine. The actual problem for reason as employed in contemporary philosophical defenses of religious belief is, then, quite specific. The fallacious reasoning in empirical realist forms of theism is constantly reinforced by specific myths which constitute the symbolic exclusion of the female other as irrational on intellectual grounds.

Yet my contention in this book is that rationality should not be assumed to be something that can be given up. Instead the sex/gender-biased symbolism, which has defined rationality, needs to be refigured. Ideally reason figured more inclusively would transcend the falsehoods, fallacies, and phantasies of partial and pernicious beliefs.

Perhaps surprisingly, Kant's vindication of reason from the eighteenth century supports the present proposal for a refiguration of rationality. The following argument from Kant, concerning reason's self-critical capacity, will be used in an inclusive refiguring of freedom:

> Reason must in all its undertakings subject itself to criticism; should it limit freedom of criticism by any prohibitions, it must harm itself, drawing upon itself a damaging suspicion. Nothing is so important through its usefulness, nothing so sacred, that it may be exempted from this searching examination, which knows no respect for persons. Reason depends on this freedom for its very existence. For reason has no dictatorial authority; its verdict is always simply the agreement of free citizens, of whom each one must be permitted to express, without let or hindrance, his objection or even his veto. (Kant 1950 [1781, 1787], 593, A738–9/B766–7)

To be fair, free citizens can and must be refigured so that 'his' objection or 'his' veto renders those of women and men of any class, race, ethnicity, or sex-orientation.[72] The male symbolism of reason may render rationality as free masculinity and irrationality as unfree femininity. It is precisely such symbolic configurations of fixed gender-identity which need urgently to be refigured if sex, race, and class (which arguably cannot be separated from gender constructions) are not to be an impediment to reason which freely scrutinizes religious belief; and to be consistent with Kant's practical reason, true belief would have to ensure the equality and autonomy of fully embodied beings.[73]

7 A Critique of Reason

It is impossible to do total justice to the significance of the scandal of circularity played out by the rationality of religious belief in empirical realist forms of theism. Already in the eighteenth century, Kant maintains the significance of a critique of pure reason. Kant's first *Critique* is a vindication of reason which could never have appealed merely to the presumed principles it proposed to vindicate; otherwise the vindication would have been recognized as circular and so would immediately have failed. No Kantian would miss the circular reasoning in empiricist appeals to the rational principles of simplicity, of credulity, of coherence which, at the same time, seek to vindicate rationality. Kant's reading of the Copernican revolution in epistemology means that no direct correspondence of rationality to reality can be presumed. Kant's use of reason is not reduced to the empirical realism of Locke or Hume which he equates with the understanding alone.

Swinburne himself criticizes Kant. According to Swinburne, Kant reduces the different forms of the arguments for the existence of God to three unnuanced types: (i) the physico-theological (or argument from design), (ii) the cosmological, and (iii) the ontological arguments.[74] While Kant contends that all three types of arguments for God's existence fail, Swinburne counters that 'Kant tends to assume that there can only be one argument of each type – whereas in fact there can quite clearly be many different arguments under each heading which are so different from each other that it would be misleading to call them forms of the same argument at all' (Swinburne 1991, 11–12). Swinburne does not accept, or is unwilling to understand, that Kant's criticism does allow for grouping different arguments under the same heading precisely insofar as they exhibit one of three distinctive types of decisive weaknesses which renders each sort and so any of them an unsound argument. These weaknesses are (i) that the universe as a whole cannot be known in-itself as evidence for a transcendent maker, as a well-ordered object in need of a designer; (ii) that the idea of the universe in need of 'an uncaused cause' is doubly unintelligible: it is wrong to assume both that the universe is an empirical thing or knowable class of things and that it can constitute knowledge of God as a cause outside of the empirical realm of causation; (iii) that existence is not a predicate which when attached to a concept adds something to that concept. For Kant, it would not matter if there were many more different arguments under each heading. All the arguments would still fail due to these three decisive weaknesses which, according to Kant, render fallacious any empirical or a priori argument for the existence of God; hence any empirical realist form of theistic argument would be fallacious.

Swinburne criticizes Kant for failing to be attentive to various possible forms of empirical arguments for the existence of God. He claims that this lack of attention results in skepticism. But it then appears surprising that Swinburne himself fails to be attentive to the various arguments formulated by Kant concerning reason and the empirical world; and these are arguments against both skepticism and dogmatism. I might admit, in order to follow Swinburne's argument, that Kant's three forms of criticism of empirical and a priori arguments for God could be, or could become, irrelevant in the light of contemporary advances in scientific observation of the unobservable.[75] However, it would follow that the empirical realist claims about God, self, and reason should not preclude serious consideration of contemporary scientific advances in philosophical psychology (including psychoanalysis and sociobiology), linguistic sciences, sociology of knowledge, even certain philosophies of science (especially of the social constructionist variety). Too often a more complete picture of human reality is sacrificed for the sake of simplicity. Certain philosophical arguments seem to have unwittingly assumed simplicity as a virtue even when it is not.[76]

The occurrence of the scandal of circular reasoning in empirical realist forms of theism is particularly worrying since this circularity is patently inconsistent with its perpetrators' nonfideist stances. Nonfideist describes a self-conscious stance of rationality as a corrective to blind faith. First, I am not persuaded that either Plantinga, on the one hand, or Swinburne, on the other hand, gets around Kant's criticisms of speculative metaphysics. In the 'Transcendental Dialectic' in the *Critique of Pure Reason*, Kant himself seeks to demonstrate that any view of principles of reason as divinely determined rules of thought which correspond to reality would lead to contradictions, including paralogisms, antinomies, and unintelligibilities.[77]

But second, and more important for women philosophers and non-philosophers than logical inconsistencies, there are unacknowledged issues of ethical truth and justice. These issues arise from the circular reasoning of privileged white European male philosophers, whose belief in a projection of their own ideal of supreme goodness and power excludes, in blindness about sex, gender, race, class of western and nonwestern women, other less privileged fathers, mothers, sons, and daughters.

Notwithstanding these problems with philosophical justifications of religious belief, my proposal is that there exist other philosophical tools which can be put to feminist use for the transformation of the religious beliefs which have been asserted but fallaciously justified. Here I mean specifically those theistic beliefs which have merely confirmed the patriarchal status quo of a genderized hierarchy of personal and political relations. Beliefs concerning evil, sin, and an all-powerful God's supreme goodness exhibit the most obvious injustices to women. The logical consequence of such beliefs is that women are to accept the gratuitous and disproportionate evil, which they have suffered for centuries, due to the implications of these theistic beliefs for their sexual, social, and spiritual lives.

But the bias against women goes even deeper; it goes to the heart of a rational enterprise which has assumed that the rational subject, in formulating hypotheses and beliefs, takes a position beyond all aspects of historicity and contingency, even his own materially conditioned status. This 'rational' position has been necessarily masculine, since it rests upon the male subject's projection of his intractable physicality and contingency onto the female other who, in contrast, is excluded as feminine from the rational enterprise.

Philosophers of religion give privilege to the male point of view by configuring, in their examples and myths, the female other as a possession, a commodity, or a thing which is vulnerable to defilement and abjection. On a larger historical scale in western mythology and theology, women have been associated with sexual desire, especially with the passion or inordinate desire (i.e. concupiscence) which, for those who follow Augustine, constitutes sin.[78] The result is the virtual eclipse of the female voice in configurations of religious beliefs concerning reason and desire, and good and evil.

Notably this eclipse is represented mythically in configurations of Eve and Mary as the Second Eve, and in configurations of the Penitent Mary Magdalene and the Virgin Mary. Unmarried women are configured as either whores or saints, while married women can never achieve the perfection figured by the Virgin Mother.[79] The following is asserted of the historical configuration of the myth and the cult of the Virgin Mary: 'There is no place in the conceptual architecture of Christian society for a single woman who is neither a virgin or a whore' (Warner 1976, 235).

In chapters 4 and 5, I will propose new uses of myth and mimesis, aiming to enable the self-reflexive, communal, and critical rethinking of entrenched positions in philosophy of religion. Philosophical positions concerning religious belief are often difficult to dislodge. This is especially true when the rational justification of religious belief is founded upon reason conceived to be disembodied and superior to desire, love, death, and so to all those realities largely excluded from philosophy but portrayed in myth.

My proposal for an alternative to a disembodied conception of rationality is not to replace rational defenses of religious belief with mythical reflections; and it is not to replace reason with desire. Instead I will encourage attempts at collapsing the opposition between a rational subject and his own materially conditioned status as projected onto the female other. This is a precarious opposition which nonetheless has characterized modern, Enlightenment rationality and so such rational enterprises as contemporary philosophy of religion.

A central challenge for a feminist philosophy of religion rests in the sexed/gendered configurations of rationality. Thus I intend to confront the feminist philosopher with the task of finding tools for the refiguring of the mythical configurations which (often unwittingly) accompany rationally justified belief. A critique of reason, in its justification of theism, would uncover the partial and biased beliefs which have been given privilege by patriarchal forms of belief. Yet I stress again that my proposal to use mimetic refigurations of sexed/gendered configurations of rationality and irrationality is not to throw out reason altogether; there are no new logical criteria to replace reason; myth does not replace philosophy. Instead it is necessary to revise and supplement the construction of theistic belief; a key source for this revision is the significant material content of belief which often appears in myth, but has been devalued.

Notes

1. Descartes 1986; cf. Williams 1978. For Descartes' place in an introduction to philosophy of religion, see Davies 1993 (1982), 9, 57–8, 66–7, 94–120, 214–20, 243–4.
2. This feminist framework is introduced in section 4 of this chapter; but it will be given critical focus, as a framework for belief, in chapter 3.
3. For example, the a priori principle of simplicity is crucial to Swinburne's arguments for theism; see Swinburne 1991 (1979), 52, 63, 102–6, 131–2, 293–9. For Swinburne, God is the simplest explanation of the universe, and simplicity is an attribute of God as creator; the principle of simplicity even appears to underlie his examples which only include male subjects; see ibid., 158, 182, 191–2. Here Swinburne makes infrequent references to women as opposed to frequent references to man as a male-neutral category; his references to women are only to women as wives, married women who are seduced, the mothers of man's children, possessions of men, or passive objects for men's seduction.

   For a contrasting, feminist account of the fundamental significance of language and the logic of predication in revealing assumptions about women as commodities in western, theistic cultures, see Irigaray 1985b, 170–91; 1993a, 112–15; 1993b, 15–22, 29–36; 1996, 69–78.

4. Ricoeur 1967; Kristeva 1982 (1980); Irigaray 1985a, 321–40, 346–58; 1993b 14–22, 45–50.
5. On the importance of Locke's original, evidentialist challenge, see Wolterstorff 1983, 137–40, 182; 1986, 38–81; 1996.
6. For more about modern epistemology and the highly nuanced debates over foundationalism, see Pastin 1975, 141–9; Alston 1976, 165–85; Clark 1990; Haack 1994.
7. Plantinga 1981, 41–51; 1983; Frankenberry 1987.
8. Franks Davis 1989, 87–92; Martin 1990, 268–78.
9. For his discussion of the role of warrant or epistemic duty as it derives from Descartes and Locke, see Plantinga 1992; 1993.
10. Feuerbach 1972, 153; 1989, 75, 197–203; Irigarary 1993c, 61–72.
11. Midgley argues that giving up certain mythological explanations of the inevitability of evil is in one sense good: in giving up myth, men and women are free to accept both the human responsibility and the rational power to fight evil. But in another sense, there is a danger: man (*sic*) could think he has unlimited power, identifying with the omnipotence of the mythical God; and if he takes over this God's-eye view, then realistic attempts at changing his own potentially pernicious beliefs and actual acts of evil can easily be thwarted; see Midgley 1984, 68–9.
12. For the original and an opposing account of the view-from-nowhere, see Nagel 1986 and Bordo 1987, respectively. And for use of the God's-eye point of view in support of ethical values, see Taliaferro 1988, 123–38. It is worth considering whether Nagel's original account has been misconstrued by both value theorists and feminists. For criticisms of idealizations which privilege certain sorts of human agents and life, creating covert gender chauvinism and exclusion of those not matching the ideal, see O'Neill 1993, 310–17; 1996, 39–44.
13. For her complete argument concerning the unacknowledged empiricist biases against nondominant races and religions, see Lazreg 1990, 327–32; and on the use by feminists of the problematical notion of experience inherited from classical empiricists' conception, see Lazreg 1994, 45–62.
14. Barbour 1974; Soskice 1985.
15. Franks Davis 1989, especially 10–14, 157–65, 168–92, 248–50.
16. This instability becomes more apparent in the light of the arguments against empiricist forms of objectivity in chapter 2 below. On the problem with universalizing the experience of the particular subject, see Lazreg 1994, 45–62; Gatens 1996, 95–9 (note Gatens' criticism of a very specific sense of abstraction on page 99).
17. To support this claim, chapter 2 argues that the empiricist methods and norms suffer from a weak objectivity.
18. In particular, certain concrete but pernicious beliefs have had immediate,

practical, and social consequences for women and sexuality, generally. For example, belief in the poisonous nature of menstrual blood has had grave consequences for theistic beliefs concerning women's anatomy and their sexual and moral relations – let alone women's access to religious rites and roles of authority in the Church. For historical documentation of the ways in which various pernicious beliefs concerning sexuality were developed by philosophers and theologians, see Ranke-Heinemann 1991.

19. Daly 1986 (1973).
20. For Irigaray's comment on women's possibly creative but necessarily temporary detour through same-sex groups, see Irigaray 1989, 73–4.
21. Daly 1987 (1978).
22. I have in mind especially those readers who have taken seriously two positions to be discussed later in chapters 2 and 3 – feminist standpoint epistemology and feminist poststructuralism, respectively.
23. However, the simplicity of the theistic explanation has also been at the center of debates between Swinburne and other theists and atheists; see Mackie 1982, 100, 129f, 149; Swinburne 1991, 293–9, Appendix A.
24. For other essays debating the coherence of God's attributes, see Crombie in Abraham and Holtzer (eds) 1987, 169–88; Holtzer 1987, 189–209; Stump (ed.) 1993, 3–5, 7–8, 204–47.
25. Mackie 1955, 200–12; also, see McCloskey 1960, 97–114. Plantinga presents a, for some, decisive refutation of this logical incompatibility in his 'Free Will Defense'; see Plantinga 1967, 131–55.
26. See Rowe 1986, 227–47, especially 245; also see Rowe 1984, 95–100; Wykstra 1984, 73–93.
27. Swinburne 1991, 218–21; 1987, 141–67.
28. Mackie 1982; Rowe 1986; Surin 1986; Martin 1990; Hampson 1990, 43–6; 1996, 49–50.
29. McCord Adams 1986, 248–67. According to Stump (ed.) 1993, 331–4, support for McCord Adams' position can be found in Aquinas's commentary on the book of Job; cf. Aquinas 1989.
30. Hampson 1990, 43–6; 1996, 49–50.
31. For examples, see Warner 1976, 50–78; Daly 1986, 44–68; 1987; Ranke-Heinemann 1991, 125–56, 177–83, 324ff; Irigaray 1994, 92, 98–100, 111–12.
32. Swinburne 1991, 8; cf. Gale 1991, 318–19.
33. Moulton 1992, 219–32.
34. Swinburne 1991, 158, 182, 191–2.
35. Concerning the assumption in this book of the unstable sex/gender distinction, see Harding 1983, 311–24; 1991, 174–6, 181–5; Braidotti 1994b, 49–67.
36. Hartsock 1983, 283ff; Harding 1993.
37. Irigaray 1993a-c.
38. Hartsock 1983, 283–310; Harding 1993; Longino 1990; Irigaray 1991b; Braidotti 1994a.
39. For a historically rich, socially layered reading of female dissent represented by

the Hindu *bhakti*-saint Mirabai, see Mukta 1994, ix–x, 1–3, 12, 182ff; cf. chapter 5 below.

40. Concerning God as a projection of ideal human qualities, see Feuerbach 1989; Irigaray 1993c, 57–72.
41. A similar irony appears in contemporary readings in the psychology of religion; see Goldenberg 1995a, 105–9. Although certain psychologists of religion fear psychoanalysis because of its supposed reductive power in relation to religious phenomena, the reverse causes Goldenberg concern: theistic conceptions of 'the sacred' easily reduce the possibilities of psychoanalytic explorations into the real complexities – especially the sexed/gendered nature – of human behaviour, feelings, thoughts, and beliefs.
42. For two very different examples, see Franks Davis 1989, 205–10, 229; Newman 1994, 15–18.
43. Lorde 1983 (1981), 94–7; Daly 1986; 1992a, 232–3. For a warning that feminism could become a new religion for the privileged woman, see Kristeva 1986, 208.
44. Daly 1986, 132–54; cf. Lazreg 1990, 326–48.
45. See Swinburne 1977; 1991; Franks Davis 1989; Prevost 1990; Martin 1990. For a different sort of philosophical theology maintaining that the highly ramified belief in the atonement (as Jesus Christ's innocent suffering of evil and death for humankind unites men and women with him) offers a practical answer to the problem of evil, see Surin 1986, 128ff.
46. I mean to reverse the premisses (concerning the expanded theism) and conclusion (the restricted theism) to generate the opposite entailment from that stated in part I, section 3.
47. Conze 1959, 40; Armstrong 1994, 37–45, 52–3, 100–5.
48. For five possible accounts of the atonement, see Blackburn 1994, 28. For more extended arguments concerning the atonement, see Swinburne 1989; Stump 1988, 61–91; Quinn 1993, 281–300.
49. Although the ramification of beliefs derived from religious experience would vary, even the unramified beliefs in empirical realist forms of theism culminate in beliefs about the incarnation of God in Jesus Christ; see Franks Davis 1989, 25, 249. Moreover very specific, largely detrimental beliefs for women surround the Virgin Mother, her immaculate conception, the virgin birth, the assumption, and the associated images of perpetual virginity and sorrowful motherhood; see Warner 1976; Schüssler Fiorenza 1995, 164–77.
50. Irigaray illustrates how, in western cultures, the hidden sacrifices of embodied women and of some men have not only been built upon Christian theism but have structured our social and economic lives; see Irigaray 1993c, 75–88.
51. For significant background on the biases of patriarchal history including the history of the dominant western form of patriarchal religion, see Ranke-Heinemann 1991; Lerner 1993, 3–17. For specific criticisms of the continuing dominance of the paradigm which has excluded religious women and men of different races and ethnicities, see Lazreg 1990, 326–48; 1994, 45–63.

52. An analogous situation in which the neutrality and fairness – indeed, the altruism – of an authority figure has been decisively questioned is the family's head of household. From the studies done for Nussbaum and Glover (eds) 1995, Nussbaum concludes that 'males [whether husband or father] are quite often neglectful of the interests of females, whether wives or children, and make decisions inimical to those interests' (6–7).
53. Swinburne 1991; 1989, 240ff; Franks Davis 1989; Prevost 1990; Alston 1991; Plantinga 1992.
54. I would like to make absolutely clear that my use of Swinburne as an example should not be taken as anything personal. I merely find his work especially useful as a contemporary example of an empirical realist form of theism which has been highly praised for its coherence and rigor, as well as most highly privileged by Anglo-American philosophers of religion. Hence it becomes highly significant to consider both the language and the power of Swinburne's theism in terms of sex/gender.
55. Swinburne 1991, 69.
56. Franks Davis 1989, 249f; Swinburne 1989.
57. Swinburne 1991; Plantinga 1992; Alston 1991; Stump (ed.) 1993.
58. Swinburne 1991; Franks Davis 1989; Prevost 1990. To consider another woman's position *vis-à-vis* patriarchal forms of theism, see McCord Adams in Stump (ed.) 1993 and in Morris (ed.) 1994. Moreover Stump's writings and influences can be considered in conjunction with Kretzmann; see Stump and Kretzmann 1981; Stump 1988; 1993, while noting the generous acknowledgment and dedication to Stump in Kretzmann 1997.
59. Note that the nature of the Héloïse complex is not strictly sexual in the sense of genital, but sexual in the sense that a privileged male identity is given to the philosophical subject at the expense of the female or possibly inferior male 'student.' This complex is both social and personal since connected with the nature of the institution of being a philosopher whose reputation depends strictly on his ideas and arguments: the philosopher needs to gain intellectual recognition supported by the faithfulness of followers of lower status, particularly students, and often by women who tend to be especially conscientious and loyal translators, editors, amanuenses of their writings; but such supportive recognition can also be sought in woman as a mistress who bolsters male identity. See Le Doeuff 1989, 100–28; 1991, 59–60, 162–5.
60. Abelard and Héloïse 1974, 66–77, 109–56; cf. Nye 1992, 1–22.
61. Le Doeuff 1991, 162–5.
62. Tomberlin and Van Inwagen (eds) 1985; Stump (ed.) 1993; Padgett (ed.) 1994.
63. Le Doeuff 1991, 162–5.
64. Being faithful and highly conscientious, Franks Davis acknowledges her debt to Swinburne and claims to modify his cumulative case with data from the religious experience of nontheists, she may, then, achieve a certain distance from her mentor. But it is highly likely that her modifications will inform and please the mentor who can easily incorporate her findings into his framework

which is, in any case, the framework of her writing. Perhaps the student/mentor exchange of ideas is one way in which knowledge grows. And I readily acknowledge that throughout her book on religious experience, Franks Davis's reliance upon and faithfulness to Swinburne's cumulative-case argument from religious experience, as well as his rational principles of credulity, simplicity, and testimony, are remarkable and praiseworthy. Yet this reliance also means that, in the end, Christian realist forms of theism are inevitably given privilege over all other forms of theism; see Franks Davis 1989, 2, 22–3, 82, 92–108, 113–17, 128, 133–4, 138, 144, 153–4, 166–70, 225–6, 228, 237–42ff.

65. Whitford 1991b, 53–62.
66. Flax 1990; Anderson 1993a.
67. Benhabib 1992; 1995.
68. If need be, I would describe myself as a reformist feminist, in the sense of seeking to refigure rationality; I would have to call myself radical to the degree that I recognize the necessity of new conceptions of desire, sexual difference, myth, mimesis – hence, generally, of embodiment and belief. Yet rather than identifying rationality as redeemably male and patriarchal, I hold to the idea that rationality can be less partial than presently configured. Cf. Harding 1993; Lovibond 1994a; Green 1995.
69. Lovibond 1994a; Benhabib 1992; 1995.
70. Daly 1986.
71. For more background on feminist poststructuralism, see chapter 3 below.
72. In an original account of reasonableness and equivalent rights, Cornell refigures Kant's conceptions of personhood and equality on the basis of his idea of practical reason. This could be applied to Kant's account of free citizens (in the block quotation above); see Cornell 1995a. Cornell defends minimum conditions of individuation consistent with (i) personhood as a conception of practical reason preserving the necessary conditions to become persons and (ii) practical reason ensuring that as 'sexuate beings' and citizens we are to be regarded as free and equal. The adjective 'sexuate' derives from Irigaray's use of *sexué* to stress the sexually specific natures of every man and woman. To quote Cornell,

    > . . . as equal citizens and, moreover, as sexuate beings, we should all be equivalently evaluated as worthy of achieving the conditions of personhood. No form of sexuate being, in other words, can be evaluated as inherently antithetical to personhood since such an evaluation would be antithetical to the idea that we be regarded as free and equal persons for the purposes of the 'as if' (as the test of rightfulness) of an original contract. (Ibid., 19)

73. In addition to Cornell 1995a, for further scholarly elaborations of Kantian practical reason in terms of autonomy, see O'Neill 1989, 75–7; 1996, 23–7, 48–65; Korsgaard 1996, 22–4, 348–35.
74. Kant 1950 (1781, 1787), 499–500, A590/B618-A591/B619.
75. Swinburne 1991, 54n2.
76. Swinburne's use of the rational principle of simplicity leads him into absurdities.

For instance, he refuses to use inclusive language on the grounds that 'man' is less cumbersome and so more simple to use. But arguably here simplicity sacrifices a true picture of human beings, since 'man' excludes sexually specific considerations of half the human race; see Swinburne 1986, 4.

77. Kant 1950, 297–570.
78. Warner 1976, 50–63, 67, 70–1; Ranke-Heinemann 1991, 75–98; Lerner 1993, 141–2.
79. Warner 1976, 25–67, 224–35.

2

Feminists and the Rationality of Belief, I: Strong Objectivity

It is by thinking and acting as 'outsiders within' that feminists and others can transform [scientific rationality] and its social relations for those who remain only insiders or outsiders.

Harding 1991, 160

1 Rationality and Epistemological Frameworks

The three feminist epistemological frameworks which have been identified in the previous chapter make it possible now to raise specific questions concerning the material conditions for sexed/gendered configurations of rationality and religious belief. My aim in the present chapter, continuing into the next, is to give further elaboration to two of these feminist epistemological positions on the rationality of belief while raising specific questions about objectivity and desire. I will focus the two chapters upon the challenges posed, first, by feminist standpoint epistemology and, second, by feminist poststructuralism for the empirical realist forms of theism which remain at the heart of the dominant approach to philosophy of religion. I intend to assess critically the significant principle of strong objectivity for feminist epistemology, followed by an assessment of the feminist criticism that scientific objectivity excludes and devalues female desire.[1] The recovery of both the content of female desire and the expressions of sexual difference becomes highly important for any feminist epistemology of religious belief; this content and these expressions have been repressed by patriarchal configurations of rational belief.

I begin this chapter by restating the central characteristics of the three feminist epistemological frameworks in terms of objectivity. First, the feminist empiricist approach is a revised form of Enlightenment epistemology; it accepts the empiricist method of justification and the empiricist goal in seeking objectivity as a form of detached thought about the world. But as a feminist epistemology, it seeks to apply ever more rigorously the empiricist method, to seek objectivity in the justification of true belief. A feminist empiricist aims to eliminate any unacknowledged biases of androcentrism or sexism in empiricist concepts and conclusions. Sandra Harding introduces the label 'feminist empiricist' to distinguish it from her own position; as a label it has its limitations as a self-ascription.[2] I use the label only to distinguish one possible epistemological strategy from the feminist strategies which I actually take up in part III. An attractive example of a modified, contextualized form of feminist empiricism is found in the writings of Helen Longino to whom I will briefly refer later in this chapter.

Second, feminist standpoint epistemologists accept neither the empiricist method nor its goal as sufficient grounds for objectivity. Their feminist claim is that both the method and the goal of objectivity are affected – to a greater or lesser degree – by biases of gender, including sex, race, and class biases.[3] Feminist standpoint epistemology aims to confront the deep and pervasive sex/gender bias which renders weak the objectivity of modern science and modern empiricism.

Third, the feminist poststructuralist approach to the question of objectivity might not strictly speaking be epistemology. But the relevant point is that the feminist poststructuralist rejects the essential structure of male rationality and its principle of objectivity. This feminist approach to the subject of Enlightenment epistemology suggests that it is self-contradictory to separate the subject from nature, even from his own embodiment.

The differences between the first and third approaches are evident in the very different empiricist and poststructuralist conceptions of language and of language's relation to reality. The conception of language implicit in the second approach, standpoint epistemology, falls somewhere between the other two.

Empiricists – at least those empirical realists who are the object of the feminist critique – assume the independence of reality from language; reality is understood as the world outside of and, to some degree, beyond the reach of language. Hence the empiricist subject who wants to make claims about absolute reality must try to represent an objective world that stands over against it. (Of course for Kant this empiricist attempt to represent reality is vain.) And ultimately, for the metaphysical realist, language remains inadequate as a tool for getting at truth, producing only inferior copies or images of a forever inaccessible and transcendent world.[4] In direct contrast, structuralists after Ferdinand de Saussure (1857–1913) and poststructuralists after Jacques Derrida (1930-) reject this naive realist conception of language. Instead they aim to overcome the empiricist metaphysical dualism of subject/object, word/world, language-user/reality.

Roughly speaking, structuralists maintain that the structure employed to organize the world and experience comes into existence at the same time as the structure of the language employed to express that experience. Poststructuralists explicitly claim that language is constitutive of reality, rather than separate from reality; concepts come into existence out of the play of differences making up language as a dynamic structure of interrelated, significant terms. According to the poststructuralist view, truth does not depend upon adequate representation of an objective world independent of language. Instead truth becomes what is acceptable within a linguistic structure of significant differences. Even the subject's conception of itself is determined within this linguistic structure of differences; language is a dynamic process and so the subject is also in-process. In addition to Saussure's structuralism and Derrida's poststructuralism, the distinctive feminist poststructuralist conception of language is informed by Jacques Lacan's psycholinguistics.[5]

Unlike either the feminist empiricist or the feminist poststructuralist, the feminist standpoint epistemologist does not make explicit her conception of language and its relation to reality. But in the light of feminist standpoint epistemologists' arguments against naive empiricist forms of realism, language would have to be assumed to mediate one's standpoint; and to mediate implies a two-way relation whereby language affects one's standpoint and the standpoint affects one's language. It also follows that the feminist standpoint epistemologist could not assume the poststructuralist account of language as strictly constitutive of reality, allowing nothing to exist prior to linguistic concepts, e.g. no objects or regularities in the world. In resisting epistemological relativism and deterministic constructionism, the feminist standpoint epistemologist assumes at least minimal properties of a commonly perceived world, which enable learning how to communicate truth and so how to acquire objectivity.[6]

Feminist empiricism, feminist standpoint epistemology, and feminist poststructuralism agree minimally that Enlightenment epistemology has determined the gender-status given to rationality as a specific set of logical principles, beliefs, and actions, exhibiting simplicity, clarity, coherence, and consistency.[7] Then, depending upon which of the three frameworks is used, the feminist would attempt (i) to purge this empiricist rationality of its sexism, (ii) to find less partial standpoints on rationality, incorporating differences of gender, sex, class, ethnicity, and race, or (iii) to subvert rationality as inherently male and patriarchal. All three approaches to feminist epistemology are different from much conventional epistemology in forcing scrutiny concerning the ethical truth and justice of specific logical, coherent, or simple beliefs and actions for women in general. But ethical and political scrutiny is especially true of the feminist standpoint epistemologist and arguably of certain feminist poststructuralists.

2 Accounts of Objectivity

One of the principles of rationality which has come under scrutiny by feminist philosophers is that of scientific objectivity; this objectivity could also be explained in terms of instrumental or nonsubstantive rationality. Both modern science and modern theories of knowledge are practices within which the dominant tradition has made objectivity crucial to their methodology and their goal. For feminist epistemologists the crucial question remains: Is objectivity gender-neutral? No agreed response exists amongst feminists. There exist different feminist arguments concerning objectivity and gender. Basically the alternatives are (i) that neither the objective method nor the goal of science and epistemology is gendered, (ii) that the method but not the goal is gendered, or even (iii) that both are gendered. My interest focuses upon the feminist standpoint epistemologists who find the method and the goal of empiricist epistemology affected by sex/gender-bias. This bias constitutes the covert and overt power of men over women, as well as male power over any marginalized other.

A feminist concern with the relationship between knowledge and power is neither new nor surprising. However, there is novel irony in the feminist standpoint epistemologist's claim that the traditional realist notion of scientific objectivity is too 'weak,' especially if the notion is also claimed to be in some sense 'male.' It then becomes imperative to work out the rationality of the strong objectivity which forms the heart of feminist standpoint epistemology. The most prolific advocate of strong objectivity is Harding. Hence her recent work in feminist standpoint epistemology is drawn upon to a large extent in what follows.[8]

By 'rationality,' in this context, is meant the substantive as opposed to highly formal logic and reasoning of the new, strong objectivity. Such reasoning aims to uncover biases in modern epistemology insofar as it has sought exclusively the necessary and sufficient conditions for justifying true belief and so for constituting knowledge. Clearly embodiment is a necessary condition even for the empiricist subject who tries to achieve a gender-neutral perspective on the world; but embodiment as a sufficient condition for knowledge remains an unresolved question. To recall the argument of chapter 1, philosophers of religion of an empirical realist persuasion have sought to justify the rationality of religious belief according to the male-neutral methods and goals of objectivity being challenged by feminist standpoint epistemologists.

On a more theoretical level, I continue to consider in some detail the philosophical accounts of objectivity which come under examination for being too weak. The point is to expose biases in both the construction and justification of belief by modern epistemology; such biases are easily seen in the ramified beliefs of empirical realist forms of theism. The ways in which the different senses of objectivity can be too weak gradually become apparent in the biases of both empiricist method and its goals. The philosophical account of objectivity investigated by feminist epistemologists is a notion which philosophers employed well before Kant introduced his distinction between objective and subjective in the eighteenth century. Feminist inquiries concerning objectivity also go back further than Locke to the foundationalist epistemology of Descartes' *Meditations on First Philosophy*.[9]

The seventeenth-century notion of objectivity offers the foundation for the two main senses of Enlightenment objectivity: the epistemological and the ontological. First, in an epistemological sense, objectivity either is or is not a property of ideas, belief, or perceptions. This sense is found in both Descartes and Locke. Then, according to Kant, to possess objectivity, a judgment must at least have a content that may be presupposed to be valid for all rational beings.[10] For certain epistemological readings of Kant, a judgment which is objective – which has objective validity – must be able to distinguish how things really are from how they seem to be to me. In more contemporary analytic terms, objectivity in its epistemological sense can be construed to be a property of mental acts and states. If this is the case, the property itself needs to be carefully specified. But any such specification is not directly relevant to the feminist epistemologist.

Second, in its ontological sense, objectivity is the way something, if it exists, is independent of any mediate or immediate knowledge, perception, conception, or consciousness there might be of it. Such material things as trees, grass, water are called objective and so possess objectivity. An entity, which has objectivity in this ontological sense, can be made the subject of an epistemological judgment of objectivity. And we could ask: Does the epistemological objectivity of a given class of assertions require the ontological objectivity of the entity or entities which those assertions apparently invoke or range over? The class of assertions which are constituted by the attributes of the classical theist's God – i.e. his omnipotence, omniscience, eternity, supreme goodness – might come under this question. The point is that to answer this question of ontological objectivity in the affirmative is to assume a realist position concerning the existence of God; to defend a negative answer is to take an anti-realist stance. The realist explains the objectivity of a belief by appeal to the independent existence of the entities in question, for instance, of a God or gods.

The question of ontological objectivity raises the difference between realist and anti-realist accounts of epistemological objectivity. In addition to its significance for the theist, this difference is important for the feminist who claims to remain in some sense a realist – at least, realist about truth and justice.[11] As Miranda Fricker cogently argues, 'political beliefs are unintelligible in isolation from relevant empirical claims about real states of affairs in the world'. Fricker continues as follows: 'What would it mean, for example, to be committed to the eradication of poverty, or of violence against women, without a realist commitment to the empirical proposition that, say, whole communities are periodically wiped out by famine, or that many women suffer domestic violence and other forms of attack by men?' (Fricker 1994, 99). A realist would establish the objectivity of a belief by appeal to the independent existence of the entities or state of affairs in question. Epistemological objectivity would then be analyzed in terms of ontological objectivity; a judgment or belief is objective (epistemologically speaking) if and only if it stands in some specified relation to an independently existing, determinate reality. A realist can appeal to the existence of determinate facts, objects, properties, events, and states of affairs. In contrast, a common intuition of different anti-realists is that for our assertions to be objective, for our beliefs to comprise genuine knowledge, those assertions and beliefs must be, among other things, rational, justifiable, coherent, communicable, and intelligible. It is not on the basis of appeal to entities (as they are in-themselves) that, according to an anti-realist, our judgments become intelligible or coherent.[12]

In addition to these epistemological and ontological issues of objectivity, there remains a further philosophical use of objectivity relevant for feminist epistemologists. Objectivity has been taken to represent the view-from-nowhere which expresses a nonperspectival account of the world. To achieve this, all self-reflexive elements must be eliminated from assertions and judgments; all references to person, tense, place must go. An account which includes references to personal characteristics, place, time, and social situation is identified as subjective, not objective. And with this last contrast, I come to the notion most frequently queried by feminists: the God's-eye view of objectivity which excludes all perspective, everything subjective, and the very social nature of knowledge.

At times, both theists and nontheists dub the view-from-nowhere to be the God's-eye view. Similarly, achieving this sense of objectivity is dubbed the God-trick. I will return to criticize both of these dubbings.[13]

3 Objectivity as Too Weak

At this stage, I would like to pose a question to Harding. In what sense(s) could the Enlightenment philosophers' accounts of objectivity, whether realist or not, whether absolutely objective and nonperspectival or not, be too weak? It is necessary to discover in what sense 'weak' is meant.

Weakness attributed to objectivity suggests that the notion in question does not possess much – or enough – of its characteristic aspects. But in what sense, if at all, could the characteristics of objectivity in its nonperspectival use – or the view-from-nowhere – render it weak? The label 'God's-eye view' implies being omniscient, omnitemporal, omnipotent: so by definition it is strong. If this is the view of the all-knowing and all-powerful, in what sense could it be weak? Alternatively take the realist notion of objectivity which appeals to the way things are and so is supported by its epistemological and ontological senses. In what way could this be weak? Furthermore any account of an impartial principle would have to be judged weak or strong according to the reliability of criteria which are used to assess the characteristic aspects of the principle at issue, in this case, of objectivity. Both the God's-eye view and the realist accounts of objectivity appear at first strong insofar as appeal is made to impartial (since divine) power and knowledge, and human neutrality, and to the way things are, respectively.

Feminist philosophers of science, in particular, have labeled such accounts of objectivity weak. Despite the criteria of being impartial and true to the facts, despite the assessment of necessary and sufficient conditions, these views are not value-neutral; hence they are not views-from-nowhere. Instead these positions hide *un*acknowledged biases supported by various (prejudiced) background beliefs which distort and render partial both their so-called objective methods and the goals of their epistemological activities. The criticism is that certain biases allow subjects to claim knowledge of the world as it is while excluding from that world the lives of women, of nondominant races, of nonprivileged classes. And the feminist contention is that this privileged perspective narrows and distorts the subject's knowledge not only of social life but of scientific 'facts.'

However, the feminist criticism that the God's-eye view is, ironically, a weak form of objectivity does *not* constitute a criticism of religious belief *per se*, as certain women academics have wrongly assumed.[14] Instead the feminist aims to demonstrate that this idealized objectivity is weak because justifying unselfconsciously partial theistic beliefs. To support their criticism, feminist standpoint epistemologists expose the domination resulting from construction of an all-powerful God's-eye view which merely reinforces male privilege, male prerogatives, and the marginalization of women, while excluding all nonprivileged others.

More generally, criticisms of weak objectivity arise from a position which claims a strong objectivity on the basis of the social nature of knowledge, including scientific knowledge. In Harding's words, '[f]eminist objectivity means quite simply socially situated knowledges.'[15] The subjects of feminist knowledges become objects of knowledge and so part of generating the culture's best beliefs: 'the same kinds of social forces that shape objects of knowledge also shape (but do not determine) knowers and their scientific projects' (Harding 1993, 64).

Although differing in other respects from feminist standpoint epistemology, Longino's contextual version of feminist empiricism similarly contrasts feminist objectivity with the empirical realist account of objectivity as conventionally conceived. The conventional account at issue for these various feminists is summarily stated by Longino: 'Objectivity is a characteristic which has been applied to beliefs, individuals, theories, observations, and methods of inquiry. It is generally thought to involve the willingness to let our beliefs be determined by 'the facts' or by some impartial and nonarbitrary criteria rather than by our wishes as to how things ought to be' (Longino 1990, 62). Longino herself has more recently offered a list of new criteria for feminist objectivity and choice of theory. Instead of supposedly impartial facts, Longino lists six criteria or virtues which she has found in feminist epistemologies. These include empirical adequacy, novelty, ontological heterogeneity, complexity of relationship, applicability to current human needs, and diffusion of power. One way or another, all of these criteria are to prevent gender from 'being disappeared.'[16]

In the end, whichever feminist epistemological position is taken up, the core problem for a feminist philosophy of religion with the conventional, empirical realist account of objectivity would be that ironically it has resulted in sex/gender-biased beliefs. For the feminist standpoint epistemologist, it has not been objective enough. The facts or impartial, nonarbitrary criteria for determining true belief have been partial and biased.[17] Moreover claims to true belief, such as belief in the associations of virginity, purity, and male divinity, on the basis of weak objectivity have oppressed women and all other nondominant classes, races, ethnicities, since derived exclusively from a privileged male position of knowledge-makers.

Briefly stated, there are at least two ways in which scientific objectivity has been shown by Harding to be weak. It is paradoxically shown to be applied, first, too narrowly and, second, too broadly.[18]

First, scientific objectivity is said to be operationalized in too narrow a way to permit the achievement of the value-free research which is supposed to be its outcome. Harding means by 'operationalized' the way in which the scientific goal of objectivity (as impartiality) determines the practice of scientific and epistemological research. A certain blindness exists in the conventional assumption that the truly scientific part of knowledge-seeking occurs only in the context of justifying belief. In Harding's words,

> The context of discovery, in which problems are identified as appropriate for scientific investigation, hypotheses are formulated, key concepts are defined – this part of the scientific process is thought to be unexaminable within science by rational methods. Thus 'real science' is restricted to those processes controllable by methodological rules. The methods of science – or rather, of the special sciences – are restricted to procedures for the testing of already formulated hypotheses. Untouched by these methods are those values and interests entrenched in the very statement of what problem is to be researched and in the concepts favored in the hypotheses that are to be tested. (Harding 1993, 70)

The above references to the restriction of real science to processes controllable by empiricist rules determines the very ideas, beliefs, and hypotheses which empiricists seek to justify.[19] This weakness recalls precisely the restrictions, the controlled methods and problems which are criticized by the feminist Lazreg who, as seen in the previous chapter, studies women and religious belief in Algeria. Lazreg identified the method of abstracted empiricism as biased against the religion of Algerian women: its method determined the very problems which preoccupy empirical realist forms of philosophy of religion. The implication is simply that Islam with its distinctive religious beliefs is devalued by inappropriate methods and problems. Preconceived ideas prohibit the listening and understanding necessary to learn from the actual beliefs of real women and from the beliefs represented in specific Muslim practices.[20]

Thus the first weakness of the conventional scientific or empiricist objectivity indicated by Harding rests on the assumption that epistemology is strictly about justification of truth claims and not about the subjects who formulate the claims, nor about the context from which hypotheses about beliefs emerge. To overcome this, the context of discovery, as well as the context of justification, should be the concern of epistemologists.

Second, according to Harding, scientific objectivity has been applied too broadly and this adds to its other weakness. Its application is to cover all social values and interests by eliminating them from the process and result of knowledge production. But is such total elimination possible? Harding contends that not all values and interests have the same negative effect upon the generation of beliefs. In particular, democracy-advancing values would generate less partial and less distorted beliefs than those justified by privileged scientists or the dominant group in society; advancing these values would rule out the hierarchy of power implicit in certain epistemological methods.[21]

Designed to overcome the weaknesses of the empiricist objectivity, feminist standpoint epistemology has two goals. It aims to produce stronger objectivity by acknowledging the situatedness of one's beliefs and generating the best beliefs possible within the paradigms of any culture. Harding argues that 'a feminist standpoint theory can direct the production of less partial and less distorted beliefs. [It] will not merely acknowledge the social situatedness – the historicity – of the very best beliefs any culture has arrived at or could in principle "discover" but use this fact as a resource for generating those beliefs' (Harding 1991, 138). Thus strong objectivity aims to construct less distorted belief than those beliefs justified by a privileged few who remain unaware of their situatedness and so their biases in the very construction of belief. However, this means that, in contrast to objectivity as conventionally defined, Harding's feminist strong objectivity involves a prima facie contradiction in terms. Objectivity is defined as socially situated.

4 Strong Objectivity

To find a philosophically intelligible account in this feminist proposal for a stronger objectivity, it is necessary to understand two main imperatives or moves. First, the subject moves outward to shift away from his or her own perspective to 'think from the lives of others.'[22] Second, the subject moves backward reflexively to examine the basic background beliefs of the subject of knowledge. The purpose of these moves toward objectivity is to gain less false and less partial knowledge, not absolute truth or impartial knowledge.

As socially situated knowledge, strong objectivity differs from the objectivism of modern science. Harding rejects objectivism but not objectivity. Only objectivism is restricted to the weak objectivity of conventional epistemology, as value-free, impartial, dispassionate and as guiding scientific research. Supposedly objectivists would maintain that without their account of scientific objectivity, justified beliefs or judgments could not be positively distinguished from mere opinion or from mere claims to knowledge. But in rejecting the objectivist objectivity for being too weak, feminists confidently challenge the view-from-nowhere; they reject a God-trick which claims absolute knowledge and value-free objectivity.[23]

So it is intriguing, even if self-contradictory, that Harding asks of her own position: Has feminist standpoint theory really abandoned objectivity and embraced relativism?[24] Or an opponent might ask: Has she given up realism and opted for social constructionism? The answer to both questions is definitely 'no' according to Harding. At least she has not given up objectivity to embrace relativism. Perhaps the problem with Harding's efforts is that she attempts to resist the charge as an epistemologist but, due to her political concerns as a feminist, fails to avoid the relativist position. Yet instead of acknowledging any failure on her part, I would like to scrutinize Harding's own defense a bit more. She could give up the unmediated facts and evidences of a naive, empirical realism without necessarily giving up realism. Nonrealism or anti-realism are not the only alternatives to naive realism.[25]

The pressing question is: If one gives up the objectivity of objectivism and so the view-from-nowhere, how can one avoid cultural relativism or, worse still, epistemological relativism? The feminist standpoint epistemologist defense is that epistemological relativism is the alternative to the view-from-nowhere if and only if one takes the perspective of objectivism; and cultural relativism, as merely a descriptive position, is not an issue for the epistemologist.[26] I might suggest a precedent for this argument: Kant accepts the perspectival nature of an empirical subject's view of the world while conceiving objectivity as permeated with a universal interest or value. Hence epistemological relativism is avoided while, on the one hand, acknowledging perspective and, on the other hand, without treating objectivity as a valueless view-from-nowhere.[27] Harding, for her part, claims that philosophers should be able to reject both objectivism and epistemological relativism by throwing out the coin which has these two sides as alternatives.

To apply Harding's claim to empirical realist forms of classical theism, consider arguing for the unramified belief in its core idea of God. The theistic arguments for the existence of God as omnipotent, omniscient, supremely good, perfectly free, transcendent, creator are premissed on the empiricist principle of objectivity as perspectiveless. In such arguments, unramified belief in this God is assumed to be objective in the sense of nonperspectival and gender-free. Implied in this assumption is that the theistic God represents the view-from-nowhere; and supposedly all men would agree with this idea of God as long as the arguments for his existence were both valid and sound. So the disputes between theists and atheists have been about the success of their arguments, and not about the background beliefs and their implicit principle of objectivity. As a consequence, these theistic arguments are built upon a concealed circularity: God ensures the idea of objectivity at the same time as objectivity ensures the idea of the theistic God. Thus the empiricist objectivity fails in precisely the ways in which the God-trick fails; it is not a view-from-nowhere. Instead it appears to be an unacknowledged idealization of the privileged man's own values, excluding all others.

According to Harding, the objectivity of objectivism begins to look like an absolutist position whose flip-side could equally be called epistemological relativism. The empirical realist form of theism not only appears to reflect the privileged male point of view but appears either absolutist or relativist which comes to the same thing due to its blindness on issues of sex/gender, race, class, and ethnicity. Thus the naive realist ground for objective knowledge is too narrow, since it excludes the context of the belief's construction as well as the limitations of the subject's perspective including the sex/gender of the subject. Stated differently, it lacks content from nonprivileged points of view.

Yet there are further questions here. In more practicable terms than the phrase 'socially situated knowledges' offers, what is strong objectivity? That is, how would objectivity as socially situated knowledges actually work? And what are the criteria for objectivity?

Strong objectivity is a socially produced and mediated value; it is characterized by a willingness to think from the lives of marginalized others and by a certain self-reflexivity.[28] To be objective is to be able to think one's claim from the perspective of another and to reinvent oneself as other.

The first criterion of strong objectivity measures the degree to which an objective claim is consistent with the nonprivileged or marginalized standpoint. A substantive logic is at work in a privileged subject endeavoring to think objectively from the lives of marginalized others. For one thing, this logic assumes that the oppressed other who lives on the margins and not at the center of knowledge-construction is forced to possess knowledge of both privileged and marginalized lives. To survive on the margin, the other must know not only his or her own situation but must acquire knowledge of reality at the center and of their oppressor. In contrast, the privileged knowledge-maker tends to have a vested interest in maintaining the authority of his or her knowledge-claims only. And so the marginalized other will have greater knowledge of social reality. For another thing, the lives of marginalized others are used as a test for truth because the subjects of those lives will have a smaller vested interest in the exclusive claims made from the center of a society to support the privileged subject. And so this other will be more free to acknowledge the greater social reality and complexity of truth.

The second criterion of strong objectivity is comparable with the transformative logic of a certain phenomenological thinking. For this, I quote Merleau-Ponty: '[This] is a way of thinking, the way which imposes itself when the object is "different" and requires us to transform ourselves. [When we] let ourselves be taught [by the object]' (Merleau-Ponty 1964b, 120). Letting ourselves be taught by the object is crucial to the logic of Harding's strong objectivity. This means that when another's view of reality is the object of my study, I must be taught by the other in order to transform myself and my beliefs. And I must not silence the other by speaking for her or him about their reality. Instead I listen to what the other tells me about their standpoint on my world in order to gain greater knowledge of reality; but I must then be willing to be transformed by this knowledge. In the process, I reinvent myself as other.

I would like to illustrate these criteria of strong objectivity by interpreting an example from the work of a leading Muslim feminist and sociologist, Fatima Mernissi. In her study of Islamic memory and women's rebellion, Mernissi acknowledges learning her greatest lessons about Islamic belief from an illiterate Arab woman of 79 years. Mernissi listens to this marginalized woman's narrative of female resistance as she recounts the tale of a faithful Muslim woman, a daughter of a merchant who marries the son of the sultan.

The tale has a coherent narrative, developing from the insistence of the sultan's son that the merchant's daughter admit that man is more cunning than woman; but throughout the tale, the merchant's daughter consistently refuses any such admission. After their marriage, the merchant's daughter is first incarcerated by the sultan's son in an underground cell; yet she manages to dig a tunnel to her parents' household. Next, each time the husband leaves their home, the young wife manages to escape through the tunnel, to disguise herself, and to become the female lover of her own husband without him recognizing her real identity. It is in order to teach her adulterous and deceiving husband a lesson that the wife disguised as a lover meets the sultan's son outside their home on numerous nights over a period of years; the husband makes love to her each time he meets her as his lover; she becomes pregnant three times and each time names the child after the place where they met. Finally the tale concludes once the husband realizes that his deceptions have been countered with the wife's far cleverer disguises; in the end, he has to acknowledge that woman is more cunning than man. The preferred moral of the tale is that a woman's behavior can prove her superior wisdom, despite any imposed conceptions of her social and sexual inferiority.

The illiterate woman who tells this tale develops a narrative which reveals to Mernissi a tradition by which women articulate and carry on resistance to male injustice even in a violent patriarchal society. The telling of tales becomes a resource for women to subvert, perhaps often in simple but subtle ways, the oppressive male identity of Islam which dominates their lives.

So from particular cases, Mernissi realizes the possibility in refiguring women's identity on a larger scale in Islam out of the actual memory of such religious narratives of dissent. Muslim women's memory of female devotion, resistance, and rebellion is largely hidden by what is learned from the patriarchal configurations of Islam; these merely inhibit privileged women from discovering the existing memory and the female identity created by dissent from within patriarchy. Against feminists whose superiority leads them to try to raise the consciousness of uneducated Muslim women, Mernissi asserts the following: 'the basic question for each woman who thinks herself a feminist is not how far ahead she is in her consciousness compared to women from other cultures, but how much she *shares* in that consciousness with women from different social classes in her *own* society' (Mernissi 1996, 16). Mernissi suggests that she can learn from a different social class in her own society; but she also assumes a principle which should apply to the privileged western feminist.[29] Her implicit principle is that in thinking from the lives of marginalized others, feminists transform themselves in realizing the biased nature of their own assumptions. In this case, the privileged feminist finds undermined the assumption 'that the Arab woman is a semi-idiotic submissive subhuman who bathes happily in patriarchally organized degradation and institutionalization deprivation' (Mernissi 1996, 13).[30]

Following this implicit principle of strongly objective thinking, even the privileged feminist scientist would claim that objectivity cannot be achieved by the realist reduplication of facts. Instead strong objectivity is the result of both the proven credibility of the knowledge claimant by marginalized others and the broad communal criticism of knowledge-claims. In short, greater knowledge is possessed by the outsiders within the dominant epistemological framework of modern science and society. 'It is by thinking and acting as "outsiders within" that feminists and others can transform science and its social relations for those who remain only insiders or outsiders' (Harding 1991, 160).[31]

The feminist epistemologist of religious belief would be concerned with the consequences for women of the theist's preoccupation with beliefs justified by the privileged Lockean empirical realists. This concern is expressed by raising questions such as: Whose reason gives justification or warrant to Christian realist forms of theism? And for whom have theistic beliefs been constructed? At first glance, these questions may suggest unwarranted assumptions about the relativism of justified belief and the social construction of reality. Notwithstanding these suggestions, the feminist standpoint epistemologist remains adamant in making a strong claim for objectivity, and even claims the possibility of greater ethical truth. Hence she intends to resist either epistemological relativism or anti-realism.

Ultimately objectivity is to be made strong by weighing all evidence for or against a hypothesis including the systematic examination of background beliefs. This latter examination renders the crucial difference between weak and strong objectivity. Yet how are background beliefs systematically examined? To repeat, the task is to construct less partial beliefs by thinking from the position of marginalized others.

I offer another example, this time from a piece of fiction. In this example, thinking is done from the fictional lives of the women in Alice Walker's *Possessing the Secret of Joy* (1992). The 'secret of joy' symbolizes certain African women's resistance to the patriarchal phantasy of male creativity and power; the phantasy is that regeneration can only be possible for those who have a phallus, the male image of sexual completion. The resistance is against the horrifying violence to women's bodies of particular, male-privileged religious rituals. Walker's symbolic portrayal of resistance by African women to this phantasy and the actual erasure of the female sex can enhance our thinking about conscious and unconscious beliefs. That is, it can enable us to reinvent ourselves as other by imagining reality from the lives of marginalized others. I am, then, to be transformed by the knowledge I gain about the reality of patriarchy and how it has distorted my own beliefs as a privileged white woman.[32] The feminist significance of imagining symbolic battles against patriarchal lineage and on behalf of a democratic vision is brought to center-stage. The goal of such imaginative thinking is utopian: to imagine a refigured vision which is not based upon the system of stratified differentiations inherent in patriarchy, especially differences of sex/gender, race, class, and ethnicity.

In part III, I will take up the refiguring of patriarchal myths. Even greater significance can be discovered in myth, as distinct from fiction, insofar as mythical figures are able to 'live many lives' in different times and places, not just in contemporary settings. The assumption, to be defended later, is that perennial myths are constantly being refigured; this has to do with the nature of myth; but the problem will be that this refiguring can work either for or against women's oppression. Feminist standpoint epistemologists do not typically employ mythical figures in order to gain less biased knowledge than they already possess; they are more directly concerned with actual, marginalized others who live alongside of them, those others who are encountered in their daily lives. However, it is my particular contention that the mimetic refiguring of mythical configurations can guide the disruption of hierarchical structures of religious belief; and this means traditional structures, which must be disrupted if feminist philosophers of religion are to move beyond deep cultural prejudices, sectarianism, or fanaticism in religious beliefs. In chapter 4, I argue that this disruption is potentially achievable by a distinctive miming of mythical configurations of religious beliefs, of the actions endorsed and the emotions evoked by these beliefs. In chapter 5, I defend the mimetic refiguring of biased religious beliefs, comparing this with dissident speech.

I am briefly anticipating my argument in the constructive chapters of part III in order to make clear at this stage my epistemological intention: to avoid, if possible, simply reproducing the biases of my own privileged position. It may be that embracing feminist standpoint epistemology leaves me trapped. The marginalized other could accuse me of doing precisely what I accuse the privileged, naive realist of doing, remaining blind to one's own biases. However, I can only reply that I am intent upon listening to the other to learn about my own situatedness and so to enlarge the narrowness of my privileged beliefs.

Consequently in chapter 5, I attempt significant applications of the two standpoint imperatives: to think from others' lives and to reinvent ourselves as other. I take specific configurations of women's beliefs, actions, and emotions as symbolic representations of the theistic devotion binding together marginalized others. First, I will let the Indian *bhakti*-saint Mirabai serve as a representative figure of dissent from class privilege, who has knowledge as an outsider within her religious devotion to both Krishna and to the common life at the margins. Second, I will have the Greek tragic heroine Antigone serve as a dissenting woman who is marginalized as an outsider within her steadfast devotion to ancient burial rites. In this way, I will illustrate the divided, religious loyalties of women on the margins, especially for those feminists who try to dissent from religious beliefs of the center, in rethinking the mythical configurations of the Hindu devotee of Krishna and the Greek devotee of familial, religious rites. What becomes interesting are the ways in which truth-claims of the center alone can be shown to be biased and prejudiced against greater knowledge and better justice; this includes dominant configurations of religious belief.

Insofar as epistemological research seeks less partial truth and stronger objectivity than presently achieved, it must begin to consider the lives of women and men of different races, classes, sexualities, and societies. I assume this to be equally true for the construction of religious beliefs as for scientific or social knowledges by feminist epistemologists. Without thinking from the lives and beliefs of the other, noncritical and nonreflexive women's beliefs remain biased toward the dominant perspective of white, privileged men. Once committed to feminist standpoint epistemology, critical, reflexive, and communal thinking from the lives of others becomes crucial. Yet this thinking implies that men (as well as women) of consciousness can be feminist; men can achieve feminist objectivity which is strong in its pursuit of how things really are, strong in truth and justice. But these feminist men, as well as these women, must be able to think from the lives of women of a different race, class, or ethnicity.[33] Otherwise we deny the logic and possibility of change to be brought about by standpoint epistemology.

5 The Subject of Feminist Standpoint Epistemology

It follows from the preceding account of strong objectivity that the subject of feminist standpoint epistemology is not unitary, homogeneous, and coherent. It is not like the epistemological and ontological subject of empirical realism. For instance, it sharply contrasts with the conviction that the truth of theism depends upon the subject's unity, the coherence of his beliefs, and the simplicity of his core belief in God as creator of a complex universe. Rather the new subject of feminist standpoint epistemology is multiply divided, often contradictory or incoherent, and complex.

In addition, unlike the subject of empirical realist forms of theism, the feminist philosopher of religion may be persuaded that it is essential to configure the actions manifesting belief in order to refigure the dominant representation of religious belief. With this in mind, I will attempt to demonstrate the necessity of an ongoing critical process of configurations and refigurations for preserving the true complexity of women's and men's beliefs. One source of this complexity is the heterogeneity of the new subjects of feminist epistemologies.

Heterogeneity and multiplicity are true of the new subjects of knowledge as both object and subject.

> [First of all] feminist knowledge has started off from women's lives, but it has started off from many different women's lives . . . Moreover, these different women's lives are in important respects opposed to each other . . . Nevertheless, thought that starts off from each of these different kinds of lives can generate less partial and distorted accounts of nature and social life.
>
> . . .
>
> [Second] the subject/agent of feminist knowledge is multiple, heterogeneous and frequently contradictory . . . It is the thinker whose consciousness is bifurcated, the outsider within, the marginal person now located at the center, the person is committed to two agendas that are by their nature at least partially in conflict . . . It is starting off from a contradictory social position that generates feminist knowledge. (Harding 1993, 65, 66)

The above paragraphs imply a movement outward to the concrete lives which serve as the objects of knowledge, and then backward to the self-divided consciousness which constitutes the subject of knowledge. This dialectical movement intends to transcend the sharp dualism of subject and object.[34]

In regard to this dialectic, I would like to stress that, because of its starting point, feminist knowledge is not exclusively women's knowledge. Feminist standpoint epistemology is not simply personal knowledge of women's own experiences. To start thinking from women's lives means beginning from lives of marginalized others who include all women and some men; later the thinker raises questions for her or his own dominant class of knowledge-makers in order to generate less distorted accounts of the natural world, social lives, and beliefs.

Another requirement stated in the above quotations is that the lives at issue necessarily conflict with one another. But how novel is this new requirement for knowledge? One of the conditions of knowledge in modern epistemology has been the disparate experiences of particular individuals. Admittedly modern philosophers have tended to abstract from particular feelings and the subjective content of personal experiences in order to achieve detached thought about the reality of human experience generally. Yet the point is that, for the feminist standpoint epistemologist, the modern philosopher has grounded his or her search for objectivity in heterogeneous intuitions and impressions. Does this suggest that strong objectivity might be read as a reform of earlier philosophical accounts of objectivity?

In particular, strong objectivity exhibits similarities with a post-Hegelian reform of Kant's account of objectivity. Kant's account draws a sharp distinction between objective and subjective; objective applies to judgments which possess a universal validity for all rational subjects. Yet Kant's objectivity cannot escape the subject which both constantly changes in its empirical aspect or standpoint and remains unknowable in its noumenal aspect (unknowable in-itself as noumenon). Hence Kant's search for objectivity seems bound up with an abstract unitary subject in only one of its aspects; and this is what Hegel identifies as his ahistorical subjectivity. Hegel criticizes Kant's objectivity insofar as it includes, at its core, a paradoxical account of the self-identical subject as both empirical and noumenal, object and subject. But Kant's account of subjectivity can also be read as inherently contradictory due to the fact that there are multiple embodiments of reason; every empirical subject embodies reason. Kant's internally and externally split, yet rational, subject is often acknowledged in post-Kantian philosophy as having a certain affinity with Hegel's philosophy.

Hegel's main criticisms, which focus upon Kant's limitation of reason in ahistorical terms and in his suppression of the sensuous nature of our attachment to others, anticipate key aspects of standpoint epistemology.[35] In turn, the feminist standpoint epistemologists seem to presuppose Kant's account of objectivity and Hegel's criticism of Kant's subjectivity. In particular they turn to Hegel's master and slave dialectic, supporting their move from the master's philosophy to thinking from the lives of the marginalized other. Harding, and Hartsock before her, each claim to follow the pattern of Hegel's master who takes the point of view of the slave in order to recognize something objective about life and death, about history and society.[36]

To draw together some of the preceding points, consider a contrast. The subject of traditional empiricist epistemology and so also of empirical realist forms of theism can be contrasted with the subjects of feminist standpoint epistemology. For the conventional subject is (i) culturally and historically disembodied, even invisible, so cultural prejudices, sectarianism, religious fanaticism can go unchecked while belief seems coherent, consistent, simple, and so on; (ii) different from the objects in space and time which it examines, and so there is the problem of various dichotomies of subject and object; (iii) transhistorical and so knowledge is discovered by individuals, not culturally specified groups, e.g. of a certain class, gender, or race, and this means that the empirical realist subject of conventional philosophy of religion is bound to be blind to historically specific beliefs surrounding the western concepts of God; and, as already noted, (iv) unitary and homogeneous, since knowledge is to be coherent and consistent. But such unity and homogeneity have been challenged by philosophers since Kant – especially by continental philosophers – who see in unity, identity, and coherence the repression of differences and exclusion of strangeness or the stranger.[37] The philosophical and ethical problems in exclusion of differences, in repression of the stranger (within), in the unity and finality of narratives are to be illustrated by configuring and refiguring religious beliefs.

To complete the contrast, the subjects of feminist standpoint epistemology are point by point different from the conventional subject (as above). Note that these contrasting points will also move the concerns of feminist standpoint epistemologists closer to feminist poststructuralists. So the new subjects are (i) embodied and visible. That is, 'the lives from which thought has started are always present and visible in the results of that thought' (Harding 1993, 63). The claims of both hermeneutical and poststructuralist philosophies are especially consistent with the critical background to this first point: 'the delusion that one's thought can escape historical locatedness is just one of the thoughts that is typical of dominant groups in these and other ages. The "scientific world view" is, in fact, a view of (dominant groups in) modern, Western societies, as the histories of science proudly point out' (Harding 1993, 63). The next chapter will begin with the above background concerning the delusive nature of the disembodied and invisible subject in order to bring together feminist standpoint epistemology and feminist poststructuralism.

The new subjects are (ii) embodied and located, and so not fundamentally different from the objects of their knowledge: 'the same kinds of social forces that shape objects of knowledge also shape (but do not determine) knowers and their (epistemological) projects' (Harding 1993, 64). As a consequence of the two preceding points, the subjects are (iii) not isolated individuals but communities of knowers.[38] Hence Harding argues that 'for one thing, what I believe that I thought through all by myself (in my mind), which I know, only gets transformed from my personal belief to knowledge when it is socially legitimated' (Harding 1993, 65).

Finally, the subjects as agents of knowledge are (iv) multiple, heterogeneous, and contradictory or incoherent. Unlike the subjects and agents of empiricist epistemology, they are not unitary, homogeneous, and coherent; this is true in two ways, externally and internally multiple. Externally the subject of feminist standpoint epistemology starts her thinking from the lives of many different women; these lives render the subject of knowledge externally heterogeneous and multiple. Internally she is contradictory in generating knowledge as outsiders within; also as an agent of knowledge this subject is not unitary but divided as subjects who are also objects of their own self-reflexivity. Yet I stress here that the important issue not directly addressed by feminist standpoint epistemology is the role of desire and sexual difference in the construction of socially legitimated belief. I will begin to address this lack in the next section of this chapter by looking more closely at desire in Hegel's master and slave dialectic.

To give a preliminary summation, standpoint epistemology offers feminists an essentially reformist position on Enlightenment reason and objectivity. This reformism renders strong objectivity and feminist standpoint epistemology attractive alternatives for a feminist philosophy of religion. More precisely, feminist standpoint epistemology is philosophically attractive for four main reasons. First, it is not built upon a naive claim to relativism. Second, its aim is not exclusive, elitist; on the contrary, it aims to understand oppression at the same time as the privileged position of knowledge-makers. Third, it upholds epistemology, objectivity, reason, and so retains concern for truth and justice; hence it is not anti-Enlightenment in the strong sense of some postmodern extremes. Fourth, it constantly struggles with the inevitability of presuppositions and prejudices. This inevitability is equally consistent with aspects of continental epistemology, of Kant's critical philosophy, of Hegel's modifications of Kant, as well as with the presuppositional claims of twentieth-century hermeneutics.[39]

Yet more thinking is necessary to work out how strong objectivity would actually function in our arguments in philosophy of religion. In particular, how can it bring in legitimate differences of sex, gender, race, class, ethnicity, without being rejected as merely politically correct jargon? I have suggested that there is a serious argument for strong objectivity. But if it is not simply a matter of using the correct terms or asking the right questions, then we need to learn how to think from the lives of others in order to achieve feminist knowledge and so less biased beliefs than philosophers justify at present.

6 What is Still Lacking for Feminist Belief

Note, first, that Hegel informs the notion of strong objectivity in feminist standpoint epistemology; second, that one of two crucial imperatives of strong objectivity is self-reflexivity; and third, that in Hegelian terms, desire reveals the reflexivity of the subject's consciousness. The feminist standpoint epistemologist's lack of attention to desire is especially noticeable in that

Hegel himself gives a crucial role to desire in self-reflexivity.[40] Thus it is important to take a slight detour and consider the role of desire in Hegel.

For Hegel, desire signifies the necessity that consciousness become other to itself in order to know itself.[41] Here consciousness signifies the emergent yet still detached subject who has not become fully aware of herself or himself as embodied. Hegel links desire with self-knowledge while self-consciousness becomes identified with desire in general.[42]

Most significant is the role that desire plays in Hegel's master and slave dialectic in *The Phenomenology of Spirit*, since this dialectic is also fundamental to feminist standpoint epistemology. To establish the integral role of desire in Hegel's dialectic, I will consider the way in which it enables the detached subject to gain self-knowledge. At the same time, I will suggest how the discrete subject of traditional epistemology can be transformed by the new self-knowledge gained from feminist standpoint appropriations of Hegel's dialectic.

Roughly following Hegel, I assert that the subject of modern epistemology, at least since Descartes, starts as a subject who does not yet know itself as embodied. To begin with, the detached, epistemological subject has a consciousness with only a theoretical experience of its object, a sense of what it must be like; the sensuous and empirical world remains distant as an object of theory and experientially unknown. The problem of consciousness for the emergent subject is how to conceptualize its relationship with the world, including its relationship with her or his own body and with other emergent subjects.

According to Judith Butler, Hegel solves this problem by calling on the experience of desire as the mode in which self-consciousness requires the sensuous and empirical world. Self-consciousness emerges as a kind of knowing that is at once a mode of becoming; knowing as becoming is suffered and enacted. In desiring some feature of the world, self-consciousness seeks to achieve the unity with the world that consciousness could achieve only theoretically and not fully. Unlike the momentary act of a discrete subject perceiving a distant and discrete world, self-consciousness is a cognitive experience taking place in an evolving sense of time. As a cognitive experience, it grasps the temporal life of the object itself. Prior to self-consciousness, the subject as consciousness could think of actual objects in the empirical world but could not think the actual process of determination and indetermination that is life itself; it could not think change.[43]

Bear in mind that for Hegel desire itself is intentional. This means that it is always desire of or for a given object or an other. And, as already stated, desire is also reflexive. This means that desire constitutes the instrument by which the self-conscious subject is both found and developed. Butler explains the implications of desire as intentional and reflexive: the conditions which give rise to desire constitute a metaphysics of internal relations; at the same time, these conditions are precisely what desire seeks to express or make explicit. In this way, desire constitutes an implicit search for metaphysical knowledge, the human way in which such knowledge 'speaks.'[44]

For feminists who seek to gain self-knowledge, desire becomes the motivation for the disembodied subject to acquire knowledge of reality from a seemingly separate and disparate world of nature. Once expressed explicitly, desire would help to alter the traditional empiricist notion of human agency to fit the new, reflexive requirements of self-consciousness. As a sensuous and self-reflexive expression of consciousness, desire discloses self-consciousness as that which participates in what it investigates. In the process of becoming, desire constantly widens its intentional aims and thereby expands the domain of reflexivity which, to repeat, it finds and develops.

In turn, Hegel says of self-consciousness that it is essentially the return from otherness.[45] In its development, desire as an expression of self-consciousness returns from its movement outward into the world of nature and becomes the constant motive for overcoming the ontological separation of consciousness and its world. Desire does not change the ontological difference between subject and world, but provides an alternative mode of conceptualizing their diremption. By recognizing its embodiment in the world, the desiring subject reveals its proper ontological structure in its relation to otherness.[46]

Now the question for the privileged feminist subject is: What kind of otherness must self-consciousness find such that self-realization mediated by this other results in self-recovery? If Hegel is correct that desire is realized in otherness and that this otherness reflects itself, then the otherness which desire seeks must be another self-consciousness. What more specifically can I say about this other self-consciousness?

Hegel's chapter on the master and the slave enacts the gradual specification of desire. In this re-enactment, self-consciousness becomes desire in particular. Initially for the master, bodily life must be taken care of, but this can be done by an other; for the body is not, at least not initially, part of his own project of identity. The master's identity is essentially beyond the body; he gains illusory confirmation for this view by requiring the other to be the body that he attempts not to be. I would suggest here that the master appears similar to the detached, privileged male subject; and certain feminists have read the other as the female sex.[47]

Hegel also describes the initial figures of both the master and the slave as configurations of death in life; death-bound desires appear in the shadows of more explicit desires to die.[48] Before their mutual self-recognition, the master and the slave turn against life in different ways while both resist the synthesis of their corporeality and freedom; but this synthesis alone is constitutive of human life. The initial situation is that the master – like the caricature of the disembodied male subject of modern philosophy – lives in dread of his body while the slave lives in dread of freedom.

As long as desire resists the synthesis of corporeality and freedom, the desire to eliminate the other motivates a mutual action of master and slave. Each self-consciousness seeks to destroy the definite boundaries that exist between them; they intend to destroy each other's bodies. However, implicit in Hegel's dialectic is the principle that whatever exists as a precondition of desire also serves as an intentional aim of desire's expression. Ultimately the desire of subjects which is a transformation of the natural world becomes the transformation of the natural selves of master and slave themselves into embodied freedoms. At this stage in its development, the notion of desire loses its earlier, reified character as desire in general – as an abstract universal – and becomes situated in terms of an embodied identity. Hence the master is forced out of his initial position in acknowledging, albeit with hestitation, that he too is tied to nature and life. And so the desiring subjects arrive at recognition of the situatedness which leads to one of the two key imperatives of strong objectivity: to think from the lives of others. Thus the master sees himself embodied like the slave, and the slave recognizes his freedom like the master in the face of life.

Arguably the Hegelian transformations of desire and of subjects of desire cannot actually develop outside of an historically constituted intersubjectivity which mediates the relation to nature and to the self. This means that subjects mutually recognize each other only in actual communities. At least for some post-Hegelians, true subjectivities come to flourish only in communities which provide for reciprocal recognition: for we do not come to ourselves alone but through the acknowledging look of the other who confirms us.[49]

I would contend that such reciprocal recognition in historically specific communities is the point where feminist standpoint epistemology introduces the second imperative of strong objectivity: to reinvent ourselves as other.[50] It is important both to understand this in terms of Hegel's master and slave dialectic, and to see desire in terms of the embodied identity of subjects who are freely recognized within historically constituted communities. This background informs my subsequent applications of both imperatives of feminist strong objectivity: (1) to think from the lives of others, and (2) to reinvent (our)selves as other.

Yet the obvious questions are: Where are the historically constituted communities rendering women and men their embodied identities? Whose lives are involved in reciprocal recognition? More specifically, to whom does 'other' refer at the heart of feminist standpoint epistemology? Harding has said that the lives of others include, for example, 'Third World' women. But this may not be enough to identify historically constituted communities of women knowers who return from otherness in order to reinvent themselves. Harding seems to lack an articulated method for arriving at the distinctive thinking of these historical others named Third World women. So what constitutes otherness? And what does our return from otherness constitute? Lazreg contends that

> I find Harding's formulation of the questions she raises about what it would mean for western feminists to 'learn from the standpoint of women of Third World descent' [Harding 1991, 245] in their musings over science and technology interesting but troubling . . . I have yet to know what it means to be of 'Third World descent'. These women's counterparts are defined as 'First World', 'North Atlantic', of 'European descent'. Although these labels are an improvement over the generic 'women of colour', they are still inadequate and beg the issue. Non-Third World women (why not?) are said to 'learn to ask different questions by starting their thought from accounts that begin in Third World women's lives'. This solution is mechanistic. Is it a matter of asking the right questions? Or is it a matter of coming to grips with the fact that First World women's lives are another modality of Third World women's lives? (Lazreg 1994, 53–4)

Harding's method may not be made fully explicit and may well sound mechanistic. Yet Harding is clear that thinking from women's lives involves struggle; and this struggle with otherness avoids the problems seen in the present chapter related to the empiricists' expressions of experience. In Harding, 'women's lives' do not refer straightforwardly to women's experiences. Nor does objectivity have to mean a completely detached form of thought about life. In this way, she seeks to overcome the deeply problematic notion of experience.

To summarize this last point, an epistemology based in discrete, individual experiences cannot give access either to knowledge of the social structures within which experience takes place or to the social antecedents of that same experience. But Harding is not speaking as a naive empiricist would about experience as the basis for knowledge. In speaking about the lives of others, she intends to situate knowledge historically and specifically.

A discrete individual, even if privileged, cannot generate true knowledge; it is necessary to have confirmation from the perspective of the lives of others.

But once the above is accepted, how are women's lives, if not experiences, accurately got at? Identifying the characteristics of women living in male-dominated societies does not necessarily constitute knowledge of women. Is there some sort of distinctive women's quality to the lives of women as other? If I am not talking about something distinctively female, it is not obviously easy to work out something distinctively other. How, in the end, do I make my thinking from the lives of others inclusive of all women, including women who differ by class, race, ethnicity? I suggested earlier that we take seriously Mernissi's criticism of feminists who fail to acknowledge the challenges posed to patriarchy by the lives of illiterate Arab women in their dissenting practices within Islam. The task is to see the hidden in order to make strange the all-too-familiar, patriarchal configurations of belief, in order to become outsiders within patriarchal frames of reference.

In addition, it is my contention that relevant linguistic and phenomenological tools are needed to fill out and support the twofold imperatives, to think from the lives of others, and to reinvent ourselves as other. Specifically I am advocating the use of myth as a tool for imagining ever-new figures of female desire, difference, and dissent while miming becomes a tool for disrupting biased configurations of beliefs.

7 A Critical Coda

It is time to draw some conclusions concerning the question of feminist objectivity. Does the rationality of strong objectivity as central to standpoint epistemology constitute a logic which can be used to assess the soundness, validity, or truth of arguments for or against religious belief? Feminist standpoint epistemologists are not really concerned with the assessment of arguments for their strictly formal, logical success. And feminist standpoint epistemology does not justify true belief by seeking necessary and sufficient conditions for truth. The feminist standpoint epistemologists would insist that even the naive empiricist must admit that embodiment is a necessary condition of the knowing subject, but the feminist standpoint epistemologists do not seem to ask the question of sufficient conditions for knowledge. Instead their question is: For whom have justified true beliefs been constructed?

Yet is this alternative question within the domain of epistemology? If I say 'yes,' this might suggest a reformed version of modern epistemologies, emphasizing ethical truth and justice over logical truth. (The answer 'no' would probably imply a question of postmodern theory which tends to be anti-epistemology; but this seems to overstate the feminist standpoint epistemologist criticisms of modern epistemological concerns, since clearly they do not reject *tout court* epistemology, reason, and objectivity.[51]) In particular, strong objectivity is not far from a reformed version of the past epistemological notion of Kant modified by Hegel and Marx. Perhaps reform is really what the feminist epistemologist intends. But if so, the subject of feminist objectivity may not be all that much stronger than Kant's paradoxical account of the subject of knowledge as both subject and object, noumenal and empirical; and if it represents a solid advance on Kant's notions of ahistorical subjectivity and objectivity, it may leave us with the problems resulting from Hegel's and Marx's criticisms of Kant's limitation of reason.[52] And yet it should not go unnoticed that feminist standpoint epistemology exhibits a crucial difference from all earlier philosophical accounts of reason and objectivity in its ethical scrutiny of biased and partial beliefs structurally and specifically against women and all marginalized others.

In the context of the argument of this book, the really important question becomes: What does a feminist epistemology of belief which hopes to employ this reformed account of objectivity still lack? I have proposed that the specific content of women's beliefs constructed by thinking from the lives of others remains unclear, if not lacking. I will respond to this potential lack in the next chapter by considering the repression of female desire. The critical point is that desire and sexual difference, although probably constituting crucial content for women's beliefs, are not fully recognized or enhanced by feminist standpoint epistemology. Here I employ female desire as a general category; but this is also compatible with the specificity of female desires. My use of a general category of desire does not necessarily exclude recognition of particular embodiments of desire, taking into account differences of gender, race, class, and creed. At least within modern philosophy since Kant, a general category can in fact be given new content by particular examples; the problem will arise with certain postmodern criticisms of any identity of particular and general in the subject.

In the end, feminist standpoint epistemology cannot offer a complete answer to my question concerning the specific material content of women's religious beliefs. Therefore, at this stage, I leave the reader with various suggestions concerning the role and content of desire in the construction of theistic or nontheistic beliefs. Despite any lack of definitive points about desire, the claim to think from the lives of marginalized others offers a point for dialogue with poststructuralists and for development with readings of sexual difference; this dialogue and development will begin in the next chapter. I also stress the proposal, to be taken up in part III, that feminist philosophers of religion employ myth and mimesis to configure and refigure belief; this would mean recognizing the role of desire and of objectivity in reinventing ourselves as other. In particular, mimetic refigurations of women's expressions of belief understood as dissident speech offer the possibility of breaking down barriers while voicing the content of our differences.[53]

Notes

1. For a different integration of feminist standpoint epistemology and feminist poststructuralism, see Hennessy 1993, 14–34.
2. Harding 1991, 111.
3. Concerning the unstable relation of sex/gender, see Harding 1983, 311–24; Gatens 1991a, 139–60; Butler, 1987b; 1990; Braidotti 1994b, 49–70; Chanter 1995, 21–47.
4. Moore 1997 presents an alternative account to this naive empiricist conception of absolute reality. He insists upon the possibility of absolute representations: although we may never produce an absolute representation of reality, this possibility is crucial for preserving the unity, substantiality, and autonomy of reality.
5. For more on psycholinguistics, see chapter 3 below.
6. Harding 1990, 83–106.
7. Hartsock 1983, 283–310; Longino 1990; Harding 1993; Irigaray 1993a; Braidotti 1994a.
8. Harding 1983; 1991; 1993. I will not assess applications of standpoint theories in psychology and moral philosophy, but for an example of the latter, see Noddings 1984.
9. Descartes 1986 (1641); Bordo 1987.
10. For Kant, content valid for all rational beings would be judged valid from both the rational vantage of human beings, who, unlike a divine being, are embodied and so not fully or purely rational, and the ideal vantage of God, who, as nonembodied, is postulated as the only fully rational being; see Kant 1950 (1781, 1787), 494–5, 522–4, 550–1, 555–61 (especially A670–89/B707–17); cf. Scruton 1996, 120, 225–6; Moore 1997. Yet it does not necessarily follow that objectivity is achievable by rational human beings who try to approximate a view-from-nowhere, especially if this approximation involves thinking as if disembodied; even if achievable, disembodied thinking would not be the same as God's nonembodied view of the world (see chapter 4, section 1, below, concerning nonembodied and disembodied). Moreover in what sorts of cases, if any, would disembodied thinking be more objective than embodied (or nonembodied) thought? The empiricist assumes that rational validity is bound

up with the universality achieved only by transcending the particularity of one's embodiment; but this is not strictly true for Kant.

11. Harding 1993.
12. For an argument against the possible anti-realism of the feminist poststructuralist Irigaray, see Assiter 1996, 54–67. Alternatively for a possible anti-realist circumspection on an otherwise realist position, see Moore 1997.
13. My simultaneous criticisms of empirical realist forms of theism and conventional objectivity are supported by examples of an assumed affinity between the God's-eye view and the ideal observer theory of values. For a contemporary philosopher of religion who defends the attributes of an ideal observer in the context of a larger defense of the theistic God, see Taliaferro 1997, chapter 5.
14. Newman 1994, 15ff; cf. chapter 4, section 1, below.
15. Harding 1993, 49, 69, 71; cf. Haraway 1988, 581.
16. Longino 1994, 476–9, 481.
17. Harding 1991, 138f.
18. Harding 1993, 70–1.
19. For an argument concerning the restrictive nature of the so-called abstracted empiricism implicit in feminist conceptions of experience, see Lazreg 1994.
20. Lazreg 1990, 326ff. For an empiricist approach to 'the conflicting claims' of religious experiences which develops a cumulative case for western theism, see Franks Davis 1989, 166–9, 189–92; and for criticisms of this approach, see Jantzen 1994, 197–9.
21. Harding 1993, 71.
22. Harding 1991, 120–33, 249f.
23. Bordo 1987; Haraway 1988, 581; Nicholson and Fraser (eds)1990, 3; Harding 1991; 1993, 57.
24. Harding 1993, 61–2.
25. Another possibility for feminist epistemology both preserves realism and avoids foundationalism by drawing upon naturalized epistemology; see Fricker 1994, 95–109. Instead of a picture of beliefs being built upon a secure experiential foundation, naturalized epistemology offers a holistic or coherentist picture in which political and empirical beliefs are interdependent; also, see Hankinson Nelson 1990.
26. Harding 1991, 139–42.
27. Code objects to feminist uses of Kant's ideal of pure reason and the consequent conceptions of objective knowledge and subjectivity; for her criticisms of Kantian formalism, see Code 1995, 208–33. In contrast, O'Neill (1989) argues for and uses the primacy of Kant's practical reason; and for her highly nuanced Kantian account of justice applied to women's lives which avoids both relativism and unjust idealizations, see O'Neill 1993, 301–23; 1995, 140–52; 1996.
28. Harding 1991, 161–3, 268–95; Hill Collins 1991, 201–15, 222–38; hooks 1990, 145–53.
29. Mernissi 1996, 13–20.

30. Mernissi also elucidates the paradox of memory which ignores the pre-eminence of women on the political stage in the first decades of Islam. During these formative years, Muslim women were disciples who triumphed in the political game as mothers and queens. Yet the history which gave enormous importance to the mothers of believers and to the wives of prophets and kings is forgotten by the later leaders of Islam – as well as by feminists – who insist that Muslim women obey only, not lead. Those who currently contest women's entitlement to political rights in the name of Islam select from the period of absolutism as embodied in and symbolized by the figure of the slave woman (*jariya*). In this reading of history, the Muslim woman's identity has been decisively excluded but Islamic memory has also been suppressed; see Mernissi 1996, 79–91.
31. The concept of 'outsider within' as the subject who generates a maximal objectivity originally comes from Hill Collins 1986, 14–32.
32. For a privileged white woman who gained firsthand knowledge about Arab women's resistance to the violence of patriarchal religious rituals, see Brooks 1996. Brooks demonstrates the real possibility of learning to think from the lives of others while reinventing oneself as an outsider within.
33. For discussion of men becoming feminists and becoming like females by religious miming, see chapter 5, section 2, below.
34. Haraway 1988; 1990 (1989).
35. For an argument against empiricist readings of Kant which fail to understand Kant's idea of a rational community of embodied subjects, his affinity with Hegel, and Hegel's advance on Kant, see Tuschling in Rossi and Wreen (eds) 1991, 181–206.
36. Hegel 1977, 111–19. For critical accounts of Hegel's master–slave dialectic, see Butler 1987a; Roth 1988, 99–119; Wood 1990, 85–93. Note that here Butler describes Lacan as disagreeing with Hegel, especially in Lacan's reading of desire as an expression of a longing for a return to origins which would necessitate the dissolution of the subject (cf. 186–204).
37. Kristeva 1991, 1, 75f, 184, 191f.
38. For an argument advocating epistemological communities, see Hankinson Nelson 1993.
39. For a collection of essays on the interface between the different schools of Enlightenment epistemology and post-Enlightenment philosophies, see Kunneman and Vries (eds) 1993, especially Bennington, 45–60; Vries, 211–56; Braidotti, 319–41; Dews, 367–77. See also Fodor 1995.
40. Harding 1991, 120f. At least the influential French reading of Hegel by Kojève gives desire a crucial role in self-reflexivity; see Kojève 1980 (1947). Cf. Descombes 1980; Butler 1987a; Roth 1988.
41. Butler 1987a, 7.
42. Hegel 1977, 104–6, 109–18; cf. Butler 1987a, 24–5, 43–4, 48–58.
43. Butler 1987a, 28; cf. Hegel 1977, 101: para. 163, 106–9, 113: para. 186.

44. Butler 1987a, 24–5. Compare this with the discussion of hysteria and the miming of female desire in chapters 3 and 4 below.
45. Hegel 1977, 105: para. 167.
46. Butler 1987a, 34.
47. Beauvoir 1989 (1949), 3, 6–7, 23, 64–5; cf. Gatens 1991b, 48–59; 1996, 29–45.
48. Compare the master and slave configurations of death in life with Irigaray's miming of woman as the figure of living death in part IV below.
49. For more on desire in Hegel, see Butler 1987a, 24–99.
50. Marx's comments on Hegel should come into Harding's account here; see Harding 1991, 120; Marx criticizes Hegel for not realizing that human activity and material life constrain what we can know.
51. Harding 1990, 83–106.
52. These problems are no longer strictly epistemological or necessarily about reason. After Hegel, intriguing questions are raised about desire and the subjects of desire; for various answers in the French reception of Hegel, see Butler 1987a.
53. See chapter 4 below; cf. Irigaray 1993a; Meyers 1994, 56–61; Braidotti 1994a, 75f, 95–110.

3

Feminists and the Rationality of Belief, II: Female Desire

what deceives some people and destroys others about belief is the way it makes us forget the real.

Irigaray 1993c, 26

1 New Content for Belief

The new subjects of feminist knowledges who seek a strong objectivity, as conceived in the previous chapter, should acknowledge their embodiment and everything which goes with being a part of nature. Nevertheless disembodiment has been assumed by advocates of the conventional scientific objectivity of empirical realism. Ironically the position of the subject of empirical realism, whether that of the scientist or the epistemologist, is said to be a disembodied position originally conceived by modern philosophers keen to use scientific method precisely to render the objectivity of true belief possible. Yet this objective position is impossible not only because the subject of empirical realism has failed to take into account the fact that 'he' too is in nature, but because he has failed to recognize the partiality of belief which remains an unavoidable aspect of his being embodied.

Irigaray confirms the impossible position of the disembodied epistemological subject. In the post-phenomenological terms of Irigaray, embodiment would mean being a mind and spirit incarnate in a multifaceted physical body which speaks, i.e. uses language, to express feelings, desires, intuitions, beliefs, reasons, or rationality.[1] On this crucial point at least, Irigaray seems both correct and compatible with feminist standpoint epistemology. She claims that

> The discourse of the subject has been altered but finds itself even more disturbed by [the Copernican] revolution than the language of the

> [premodern] world which preceded it. Given that the scientist, now, wants to be in front of the world: naming the world, making its laws, its axioms. Manipulating nature, exploiting it, but forgetting that he too is in nature. That he is still physical, and not only when faced with phenomena whose physical nature he tends to ignore. As he progresses according to an objective method designed to shelter him from any instability, any 'mood', any feelings and affective fluctuations, from any intuition that has not been programmed in the name of science, from any influence of his desire, particularly his sexual desire. (Irigaray 1993a, 125)

The crucial problem for women, according to the above passage, is that the modern epistemological subject stands over and against nature. In modern epistemology, nature has included the physical world but not the objective method used to study this world; and the scientist's objective method does not include feelings, moods, desires, or any emotions associated with women. Feminist philosophers such as Irigaray offer the philosopher of religion insight concerning the possible role of desire in a new, more inclusive epistemology of religious belief. In contrast, the theist who follows the modern scientific subject not only excludes his own physical embodiment from his objective method of justifying true belief, but is unable to recognize the significant role played by feelings, and spiritual and sexual desires in the justification of religious belief. Instead desire has been unconsciously projected onto the female other by the epistemological subject; nevertheless she serves as a pretext for experiences of the divine, especially in love-making.

Irigaray describes how this is so:

> She is brought into a world that is not her own so that the male lover may enjoy himself and gain strength for his voyage toward an autistic transcendence. In his quest for a God who is already inscribed but voiceless, does she permit him not to constitute the ethical site of lovemaking? A seducer who is seduced by the gravity of the Other but approaches the female other carelessly, he takes her light to illuminate his path. Without regard for what shines and glistens between them. Whether he wills it or not, knows it or not, he uses this divine light to illuminate reason or the invisibility of the 'god.'
>
> In the meantime he will have taken from the beloved woman this visibility that she offers him, which strengthens him, and will have sent her back to darkness. He will have stolen her gaze. And her song[2] . . . The male lover steals her desire from her to adorn his world – which

> predates love – to spark his pleasure and aid his ascent . . . (Irigaray 1993a, 209–10; cf. Irigaray 1991a, 171–7)

In the above passage, Irigaray's language is both evocative and provocative. The use of sexual metaphors helps us to see the way in which female desire has been needed, used, and then eclipsed in love-making. The specific content of Irigaray's words provoke us to question 'his' theft of 'her' desire which prevents him from seeing the divine light between them as two subjects in love. Instead her song and her light are stolen to aid his ascent, igniting only his pleasures and illuminating only his path.

In this chapter, I aim to study feminist poststructuralist accounts of the role of female desire and the function of the maternal in experiences of the divine, especially with reference to the infinite. In addition to Irigaray, who is both a philosopher and a psychoanalyst, I am placing the semiotician and psychoanalyst Julia Kristeva, who will be given special attention in this chapter, within the framework of feminist poststructuralism. Yet each of these women has objected at times to the label 'feminist' and they each would disagree in their own ways with particular poststructuralist concerns.[3] However, I use the category feminist poststructuralist to emphasize a distinctive position informed by critical engagement with Jacques Lacan (1901–81) and, to a certain degree, with Jacques Derrida on issues of sexual difference and female desire.

Minimally Derrida offers feminists the philosophical tools for a critique of both the autonomous subject and the dominant form of metaphysics. The latter he calls logocentrism because it focuses on a singular logic or rationality of identity while excluding binary differences. Roughly speaking, logocentrism privileges reason while excluding desire, form while excluding matter, unity while excluding multiplicity, and so on. Lacan offers feminists the psychoanalytic tools to account for the specifically masculine rationality in the logocentric constitution of the social-symbolic order which represses both femininity, including the maternal, and sexual difference, including desire. For the feminist poststructuralist, the rationality of belief has been determined by the male symbolic order, while desire is repressed and so excluded by this order. Yet desire is also potentially expressible as the sexually specific discourse of the forgotten love of the female other.

Within the patriarchal social-symbolic order, desire appears in the breaks or ruptures of consciousness, giving indications of the repressed content of a religious belief. To explain this, I turn to Judith Butler again. I have selected certain of Butler's concise yet critical statements concerning Lacan's difference from Hegel on desire. Notice that, despite Lacan's criticisms of Hegel, Butler also discerns their common ground:

> For Lacan, desire can no longer be equated with the fundamental structure of human rationality; Eros and Logos resist an Hegelian conflation . . . Desire is that which consciousness in its reflexivity seeks to *conceal*. Indeed, desire is the moment of longing that consciousness may be said to suffer, but which is only 'revealed' through the displacements, ruptures and fissures of consciousness.
>
> . . .
>
> Lacan's criticism assumes that Hegel's subject, in fact, 'knows what it wants' . . . The [Hegelian] subject itself, however, does not know what it wants from the start, although it may implicitly *be* all that it comes to know about itself in the course of the *Phenomenology*.
>
> . . .
>
> And yet, for Lacan, Hegel's formulation is not wholly wrong . . . Desire [in Lacan] maintains something of the transcendental pursuit of presence . . . seen in the Hegelian thinkers.
>
> . . .
>
> For Lacan, desire is still in search of (Hegel's) Absolute, but this desire has become specified as male desire, and this Absolute is understood to be the fantasy of maternal fulfillment that women are obliged to represent . . . It makes sense, then, to ask whether Lacan has not rediscovered a religious dream of plenitude in a fantasy of lost pleasure that he himself has constructed. Although Lacan understands himself to have refuted the possibility of a dialectical pursuit of plenitude, a seamless web of internal relations, the belief in such a state is evident in the nostalgia that, according to Lacan, characterizes all human desire. (Butler 1987a, 186, 196, 197, 203–4)

With the above statements in mind, I move on to discover the ways in which continental feminists reappropriate desire following both Hegel and Lacan.

The distinctive significance of the feminist poststructuralist engagement with Lacan is obvious in Irigaray's provocative writings on desire, sexual difference, love, and religion. Her writings have had a diverse reception but at the present moment excitement over her work grows ever stronger, especially for those seeking to uncover the specificities of female desire.[4] Both Irigaray, born in Belgium (1930), and Kristeva, born in Bulgaria (1941), live and practice psychoanalysis in Paris where they were each educated in Lacanian psychoanalysis or, more accurately, in psycholinguistics (discussed in section 3 of this chapter). Yet the two women have made different and distinctive contributions to the intellectual world, each having produced significant works for psychoanalysis, philosophy, and women's studies. All of their works impinge, to a greater or lesser degree, upon religion.[5]

In Kristeva's work, I find the implicit query: Do women in the light of their maternal function[6] remain pretexts for experiences of a different and holy being? I will suggest that Kristeva's advance on Lacan's account of the mother is to free the maternal from the unknowable, feminine desire: she maintains that the mother is not an object of the child's desire as much as a function. The maternal function is to contain the conflicts which occur between the biological and the social dimensions of psychosexual development.

Before substantiating my reading of Kristeva, it is necessary to comment briefly on the feminist poststructuralist use of sex/gender terms of 'female'/'feminine' and 'male'/'masculine'. In French, the language of Lacan and Derrida as well as Irigaray and Kristeva, there is only one adjective to describe both female sex and feminine gender (*féminin*). So translators face a great difficulty in choosing the appropriate English terms for being gendered or sexed: when to use 'masculine' and not 'male,' or 'feminine' and not 'female' is uncertain. Yet the overriding point to bear in mind is that the sharp distinction between sex and gender which was drawn by certain Anglo-American feminists from the 1950s to 1970s is decisively challenged by Kristeva and Irigaray; they undermine the distinction between biological given and social construct.

As pointed out in part 1, gender appears to be redundant for feminist poststructuralists who instead speak of seeking sexual difference. In this century, Anglo-American feminists defined gender as a socially constituted norm; but today other feminists are also claiming that sexual identity and nonidentity are constituted by the patriarchal social-symbolic order. For these latter, the definition of women's sexual identity is not biologically given but is constructed by the male; at the same time, sexual difference and with it specifically female desire are repressed. The difference between a male construction of female desire and a woman's sexually specific account of female desire cannot, then, be recognized (even by women themselves) until women are free to express themselves as subjects in love. In discussions of feminist poststructuralists, the social-symbolic order of a patriarchal culture is not just called masculine: it is male. The social variable of masculinity cannot be separated from the material of sexual identity. No clear line can be drawn between masculine and male as conditioned by a dynamic linguistic process of a patriarchal social-symbolic order.

However, certain Anglo-American feminists still have trouble seeing that this collapse of the sex/gender distinction by eliminating gender does not mean opting for an essentialism of Woman. But in fact there can be no fundamental form 'Woman' in the philosophical thinking of continental feminists which follows after both phenomenology and psychoanalysis.[7] To guide those readers who seek more background on Kristeva's and Irigaray's respective accounts of religious belief, let me offer a minimal amount of psychoanalytic perspective on desire and rationality. Neither Kristeva nor Irigaray can be understood without some knowledge of the decentering of reason attempted by Lacan and, before him, by Freud.

2 Desire and the Rational Subject

Whether philosopher, feminist, or feminist philosopher, the poststructuralist critic challenges the exclusive privilege given to the rational subject in modern epistemology. The poststructuralist challenge is evident in such phrases as decentering the subject, the dethroned subject, or the death of the rational subject.[8] Interestingly Freud's theory of unconscious desire seems to anticipate this demise of the privileged, rational subject in claiming that 'the ego is not even master in its own house' (Freud 1991 [1915], 326).

My intention is not to oversimplify the development of psychoanalysis. I acknowledge that the corpus of Freud's work on the mind is complicated, including writings on the unconscious, the id, ego, superego, and the repressed. In fact it is important to stress that after Freud the complexity of the relationship between reasoning and desiring becomes more and more significant as modern thought develops. Here it remains just possible and ultimately important to notice some of the ways in which Freud anticipates the continuing resistance by other (male) empirical ego psychologists and certain empiricist philosophers to the discovery of unconscious desire as that which, metaphorically speaking, dethrones or decenters the rational, thinking subject. This resistance is apparent and significant for us in the tendency of empiricists to dominate the field of philosophy of religion; for example, it is evident in their control over the epistemology of religious experience.[9]

Freud's still timely statement on the reasoning subject who is decentered by desire seems almost prophetic in its challenge to naively positivist and empiricist claims to knowledge. The ambivalent acceptance of this challenge remains significant.

> But human megalomania will have suffered its third [after Copernicus and Darwin] and most wounding blow from the psychological research of the present time which seeks to prove to the ego that it is not even master in its own house, but must content itself with scanty information

> of what is going on unconsciously in its mind. We [psychoanalysts] were not the first and not the only ones to utter this call to introspection; but it seems to be our fate to give it its most forcible expression and to support it with empirical material which affects every individual. Hence arises the general revolt against our science, the disregard of all considerations of academic civility and the releasing of the opposition from every restraint of impartial logic. (Freud 1991, 325–6)

The feminist psychoanalyst also challenges the binary opposition between masculine and feminine, male and female, which remains evident in modern thought. With the opposition masculine/feminine, the masculine, like the rational in rational/emotional, tends to be privileged over the feminine. But Freud, who was anything but a feminist psychoanalyst (a contradiction within his terms), does not dethrone the masculine. Instead he identifies the feminine as the dark continent; he remains convinced that femininity is so deeply embedded in the recesses of the unconscious that nothing can be discovered about it. Predictably this dark continent of femininity is precisely what, after Lacan, Kristeva and Irigaray seek to discover or uncover.

Thus a key issue for feminist poststructuralism is that of the dethroned, rational subject. A decentering of the rational subject leads directly to questions of sexual difference. Some of these questions about the subject of rationality were raised at the outset of chapter 1. For instance, does the rational subject represent the ideal attributes of masculinity while repressing femininity as that which must be excluded to achieve identity, unity, and mastery?

I have found illuminating the attempts by poststructuralists to expose the ways in which modern philosophy has precariously given privilege to oppositional thinking, as well as to the first term of oppositions such as rational/emotional, formal/material, subject/object. I use 'precariously' to stress that in one version of this privileging, the rational subject has had to project onto another aspects of its materially conditioned status. While functioning as a physical being, he claims to think as a disembodied subject. The privileging of the rational over the emotional means that modernity has tended to be reductive in valuing a person who, for instance, is rational about beliefs and not emotional (which in that context would mean irrational).

At least since Descartes wrote his philosophy in the seventeenth century, modern philosophers have employed reason to arrive at the justified true belief which represents knowledge. According to the dominant tradition of western philosophy, Descartes becomes the symbolic father of modern philosophy and so of epistemology. The convention of modern epistemology is to equate justified true belief with knowledge. After Locke, philosophers find themselves with an epistemic duty to believe only what can be rationally justified in the light of evidence. Then in the eighteenth century, Kant claims that religious belief must also always be understood within the limits of reason alone; ultimately these limits render problematic the content of the rational subject's belief. Notwithstanding these issues in the history of modern philosophy, my present aim is not to rule out Descartes, Locke, Kant, or reason itself as a consequence of the problematic position of the rational subject. Instead it is to push back the limits of reason and expose its repressed content.

In other words, this chapter offers no proposal for feminists to privilege desire over reason; neither is the proposed feminist philosophy of religion to be anti-epistemology. Instead my intention is to take seriously the feminist poststructuralist attempts to distinguish sexually specific discourse in order to uncover what has been buried and excluded: female desire and sexual difference.

Lacan's rereading of Freud in the terms of structural linguistics raises the question of language as discourse. Language is a system of signs and symbols which, like the unconscious in Freud, decenters man. For Lacan, man speaks; but symbols have made him man.[10] Hence language as a symbolic and social system becomes crucial in defining the adult male; language constitutes his sexual identity and structures the social-symbolic order which the child enters when he learns to speak. The Symbolic is Lacan's technical term for the system of cultural symbols, signs, images, and representations of all kinds – including language – which form the individual as a subject. The Symbolic privileges the father/son symbolism of patriarchal religions.

Prominent in the writings of both Kristeva and Irigaray are criticisms of the general constitution of the masculine and fundamentally male Symbolic, making up the symbolic system of patriarchy. Their criticisms take the form of readings which attempt to subvert the language and texts of religious and philosophical discourse; they aim to subvert the very language which constitutes the masculine social-symbolic order of our world. Such subversive criticism is evident in their various attempts to uncover the repressed discourse of maternal desire in religious myths. Yet despite their efforts at subversion of the Symbolic, both Kristeva and Irigaray remain to some degree dependent on Lacan.

3 Sexually Specific Discourse and the Numinous

Kristeva and Irigaray both follow Lacan in employing psychoanalytic and psycholinguistic principles in their, however different, readings of patriarchal religion. Psycholinguistic means a focus upon language as the condition for all possible meaning and value. In assuming the poststructuralist account of language, psycholinguistics neither analyzes language as an empirical object nor analyzes the different uses given to particular words in representing the world. Instead it studies language as a dynamic structure or a process which constitutes subjectivity and sexual identity. The development of this linguistic process enables the child's individuation and entrance into the social-symbolic order of (patriarchal) culture.

The important theory which Lacan's psycholinguistics adds to Freudian psychoanalysis is that of the mirror stage of a child's development. The mirror stage marks the shift from the pre-oedipal position of love relations with the mother to the oedipal order of relations; this is the stage at which the subject enters language and so culture as a signifying and social order. Kristeva illustrates the way in which the pre-oedipal position of unity with the mother is recalled in, for instance, religious symbolism of the maternal.[11]

Prior to the child's differentiation from the mother is a state of unity. This state exists only before there is knowledge of the difference between subject and object as child and mother. This pre-cognitive unity is supposedly denied yet ambivalently desired in experiences of a different being. Kristeva returns to Freud to examine the significance of the break with the pre-oedipal position for the unconscious and so for desire:

> [Freud] discovers [the paradoxical logic] in the uncanny strangeness of our unconscious. In the beginning[12] was hatred, Freud said basically (contrary to the well-known biblical and evangelical statement), as he discovered that the human child differentiates itself from its mother through a rejection affect, through the scream of anger and hatred that accompanies it, and through the 'no' sign as prototype of language and to all symbolism. To recognize the impetus of that hatred aroused by the other, within our own psychic dramas of psychosexual individuation – that is what psychoanalysis leads us to. It thus links its own adventure with the meditations each one of us is called upon to engage in when confronted with the fascination and horror that a different being produces in us. (Kristeva 1993a, 29–30)

The last sentence in the above is crucial. Kristeva suggests that fascinating and horrifying confrontations with a different being recall the childhood experience of undifferentiated being. Feelings of fascination and horror are produced by awareness of one's differentiation from the other and of one's finitude; this fascination recalls the experience of undifferentiated being as the earliest sense of the infinite.[13] The original state of undifferentiated being is in a sense ended by negation, by the 'No' of rejection. Yet this state remains latent and so can evoke the feeling of the uncanny as familiar and unfamiliar, as fascinating and horrifying mystery, since signifying the loss of identity in the infinite.

Uncanny feelings have been described by various philosophers of religion. For instance, the German philosopher Rudolf Otto (1869–1937) aptly describes the ways in which the nonrational factor in experience of a personal deity, i.e. the holy (*das Heilige*), produces distinctive feelings of mystery, horror, and fascination.[14] Otto's classic rendition of experiences of the holy, in relating the nonrational factor of the divine to the rational, identifies the numinous centrally with the feeling of an object outside of the self. The numinous is only known in terms of those feelings of the uncanny by which it can be reflected in the mind.[15]

Otto uses the Latin words *mysterium tremendum* (terrifying mystery) to describe the horrifying sense of the object which evokes the feeling of the numinous.[16] But this feeling of the numinous is, in another sense, fascinating, rendering it uncanny (*ungeheuer*).[17] *Mysterium tremendum et fascinans* includes (i) an awe, dread, or terror before the numen or numinous other, (ii) a completely overpowering presence of majesty or power, (iii) an intense and unbearable energy or urgency, (iv) the sense of a *wholly* other numen, or (v) a fascination with or attraction to the numen followed by rapture upon contact with it.[18] According to Otto, the numinous other can evoke one or all of these.

In retrospect, it could be argued that Otto's feeling of the nonrational factor of the divine in relation to the rational is evoked by the repressed experience of the unconscious stranger with which all adults continually struggle. Keeping in mind Otto's account of the numinous other, I return to Kristeva's post-Freudian identification of the repressed other with the uncanny other and the associated feelings of uncanny strangeness.

> the builder of the *other* and in the final analysis, of the *strange* is indeed repression itself and its perviousness. 'We can understand why linguistic usage has extended *das Heimliche* into its opposite, *das Unheimliche*; for this uncanny is in reality nothing new or alien, but something which is

> familiar and old-established in the mind and which has become alienated from it only through the process of repression'.[19]
>
> . . . Under certain conditions, however, the repressed 'that ought to have remained secret' shows up again and produces a feeling of uncanny strangeness. (Kristeva 1991, 184)[20]

From the above, it would appear that feelings associated with experiences of the wholly other have their source in the repression of the childhood experience of and separation from undifferentiated being. At least Kristeva's description of the strange other appears consistent with Otto's feeling of the numinous as uncanny, as fascinating and horrifying mystery.

More than either Otto or Freud, Kristeva helps me to locate the origin of the differences within and between each of us: in our early relations to the mother. Such differences are concealed at the moment of the break with the mother, yet emerge as the sexually specific feelings of fascination, horror, and mystery evoked by the uncanny other.[21] The fascinating specificity of mystical feelings depend upon the sexually specific relations of male or female to the mother. Moreover Kristeva links the formation of adult identity with the constitution of rationality. The relationship between the repressed maternal and the autonomous, arguably male, identity is mirrored in the philosophical account of the relationship between the nonrational and rational.

Her dual accounts of autonomous identity and of rationality can be compared with the classic account of reason which, as proposed by various feminists, goes back to the Pythagorean table of opposites in ancient Greek philosophy. Similar to the earlier mentioned feminist readings of ancient philosophy, Kristeva draws a distinction between patriarchal reason and maternal desire, associating the nonrational infinite with the maternal in terms of Plato's *chora*.[22] The maternal as *chora* is the receptacle of undifferentiated being and so opposed to the differentiated identity of an adult. In constituting early childhood experience, the *chora* represents the place of being one with all being rather than having a distinct, adult identity – traditionally as finite and male. For Kristeva, the *chora* connotes the unrepresentable body of the mother; the maternal body itself is easily associated with the infinite as that which is repressed.[23] The problem, then, lies in trying to allow the sexually specific discourse concerning this repressed desire to emerge, to speak for men and women.

Both Kristeva and Irigaray are preoccupied with the sexually specific discourse which has been repressed yet emerges as desire, pre- and post-oedipal, in accounts of the infinite, the uncanny, the mystical.[24] What remains essential for their respective psycholinguistic refigurings of patriarchal beliefs is Lacan's advance on Freud in providing the conceptual tools for scrutinizing sexually specific discourse. This is discourse – at least potentially spoken language – whose dynamic structure emerges out of the unconscious as specifically male or female in relation to the mother. Sexually specific would have to do with material, not formal relations, and with bodily distinctiveness, not with an indistinct or general experience.

Kristeva sees discourse of and/or about maternal desire emerging in religious texts written by men, such as Augustine.[25] But Irigaray is adamant that sexually specific discourses on female desire are expressed strictly by women; and, for her, this is not necessarily maternal desire. Their common ground is that Kristeva and Irigaray, each in their own ways, seek to recover the sexually specific discourse which emerges from the pre-oedipal position. Problematically this position may only break through the Symbolic in holiness or hysteria, mysticism or madness, in the form of what 'returns' but should be repressed. In chapters 4 and 5, I will consider the possibility of expressing female desire in the mimetic refiguring of ancient myths including, following Irigaray, narratives of matricide.[26]

If there is to be a viable philosophy of religion seriously informed by feminist poststructuralism, especially by its post-Lacanian insight into the sexually specific discourse of mystical experience, it would have to be post-patriarchal. Or at the very least it would be patriarchal in the process of transformation. I mean by 'patriarchy,' in this context, both the sex/gender differentiation of man from woman and the sex/gender stratification or hierarchy of father/son as superior to mother/son, mother/daughter, woman/woman. Moreover the gender stratification of patriarchy involves by implication a hegemony insofar as particular relationships of father/son are privileged over others; patriarchal means privileging not only the father/son relationship as superior over mother/son, but also the king (and king's son) over the nonprivileged subject (and his son), the master (and his son) over slave (and his son).

4 Post-patriarchal Philosophy and Religion

Although Kristeva and Irigaray both seek to subvert patriarchy to some degree, neither intends to eliminate religious belief completely. Yet when looked at more closely, the writings of Kristeva and Irigaray exhibit only a superficial overlap. They differ fundamentally on their views of men's relation to femininity and female desire. Irigaray is especially distinctive in her clear insistence upon women's unique need for a female divine in order to define their subjectivity. Kristeva seems content to seek to transform patriarchy at the gaps and openings in texts where the maternal breaks through the Symbolic.[27] In contrast, Irigaray is doing something more in her highly disruptive and mimetic refiguring of Freud and of the history of male philosophers.[28] In brief, the respective works of Kristeva and Irigaray both impinge upon, if not seek to subvert, patriarchal religion; but the subversion of male language is especially the aim of Irigaray. My concern remains with their common, however distinctive, criticisms of patriarchy's unacknowledged debt to the maternal.

In regard to this debt, an important focus in Kristeva is upon motherhood. In Irigaray, the focus is upon the mother–daughter relation insofar as it can tell us something about repressed female desire. So Kristeva and Irigaray focus differently upon the missing or devalued element in patriarchy's account of the maternal, yet crucial for each is the pre-oedipal position in Freud. They each write about the loss of that relation to the mother, how that lost position of the mother–child unity continues to emerge in language, and how that original relationship can be allowed new expressions. The expressions of female desire, both of and for the maternal, appear in Kristeva in the transformative possibilities of psychoanalysis for religion, and in Irigaray in the subversion of the masculine divine.

Parisian psycholinguistics fostered Kristeva's work on a psychoanalytic discourse of love premissed upon a confidence in the analyst. In turn, recognition of such confidence led to Kristeva's more specific reflections upon the Christian belief in a loving, protective father as essential to entry into a religious discourse. The main subtext for Kristeva's reflections on psychoanalysis and religion is Freud's *The Future of an Illusion*. 'Our God *Logos*' is the key to Freud's psychoanalytic cure.[29] Here *Logos* signifies the 'talking cure,' in which the word passing between the minds of the analysand and the analyst confronts illusion. Kristeva combines 'In the beginning was the Word . . . the Word was God' (John 1:1) and 'God is love' (1 John 4:8) to write *In the Beginning was Love*, proposing that 'it is want of love that sends the subject into analysis, which proceeds by first restoring confidence in, and capacity for, love through the transference, and then enabling the subject to distance himself or herself from the analyst' (Kristeva 1987a [1985], 3). Kristeva pushes beyond Freud's idea of religion as an unshakeable illusion by focusing upon the 'transitory, ludic illusions' in a discourse of love (ibid., 9). To give illusion its proper therapeutic and epistemological value, the successful analysand must be able to respond to an urge to create illusions while recognizing their true nature.[30]

In the early chapters of *In the Beginning was Love*, Kristeva argues that psychoanalytic discourse should be a discourse of love which has the potential to replace the reified discourse of faith. The aim is to get behind static linguistic representations in order to discover pre-linguistic traces of another space of experience. Kristeva names the receptacle of these traces 'the semiotic' from the Greek *semeion*, for signs. This concept, as already noted, derives from Plato's *Timaeus* where he spoke of the unnameable, unstable receptable – the *chora* – existing prior to the nameable form of the One.[31] The image of the *chora* and its pre-linguistic signs enable the status of the unconscious, emotional traces not grasped by the conscious, rational mind to be specified. The semiotic stands for something preceding, underlying, and, at times, breaking through language understood as the order of signification. For example, the semiotic is suggested in Augustine's symbolic expression of 'sucking the milk [God] givest' (Kristeva 1987a, 24).

The semiotic contains pre-signifying biological and psychical energies and as such is distinct from, yet always related to, the order of signification; the order of signification is called the symbolic. The semiotic and the symbolic are different dimensions of language, as pre-signifying and signifying orders, respectively. Together they make language a dynamic, never static, signifying process. At the same time, this implies a new model of the human subject-in-process in which language is not divorced from its pre-linguistic source in the body. Kristeva's model works to explain how illusions are constituted by language yet can be confronted by decentering the conscious subject with recognition of an unconscious, semiotic space.[32]

Accompanying Kristeva's elucidation of the semiotic is an implicit critique of the God of patriarchy. This critique builds upon Lacan's theory of the mirror stage in a child's development. Kristeva appropriates Lacan's theory to identify the vital role played by the child's identification with its own image, seeking to enlarge and articulate the distinctive role played by the nascent self's identification with an imaginary father. These identifications eventually lead to separation from the mother and formation of self-identity. For the successful formation of its identity, the subject must operate within an imaginary stage in which it strives to see itself reflected in its relations to others. Moreover like pre-oedipal relations, imaginary identifications return in adult life in certain privileged moments, notably in love relations.

According to Kristeva, signs of the maternal in religious symbolism recall the pre-oedipal position of love relations contained by the semiotic.[33] And love in psychoanalytic discourse seeks to achieve a transference relation built upon the identificatory structure of (the child's) narcissism. But when Kristeva extends her idea of an imaginary father into religious discourse, she proposes a potentially heretical notion: the Freudian father of individual prehistory becomes the third term mediating between mother and child in religious phantasies.[34] This mediating third term – or Third Party – gives the subject an ego-ideal which makes possible the transition to the symbolic order of language, but also to acceptance of the other, even the authoritative Other represented by 'God the Father Almighty' in the Catholic creed of 381 CE.

Thus in brief, Kristeva studies the situation of analyst and analysand, discovering a similarity of roles between the Christian God in the life of the believer and the imaginary father in the psychological development of the subject from child to adult. She draws an analogy symbolically between the believer's faith in a loving God and the analysand's trust in the analyst who represents the loving father; faith in both cases exhibits its dual religious and economic meanings, implying a confidence in the other as well as an offering which will be returned.

Her reflections on faith and psychoanalysis develop an earlier interest in rendering psychoanalytic discourse into a discourse of love which situates itself in the space previously filled by religious discourse.[35] The imaginary father or the third term, although emerging at a pre-linguistic stage, enables the speaking of love; this is the paternal–maternal function knit to a semiotic space. Catholic symbolization of Christian faith is especially significant in representing the paternal and maternal functions in the linguistic constitution of identity.[36]

Yet an apparent paradox might lead one to reject Kristeva's proposal that a semiotic dimension precedes all linguistic unities, binary oppositions, and symbolic hierarchies: the semiotic, although pre-linguistic, can only be articulated linguistically. What has to be proven is that the semiotic as pre-linguistic exists and can be recognized as subverting the symbolic order of language in creative poetry and mystic expressions. For example, the semiotic may be glimpsed in Augustine's recollection of the nourishing mother with images of God as suckling the infant with milk that does not perish. But then, what does it mean to say that this is the creative or mystic expression of an imaginary father?

The semiotic as the receptacle of undifferentiated being is premissed upon an unrepresentable space shared by the bodies of mother and child; this precedes all stable subjectivity and separate identity. If it exists, the semiotic space could not be restricted to women only. Instead men and women should have access to an early experience of both the maternal and paternal functions. After Kristeva, a modified configuration of faith in the existence of an other could be grounded in a conglomerate of maternal and paternal functions; the love of the other would be signified as neither the one nor the other sex, neither exclusively maternal nor paternal.[37] Such a configuration of faith in the other's love could help us to account for both the linguistic formation of our sexed/gendered identities and belief in the otherness constitutive of our differences.

Yet there are additional dangers for women in using Kristeva's psychoanalytic account of faith both to understand Christianity and to replace it after the demise of belief in the Christian God. In particular, despite possible modifications, Kristevan psychoanalysis can be read back as a lay religion retaining a patriarchal structure of power relations.[38] Problematically, if this form of psychoanalysis replaces Christianity while still employing its only potentially modified patriarchal figures and images as its model for ego formation, then women may move beyond traditional faith in the Christian God but may not move decisively beyond patriarchy and so not beyond dependency upon father-figures.[39] Much weight rests upon the extent and implication of Kristeva's modification of patriarchy. After all, for the feminist poststructuralist, a problem with Christian realist forms of theism would be precisely its patriarchal exclusion of difference and desire.

Typically the psychoanalyst would be concerned about replacing the supports of Christianity for the wounded subject who suffers the loss of religious belief in his or her God; hence the subject (the analysand) needs something or someone to replace the loving father, the nourishing mother, and the priest as the human intermediary in Christianity.[40] The danger is a new form of secular patriarchy. Isn't there a way to go beyond the injustices, biases, and exclusions of patriarchal religion or irreligion? Certain feminist theologians have sought in Kristeva the means to transform the patriarchy of traditional Christianity without putting an end to Christianity itself.[41] However, if Kristeva uses psychoanalysis as a new, secular form of religion to replace Christianity without overcoming patriarchy, then it is highly unlikely that her practice would be ultimately compatible with a feminist philosophy of religion.

And yet Kristeva offers definite possibilities for feminist philosophers who seek to explore the formation and repression of sexual difference; if critically pursued, such exploration can lead to understanding the unconscious construction of difference and its potential for subversion of the dominant forms of patriarchy.[42] In particular, when Kristeva's study of the myth and the cult of the Virgin Mary is placed alongside her account of melancholy and mourning for loss of the mother, I find that Kristeva struggles to transcend the fixed sexual identity and the hierarchy of sexed/gendered roles which characterize patriarchy.[43] In contrast to love (*agape*), whereby the subject is drawn out of itself by the other, melancholia reflects a subject turned inward, unable to form an autonomous identity – let alone a non-narcissistic relation to the other.[44] For Kristeva, melancholia is characterized by the refusal of language, of meaning, and generally of the social-symbolic order.[45] In other words, the melancholic subject refuses the patriarchal ordering of the world.

Kristeva suggests that learning language, entering the social-symbolic order of patriarchy, is equal to matricide. Melancholia signifies a refusal, the refusal of matricide. But this also means a refusal to accept the social-symbolic in its representation of God as father, as well as the impossible ideal of the virgin mother. In contrast, the healthy person, who functions normally within the world as an autonomous individual, must accept the death of the mother, mourning her loss. And in the struggle of a woman, in particular, to accept the loss of female desire, the myth and cult of the Virgin Mary has served to alleviate feminine paranoia. In the end, patriarchal myths seem necessary for the healthy, autonomous individual to live within the social-symbolic order of modern, western societies.

From a study of Kristeva, the main way to refuse patriarchy, including patriarchal configurations of religious belief, would be to accept the madness or psychosis of melancholia. The obvious problem is that madness by definition means irrational while psychosis means not being able to recognize reality or to give meaning to life. Either way, this particular form of refusal by which the subject avoids both burying the maternal body and reasserting the paternal power of patriarchy does not appear to offer a possible ground on which to build a feminist account of rationality.[46]

5 On the Buried Maternal

To overcome the potential incompatibility of feminist philosophy as a generally inclusive enterprise and Freudian psychoanalysis as a deeply patriarchal structure, allow me to focus in more detail upon the feminist poststructuralist preoccupation with the maternal. Both Kristeva and Irigaray articulate the unexpressed debt that the patriarchal symbolic order owes to femininity, especially to maternity. In this context, femininity is dependent upon but not equated with maternity. Each in their own ways, Kristeva and Irigaray seek out the buried maternal, pre-oedipal bedrock which underlies the paternal and phallic law; the phallic law or phallus is the symbol *par excellence* of male completion, signifying what is lacking in the other. And in attempting to unearth the buried maternal, these women seek to undermine the social-symbolic order as exemplified in the phallic law of the father which constitutes patriarchal society. Their feminist aim is to disrupt the Lacanian Symbolic as what gives the world its meaning and law – what is embodied in the Name-of-the-Father.

Despite her reliance on patriarchal images and symbolism, Kristeva suggests that Christian belief with all its history and heritage must be understood as the outcome of ancient battles of matriarchies against patriarchies. The question remaining for Kristeva is: What difference might be made by transforming the theistic concept of God into a Third Party who is sexed/gendered as both parents? This would be the nourishing, loving, and protective father who incorporates the maternal and the paternal functions in the transition and separation from the psychosexual to the social-symbolic order. Having something to offer here, Irigaray calls for further transformation of theistic belief in the mimetic recollection of ancient battles between matriarchies and patriarchies.[47] Irigaray's transformation of the present in conjunction with the recollection of the past aims to touch upon some potential answers to unresolved and repressed questions about patriarchy, the divine, and female desire.

For Irigaray, the decisive problem with patriarchal religions – notably Christianity – is simply that patriarchy excludes women from the divine. Her stronger claim is that all of western culture rests on the murder of the mother: 'the whole of our society and our culture . . . function on the basis of a matricide' (Irigaray 1991b, 36).[48] Irigaray's account of the bodily relationship to one's mother seeks to expose the debt which patriarchy owes to the maternal.

According to Irigaray, women have served as a pretext and an excess for male experiences of the divine. For example, it is through women's bodies that men mediate their experience of the divine. Irigaray contends that a woman's body is eaten at the Eucharist, since it is through the body of a woman that God becomes a man. Yet this vehicle of woman's body is suppressed in its sexual difference.[49] For another example, women under patriarchy serve male desire as desire for the self-same. Irigaray contends that, in love-making, women's desire is repressed for the advances of patriarchy when the sole aim of love (*eros*) is procreation.[50] According to Irigaray, sexual identity is male sameness, while the social construct of the masculine is divinized in the ideal attributes of a God who reigns supreme as father. Thus together male self-sameness and masculine divinity repress sexual difference, while the female other bolsters (male) identity and (masculine) divinity. In the end, the woman(–mother) remains only 'the other of the same', as the mirror which makes possible male sameness.[51]

Concerning a God for men and the reduction of women to maternity, Irigaray claims

> The linguistic code, like the modes of exchange, like the system of images, and representation, is made for masculine subjects. Thus God is father; he begets a son, and for this purpose he uses a woman who is

> reduced to maternity. This has been the most abiding structure of religious and civic traditions for centuries: a relation between men, or in man . . . through a woman. (Irigaray in Mortley 1991, 64)

If I remember the debt which patriarchy owes to the mother, I can understand Irigaray's contention that '[The father forbids] the bodily encounter with the mother' (Irigaray 1991b, 34). But it is not enough to acknowledge that patriarchal religion owes its life to the maternal; it is also necessary to transform the rationality of religious belief so that the maternal, including the material content of desire, does not merely bolster the paternal as formal and rational. So Irigaray seeks to subvert, for instance, the traditional reading of the Eucharist. In recalling the debt of patriarchy,

> perhaps we might remind him [the priest or male minister] that he would not be there if our body and our blood had not given him life, love and spirit. And that it is us, women-mothers, that he is giving to be eaten too. But no one must know that. That is why women cannot celebrate the eucharist . . . Something of the truth which is hidden therein might be brutally unmasked.
>
> Humanity might be washed itself clean of a sin. A woman celebrating the eucharist with her mother, sharing with her the fruits of the earth she/they have blessed, could be delivered of all hatred or ingratitude towards her maternal genealogy, could be consecrated in her identity and her female genealogy. (Irigaray 1991b, 45–6; cf. 1993c, 21)

Writing with Roman Catholic priests in mind, Irigaray is suggesting that to allow women to become priests would not automatically eliminate patriarchy. But if they were allowed, would they think of matricide when administering the sacrament? Do female Anglican priests or other female ministers think of this? In any case, what does Irigaray mean in suggesting that women treat the Eucharist as a matricide? She must be suggesting that we also think back to and before the time of the symbolic murder of the mother by patriarchal myths: to remember the ancient myths of mothers and daughters, goddesses of nature and fertility, is to exhibit gratitude for our maternal ancestry.

In the light of Irigaray's charge of matricide and so patriarchy's lack of maternal genealogies of mother–daughter, it would be helpful to explore her other, more positive references to divine women, love between subjects (including men and women, and women and women), and the sensible transcendental.[52] One certainty is that the existence of the idea of divine women becomes crucial to unearthing the buried maternal and to expressing sexual difference. This idea of divine women serves in the actualizations of the potential to which women can aspire. And so it allows women to become subjects. In love between two subjects there is, then, the possibility of creating a mediation. This would be both sensible – part of experience – and transcendental – ground of experience. The sensible transcendental, then, is to be a bridge to and a space for the divine.[53]

The difficulty is that at least three different philosophical sources for these terms of a sensible transcendental and of a love between two subjects would have to be scrutinized in order to understand fully Irigaray's proposed means to disrupt exclusively male discourse concerning the divine. And only after such scrutiny might women philosophers truly know how to unearth the buried maternal and, in turn, how to become divine women. So a fully adequate scrutiny of Irigaray's philosophical sources on divine women is really a topic large enough for its own book. And I have not proposed to do theology or to construct an account of the female divine. Instead as a philosopher, I have been concerned with questions of epistemological method and the content of beliefs. I am endeavoring to scrutinize the biased justifications of belief, while asking questions about the source and nature of the rationality which constitutes our sexed/gendered, religious beliefs.

However, my suggestion is that a feminist philosophy of religion would also encourage study of three sources which inform Irigaray's assertions concerning the existence of the feminine divine. These are (i) Ludwig Feuerbach (1804–72) on the projection of man onto God; (ii) Emmanuel Levinas (1905–95) on alterity, infinity, and love, (iii) ancient Greek philosophers on (a) the four primary elements of the cosmos, i.e. air, earth, water, and fire,[54] and (b) references to Greek gods and goddesses. Moreover it is important to work out the ways in which Irigaray disrupts these very sources by refiguring their sexed/gendered hierarchies, at the same time as she builds upon their newly refigured significance for women and men.

Yet my point is that, even after such study, it would remain doubtful whether Irigaray's own numerous provocative pieces on women and divinity, on becoming divine women, could ever be brought together without distortion or reduction for the purposes of constructing a new model for theism of a specific female deity or specific deities.[55] Put simply, I would not advocate trying to turn Irigaray into a feminist theologian. Hence it has seemed far wiser, especially in the context of philosophy of religion, to leave her suggestive passages as philosophical fragments and allow them to inspire feminist philosophers – very possibly including male feminists – in whatever ways appear appropriate for the transformation of patriarchal belief. The dual ethical and epistemological implications of

Irigaray's texts for women and men have been demonstrated elsewhere.[56] So the implications of her work for a feminist philosophy of religion could be similarly grasped without having to construct a theology of divine women.

The significant question provoked by Irigaray for philosophers of religion generally is: In what sense, if any, can one say that the female or feminine divine exists? The concluding chapter returns to the question of the existence of a personal deity. But for the moment, let me say that 'exist' could mean a real or an empirical existence; for example, it might be meant in the sense of the simple assertion that this book exists or that the ground we walk on exists. But it could also mean an ideal existence in the sense of the projection of a goal for which one strives. This ideal cannot be pointed to: not like one could point to this page of paper to know it exists. Instead this ideal is known to exist in a practical sense as it functions in one's thinking and living. Or it could mean exist in the fictional sense of what is pejoratively called a mere fiction; this means something like a fairytale, or even a good novel, which has been made up. Alternatively the feminine divine could exist in a mythical sense; this is not simply to imply the sense of a nonliteral account which is claimed by modern science to be empirically false, but is to suggest a configuration which serves to constitute a people's meaningful, qualitative identity. In this light, myth is comprised of both a narrative core of constancy and a marginal variability, allowing for constantly different interpretations.[57] Furthermore it could mean exist in the sense of an illusory idea which has been created – unconsciously – from fear of the contingencies and losses in life. Or, finally, it could mean exist in the sense of being a historically specific conception which endures for a time due to ignorance and need; this historical conception would serve a purpose only until, for instance, something inexplicable is explained or some temporary structure (of male discourse) is discarded. Some of the preceding senses of existence may overlap in Irigaray's account of divinity. And the very possibility of multiple meanings for 'exist,' as used in accounting for a personal deity, should be kept in mind.

I will develop Irigaray's provocative writings concerning divinity and sexual difference, along with the implications of the feminist standpoint epistemologist call to reinvent ourselves as other, in parts III and IV. This means, first, elucidating mythical configurations of religious belief and female actions and desires and, second, proposing the possible mimetic refiguration of these beliefs and actions, at the same time as miming the other's unspoken desires. However, I do not propose to justify the empirical existence of female goddesses or any metaphysical trinity of the feminine divine. Instead I will take the accounts of actual and mythical women, who act out of devotion to a deity or a divine duty, as illustrations for disruptively transforming patriarchal appropriations of reason, desire, and religious belief.

6 A Feminist Modification of Rational Belief

So far in part II, I have sought the rationality of religious belief for a feminist philosophy of religion in the light of feminist standpoint epistemology modified by feminist readings of Hegel, Freud, Lacan, and poststructuralism. What emerges, first, is the inadequacy of religious belief justified according to the formal or instrumental rationality and objectivity of empirical realism. Such belief appears inadequate in terms of its weak objectivity and its lack of material content, including female desire and, more generally, sexual difference. The consequence is biased, partial, and, ultimately, false beliefs.

Second, it becomes clear that a newly proposed feminist philosophy of religion, unlike Christian realist forms of theism, could not be merely descriptive and formal. It must, by necessity, include a prescription for change. Change would have to be prescribed insofar as patriarchal forms of religion need to be rethought not only for their sex/gender differentiation and gender stratification, but for their privileging of a precariously conceived rational subject; this subject is precarious because defined by the exclusion of its own materially conditioned status, an exclusion which is manifest in his privileged manner of thinking.

New thinking from the lives and beliefs of marginalized others, as well as new visions, become essential for the transformation of philosophy of religion. But caution is necessary here. I reiterate at this stage that such thinking must not involve silencing the other. Instead listening must transform both the objects of our thinking into subjects of thinking and the new thinking subjects into communities which long for spiritual and sexual change. I turn to bell hooks for some powerful insight on the dangers and possibilities in this thinking from the lives at the margins:

> Often this speech about the 'Other' is also a mask, an oppressive talk hiding gaps, absences, that space where our words would be if we were speaking, if there were silence, if we were there. This 'we' is that 'us' in the margins, that 'we' who inhabit marginal space that is not a site of domination but a place of resistance. Enter that space. Often this speech about the 'Other' annihilates, erases: 'No need to hear your voice when I can talk about you better than you can speak about yourself. No need to hear your voice. Only tell me about your pain. I want to know your

> story. And then I will tell it back to you in a new way. Tell it back to you in such a way that it has become mine, my own. Re-writing you, I write myself anew. I am still author, authority. I am still the colonizer, the speaking subject, and you are now at the center of my talk.' Stop. . . .
>
> Silenced. We fear those who speak about us, who do not speak to us and with us. We know what it is like to be silenced . . .
>
> This is an intervention. A message from that space in the margin that is a site of creativity and power, that inclusive space where we recover ourselves, where we move in a solidarity to erase the category colonized/colonizer. Marginality as site of resistance. Enter that space. Let us meet there. Enter that space . . .
>
> I am located in the margin. I make a definite distinction between that marginality which is imposed by oppressive structures and that marginality one chooses as site of resistance – as location of radical openness and possibility. . . . We know struggle to be that which pleasures, delights and fulfills desires. (hooks 1990, 151–3)

A struggle that fulfills desires involves not silencing the other (as colonized) but possibly being silenced as colonizer in order to be changed by awareness of the sexual, racial, and class structures which deeply divide us. In the process of struggle lies the possibility of real change by which racially and socially differentiated subjects discover and give expression to female desires, spiritual and sexual.

Third, there is the task of collapsing any remaining hierarchy of binary terms such as 'colonizer'/'colonized.' This means a value hierarchy which divides thinking against itself, alienating the rational subject himself or herself from his or her own nature, his or her body, and his or her emotions. Subject/object, rational/emotional, culture/nature, mind/body form a value hierarchy when the binary oppositions wrongly and unfairly give greater value to the first term in each opposition. The task of collapsing hierarchical assumptions is continued in the next chapter with a focus upon reason and desire. My aim is to undermine lingering oppositions between reason and desire in configurations of religious belief by working out the means to refigure beliefs mimetically.

Finally, far from being non-moral or relativist, Kristevan and Irigarayan poststructuralist accounts of belief, as well as a feminist standpoint epistemology of belief, offer the material for a feminist philosophy of religion which would be highly ethical in confronting the injustices of patriarchal religions. The combination of strong objectivity and newly discovered female desires should offer significant material to supplement and so transform philosophy of religion. By 'transform,' I mean a change from strictly assessing the justification of true belief to rationally assessing the construction and refiguration of religious belief. This will involve both refiguring belief to allow it to become nonexclusive and open to sexual difference, and configuring truth without fearing or repressing desire. In addition, this implies figuring love which does not manipulate and abuse but seeks to change our grasp of nature, of the divine, and of the relations between mothers and daughters, mothers and sons, women and men of any race, class, ethnicity, or sexual persuasion.

Notes

1. For feminist poststructuralist background in, and criticisms of, phenomenology, see Chanter 1995, 35f, 177–80, 225–30.
2. See the account of Mirabai's song and its betrayal in chapter 5 below.
3. Todd (ed.) 1983, 231–45; Mortley 1991, 63–78; Chanter 1995, 35–8.
4. Grosz 1993b, 199–214; Schor 1994, 3–14; Chanter 1995, 1–13.
5. Berry insists upon the intersection of key aspects of Kristeva's and Irigaray's works, especially their redirecting of intellectual interest to the complex relationship between love and the category of woman; see Berry 1995, 223–40, especially 224. Berry also notices a strikingly new concern in both Kristeva and Irigaray: to reassess and redefine the relevance of the degraded sphere of feeling, especially its relevance for thinking about themes such as the sacred, the uncanny, and the numinous.
6. Kristeva 1980 (1977), 237–43.
7. See Kristeva 1986, 188–213; Irigaray 1993b, 9–14. For the debates about essentialism, see Schor 1994, 57–78; Chanter 1995, 21–47.
8. Flax, 1990, 31–4; Anderson 1993a.
9. Franks Davis 1989; Alston 1991; Plantinga 1992; Anderson 1996a, 112–30.
10. Lacan 1977.
11. Kristeva 1987a (1985), 24–5; also, see Berry 1995, 224–7, 230–1.
12. This 'in the beginning' could be followed by 'of one's individuation or one's (sexual) identity.' For a fuller account, see Kristeva's discussion of Freud and uncanny strangeness in Kristeva 1991, 181–92.
13. The earliest sense of the infinite in relation to the mother could also lead to an experience of the infinite being expressed with various images of the maternal. And for a reading of images of maternal power in prominent theologians' expressions of God's infinitude, see Goldenberg 1995b, 108–15.
14. Otto 1923, 5–40.
15. Otto 1923, 11–12, 40; cf. Underhill 1930 (1911).
16. Otto 1923, 12–25.
17. Otto 1923, 39–40.
18. Otto 1923, 13–29.
19. Here Kristeva cites Freud 1961, 241.
20. For further reflection, see Kristeva 1991, 181–2; cf. Otto 1923, 5–49.

21. Kristeva 1991; 1993a.
22. Kristeva 1987a, 5; cf. Plato 1977, 67–70. For other references to Plato's *chora*, see Aristotle 1984 (1912–52), II, 986a-b; Flax 1983, 255–8; Le Doeuff 1989, 113; Hegel 1968, vol. 1; Irigaray 1985a, 243ff; Whitford 1991b, 59–60.
23. Kristeva 1984 (1974), 25, also 19–106; Lechte 1990, 128–30.
24. For some relevant texts, see Kristeva 1986, 160–86; 1987a; Irigaray 1985a, 191–202; 1993c, 25–35, 61–4; cf. Berry 1992; 1994; 1995.
25. For more on Augustine from Kristeva, see the next section. And for other instances of discourse on maternal desire in religious texts, again see Goldenberg 1995b.
26. Irigaray 1991b, 34–46. Goldenberg explores the important role of matricide for feminist theology in King (ed.) 1995, 158–60.
27. See Kristeva 1995, 117–18. For more discussion concerning Kristeva's reading of the maternal in the gaps of a text, see Anderson, forthcoming.
28. Irigaray 1985a; 1991c; 1992.
29. Kristeva 1987a, 3, 11; cf. Freud 1973 (1931), vol. 21, 53.
30. Kristeva 1987a, xi, 21; Berry 1995, 224–5.
31. Plato 1977, 67–70; Kristeva 1987a, 5.
32. Kristeva 1987a, 9, 26–7.
33. Kristeva 1987a, 24–5.
34. See Freud 1971 (1923), vol. 19, 31; Kristeva 1986, 244; 1989 (1987), 13, 23–4, 257.
35. Kristeva 1986, 238–71; 1987b (1983).
36. Kristeva 1987a, 40; cf. Kristeva 1986, 244, 251, 257–62; 1989, 13, 23–4, 257.
37. For different accounts of the role and the sex/gender of Kristeva's imaginary father or Third Party, see Weir 1993, 87–90; Dews 1993, 372–7; Berry 1995, 224–7.
38. Kristeva 1987a, 58.
39. Recall from part I, Le Doeuff's claim concerning the Héloïse complex and the importance for women philosophers to gain autonomy; cf. Le Doeuff 1991, 59–60.
40. Weir 1993, 84–91.
41. Chopp 1993, 31–48; cf. Anderson 1993a.
42. Young 1990a, 124, 129–36, 142–55; Weir 1993; 80–1, 87–90; 1995, 275–82.
43. Kristeva 1986, 160–85; 1989, 3–10, 28–9, 221ff.
44. Kristeva 1989, 5–13.
45. Kristeva 1989, 33–44.
46. For criticism of the Kristevan attempt to use (the melancholic or poet and) the semiotic in order to disrupt the Symbolic, see Butler 1990, 85–91.
47. Irigaray 1993b, 17–21; 1994, 4–14, 100ff. Berry finds a significant affinity between Kristeva's account of the figure of the imaginary father of individual prehistory (or the Third Party) and Irigaray's account of the angel as a bearer and facilitator of love; see Berry 1995, 224; cf. Irigaray 1993c, 23–53.

48. Already in ancient Greek myths such as *The Oresteia* the mother becomes a devouring monster; see Irigaray 1991b, 40f; Warner 1995, 3–24.
49. Irigaray 1991c, 164ff. See John 1:1–18; Jasper 1996.
50. Irigaray 1991a, 172–7; 1993a, 187–96.
51. Irigaray 1993c, 111.
52. Irigaray 1991a, 167–77; 1993a, 129; 1993c, 57–72.
53. Irigaray 1993a, 129; 1993c, 72.
54. For a study of the Greek sources and background to Irigaray's account of air, earth, water, and fire, as centrally found in *Elemental Passions*, see Canters, forthcoming.
55. For a helpful piece on Irigaray and divine women, see Grosz 1993b.
56. Cornell 1991; Whitford 1991b; Chanter 1995.
57. See chapter 4, section 2, below.

III

Refigurations of Belief

4

Myth, Mimesis, and Religious Belief

It is idle to revive old myths if we are unable to celebrate them and use them to constitute a social system, a temporal system. Is this in our power?

Let us imagine that it is possible.

Irigaray 1993c, 81

1 Reason, Embodiment, and Belief

Typically, contemporary philosophers of religion have accepted modern philosophy's privileging of reason above desire and emotion. And in general, modern empiricist philosophers building on the model of Cartesian foundationalism have sought to account for the disembodied identity of the rational subject, but not the embodied identities of sexually specific subjects. So philosophical cases are still made today for retaining or restoring the rationality of religious belief of the disembodied subject as a necessary warrant for articulating knowledge of God. In its crude form, the naive empirical realist argument is that desire and the body only hinder reason in its justification of true belief.[1]

To understand the development of my argument from chapters 1–3 into part III, the reader should remember that at least the naive, if not the critical, empirical realist forms of Christian theism presuppose in their use of reason and objectivity a subject who can be disembodied in his or her thinking.[2] In this first section, I will try to make more explicit the problems for a feminist philosopher of religion with this conception of the disembodied subject.

I have already criticized a form of empiricist objectivity for being weak. This objectivity assumes an instrumental form of ends-justifies-means reasoning only, and fails to take into account the full embodiment of the reasoning subject, especially this subject's own dependence upon others for adequate, rational knowledge of the reality of embodied beings.[3] I have also demonstrated that Anglo-American philosophers of religion take up an epistemic duty in seeking to justify rationally empirical realist forms of theism. The problem is that largely unacknowledged circular reasoning assumes a patriarchal form of theism and, then, claims to justify rationally a set of objective, coherent, credible, and simple beliefs about God; or, if not to justify with evidence, reasoning is used to warrant noninferential claims about God as properly basic beliefs. The hegemony of such sets of beliefs has prevented recognition of the, in fact, unselfconsciously biased constructions of traditional theism. On a larger scale, the hegemonic use of Enlightenment reason in the construction of rational beliefs generally has allowed violent and oppressive consequences for women, nonprivileged persons, animals, and nature.[4]

However, despite their circularity, rational defenses of traditional theism have been pursued in a highly sophisticated manner and with great integrity. The problem for women is that this circularity impinges on questions of embodiment in contemporary defenses of the unramified beliefs at the heart of empirical realist forms of Christian theism in particular, and equally of empirical realist forms of atheism. 'Unramified' means restricted to certain core theistic beliefs which, supposedly, can be compatible with other forms of religious belief. The degree to which formal rationality can avoid circularity and rationally justify belief in the existence of a personal deity, notably the Christian God, is open to philosophical debate. More specifically there is the question of the deity's own embodiment. It would seem that the God of empirical realist forms of theism is probably more appropriately described as nonembodied rather than disembodied. Yet the degree to which God can be conceived to be embodied or disembodied has been debated.[5]

Nonembodied is different from disembodied. If, unlike human beings, the God of Christian theism is nonembodied, this would imply not having (and never having had) a substantial body like men and women have, but possibly having a personal relation to material objects and subjects. By contrast, 'disembodied' literally means no longer in a body; reason is separated from the body so that corporeal relations do not affect one's perspective. Disembodied, then, implies no personal perspective on the world and no concrete relations (of one's body) to other persons or to any specific material objects affecting rational knowledge. Both the limitations associated with having a body and the impersonal nature associated with being disembodied tend to lead certain Christian realist philosophers to reject the ideas of their personal God being either embodied or disembodied.[6]

Whether in defending or attacking other forms of theism, the dominant empiricist form of Christian theism has ultimately privileged unramified religious belief. But the unramified belief is necessarily, however covertly, accompanied by specific ramified beliefs.[7] 'Dominant' refers to the empirical realist view of God held today by powerful representatives of philosophy of religion. And 'ramified' describes the more elaborate, concrete beliefs which necessarily accompany the abstract core beliefs in the God of traditional theism. The ultimate significance of ramified beliefs highlights the concrete implications of traditional theism for embodied human beings.

The dominant empirical realist constructions of religious belief are often unstable. Their construction depends upon an individual's perception – or some form of subjective apprehension by the senses – of immediate experience. But such discrete experience appears inappropriate for justifying claims about a transcendent God. And the rational arguments for their justification are generally fallacious in terms of their own logic. By 'inappropriate,' I mean that belief in the existence of, to take a crude example, a glass of water can be justified by an individual's perception or some form of empirical evidence, including observations of the hardness of the glass and the taste of the water; but, here following Kant, I would still maintain that empirical belief justified by perception cannot serve as a proper example for constructing knowledge of a supremely good, all-powerful, transcendent, but personal God.[8] By definition, this theistic God could be given neither an empirical referent nor a coherent sense, without assuming much more than either sense perceptions of empirical material or reflections upon subjective perceptions could offer.[9] 'God' has neither an empirical referent like a glass containing water nor a coherent sense as a belief about intensely subjective experiences such as having a vision of childhood when drinking water out of a certain sort of glass.

Yet my real concern is the much larger problem that no matter how elaborate the empirical observations, or the noninferential beliefs, about the material world, and no matter how sophisticated the cumulative-evidence arguments from religious experiences (of God) might become, the empiricist subject would still lack adequate, self-reflexive principles for scrutinizing the rational beliefs of embodied beings. The empiricist principles are inadequate because blind to the larger biases of their very own epistemological framework in their formally rational defenses or warrants of religious belief, whether theistic or atheistic. The empiricist principles applied to theistic beliefs tend to be based upon a weak objectivity idealized as the God's-eye view. Arguably this is not in fact a view-from-nowhere but a blindly partial projection of the ideal man's view of reality.[10] Yet these weakly objective principles dominate precisely because the privileged representatives of the contemporary field of Anglo-American analytical philosophy of religion have a vested interest, however unconscious, in retaining the exclusive beliefs of the powerful at the center of academic life. The consequence is that prejudiced and partial beliefs become entrenched. Moreover using the pretense of rigorous arguments, the authority of a particular male mentor in philosophy ensures the 'correctness' of beliefs.

Notwithstanding the philosophical obligation to scrutinize the rationality of religious beliefs, my general contention is that the epistemic duty of the philosopher of religion should also imply an imperative to construct less partial and less biased beliefs than those assumed by any group of privileged believers. The construction of less partial beliefs would aim to be rationally – logically, morally, and emotionally – adequate for the complex reasoning, feeling, desiring, intuiting, believing capacities of multiple subjects. In chapters 2 and 3, I considered the rationality of feminist objectivity and female desire, respectively, for the construction of religious belief. The crucial difference which emerged for a feminist philosophy of religion is the desire to transform such hidden assumptions as a disembodied conception of rationality. This means rejecting any rational enterprise which vainly tries to achieve truth, objectivity, and impartiality from a God's-eye view of privileged male-neutral reality.[11]

At this stage, elucidation of specific religious beliefs can help to tease out underlying, but often self-contradictory, assumptions inherent in empirical realist forms of theism. In fact the ramified beliefs, from which the unramified beliefs seem to be abstracted, are riddled with logical inconsistencies. Yet such inconsistency is precisely the sort of thing empirical realists seek to untangle and render coherent. And, as already indicated, the feminist epistemologist finds both the unramified core belief in God and the more specific, ramified theistic beliefs biased and often unjust.

To illustrate the above issue of inconsistency, allow me to consider the logical difficulties with the ramified beliefs making up the Christian theist account of an incarnation of a personal deity in human form.[12] Even without highly technical arguments, the belief in, or truth-value of, a deity being born with a male body of a human mother would seem incompatible with the assumption that greater value be given to man's disembodied reason, approximating the absolutely correct God's-eye view. The truth represented by, on the one hand, a deity as the incarnate *logos*, or the embodied word of reason, born of a woman and, on the other hand, the assumption of reason seeking truth in separation from a female body would also seem, at least prima facie, contradictory.

So perhaps the belief in a deity born of a woman who is a virgin aims to go beyond this alternative. Yet this creates new logical and experiential difficulties. In particular, it can be argued that giving superior value to this humanly impossible mother, along with the assumption of the most empirically objective method and logically coherent reason being separate from a body, would be self-contradictory of human beings themselves who are nevertheless embodied, hence both reasoning and desiring. The value given to an impossible virginity, resulting in the implicit devaluation of the sexual act, remains debatable for fully embodied beings.

Thinking about the specific belief in Christ's virgin birth, could belief in Mary's virginity have a coherent literal or symbolic meaning for a philosopher? Would this belief support giving priority to a disembodied and so impersonal rationality? Belief in a divine incarnation, whereby the deity becomes a man by being born of a virgin mother, could be part of the male imaginary: disembodiment could be the desired ideal of the self-same male subject, whereby the debt to the mother is repressed.[13] Interestingly such belief was already popular in ancient Greek mythology as well as in classical philosophy.[14]

Yet permit me to elaborate the stronger objectivity which can be gained here concerning embodiment by bringing in feminist standpoint epistemology. In this elaboration, notice the challenge posed for empirical realist forms of theism by this feminist form of objectivity. To reiterate, strong objectivity is comprised of two main moves: first, the new subjects move outward to shift away from the privileged subject's standpoint to think from the lives of others; second, the new subjects move backward – reflexively – to re-examine the basic background beliefs of their own originally privileged position as a subject of knowledge. The goal of these moves toward objectivity is not to achieve absolute truth nor impartial knowledge, but to gain less partial knowledge than the subject has from his or her privileged perspective on reality. Instead of justifying true belief and refuting skepticism in the manner of conventional epistemology, feminist standpoint epistemologists aim to gain knowledge by scrutinizing the credentials of knowledge-claimants and putting knowledge-claims under communal criticism from the perspective of the outsider. Hence with regard to belief in the virgin birth of a male god, the feminist standpoint epistemologist would reject any knowledge-claim which is biased against half the human race. The epistemological criteria of strong objectivity would ensure that greater falsehoods and injustices were not created for women (than for men), or for those men who innocently suffer on the margins created by the beliefs of privileged individuals and groups.

The virgin birth has been one of the biased beliefs constructed and justified as true by men. It renders women an impossible, religious ideal (virgin motherhood), which could serve only to keep them unfairly humbled, submissive, and defiled under patriarchal power.[15] Claims to theistic knowledge, based upon this ramified belief in the virgin birth of a male god, support a male ideal of divinity as well as the impossible ideal for women of a virgin mother. As Irigaray asserts, 'Women, traditionally cast as mothers of the gods, have no God or gods of their own to fulfill their gender, whether as individuals or as a community' (Irigaray 1993c, 81).

The construction of the ramified belief in an incarnate male god and a virgin mother results in the subjection of women due to their biological sex and in the lack of a god(dess) for women. This construction can be given various historical accounts. Generally this history includes mythical stories; myths have both accompanied classical philosophy and conditioned beliefs about the divine. Here is a possible account:

> In the pre-Christian Roman empire virgin birth was a shorthand symbol, commonly used to designate a man's divinity . . . The Christian religion was unusual in using the idea to set an enduring seal of approval on asceticism, but its use of virgin birth as the key to the argument that Jesus was the son of God was classical in spirit, and dependent on longlasting and erroneous ideas about human generation that were also inherited from classical philosophy.
>
> In his *Metamorphoses*, Ovid wickedly tells the story of the conception of Bacchus, who was born of a mortal, Semele, after a visit of the god Jupiter. Juno is jealous and, disguised as Semele's nanny, she calls on the girl, and shakes her head and sighs at her story, saying: 'I pray that it might be Jupiter! But the whole business disturbs me: many a man has made his way into an honest girl's bedroom by calling himself a god.' (Warner 1976, 34–5; cf. Ovid 1955, 81)[16]

In this way, myth has played a crucial role generally in the origin of male-biased, theistic beliefs. Moreover when left unquestioned, myths about the divine can generate their own deleterious consequences in the form of further, ramified beliefs. A consequence of the preceding belief about human generation is that 'Different cultures have used virgin birth to assert man's natural distinction and closeness to the higher orders. . . . it was [the] shift, from virgin birth to virginity, from religious sign to moral doctrine, that transformed a mother goddess like the Virgin Mary into an effective instrument of asceticism and female subjection' (Warner 1976, 49). It is not only that belief in the virgin birth of a male deity leads to the subjection of the female other; but the theistic account of human incarnation also leads to the self-contradiction of the male subject who, with his conflicting beliefs about embodiment and reason, projects his own material condition onto the female other. Again this projection occurs because to gain identity and rational autonomy, men have separated themselves from desire and the so-called mysterious powers of 'femaleness.'

Implied in the impossible ideal of a virgin mother is a devaluing of all human mothers and of human relations involving sexual intercourse. The real implication for women and nonprivileged others is the rendering of the male deity, who becomes incarnate as a man, superior to all other human males. Hence there is an in-built hierarchy of relations determined by the father's status as divine. At the same time, in the light of this belief concerning God's relation to man as represented by the Christian account of incarnation, any sort of mutual relations between man and woman (as mother or wife) seem to be doubtful; the woman seems to be merely a vehicle of new life, while the man and his paternal line determine the child's status in that life.

Moreover if I now return to the empirical realist's own test of logical coherence, the beliefs making up the theist's account of a god born in male form seem dubious; and these beliefs hardly support the assumption of a disembodied rationality as more objective, since impersonal, than embodied rationality. The various contradictions generated by placing the assumption of a disembodied subject of reason alongside specific beliefs, such as beliefs in an incarnate deity, do not suggest that reason itself would be made more coherent as impersonal. It certainly would not make reasoning or the rationality of belief more just.

Instead I would argue, given that to be human is to be embodied, that knowledge which is human must be, to be true to itself, knowledge as embodied. If being rational is said to be being separated from the body, then achieving rational human knowledge would seem to be logically impossible. Since human knowledge necessarily involves embodiment, it could be that the difficulty with rational human knowledge lies in the definition of 'rational.' Why should being rational mean being separate from the body? Or why should reason be separated from desire, and mind from body? Ultimately why should 'embodied reason' be thought a contradiction in terms? The biased beliefs and prejudiced assumptions concerning disembodied reason have allowed modern philosophers to argue that reason must be symbolized as disembodied; and that belief can be justified as true by human idealizations of pure reason.

Again these arguments on a supposedly disembodied conceptual level reflect circular reasoning.[17] They assume what needs to be proved: that truth has its ultimate ground in both the (ungrounded) idealization of God as supremely good, purely rational, bodiless, and omnipotent, and the idealization of virgin motherhood. The result of assuming such idealizations is the ramified beliefs of (different forms of) theism, including the various pernicious beliefs which devalue women's bodies as mothers, lovers, and sexual partners. And these beliefs cloud the truth about human embodiment, reason, women and men. Such contradictions and mystifications of human reason are precisely the objects in need of feminist critique.

There are decisive difficulties with the conception of a disembodied rationality, including its incoherence with itself and its incompatibility with specific theistic beliefs. Hence extreme caution should be taken by feminist philosophers of religion to avoid any careless misunderstanding of the feminist standpoint epistemologist's criticism of the 'God-trick.' This trick is a metaphor for the disembodied objectivity sought by naive empirical realists. The God-trick is supposed to achieve omniscience as disembodied, as the impersonal view-from-nowhere. And yet, as already suggested, theistic arguments for a nonembodied God have been stronger than any argument for a deity being disembodied. In the end, it is odd that either the disembodied or the nonembodied alternatives are thought to be the ideal epistemological standpoint for embodied subjects.

In the light of the incoherence of disembodied reason, can we expect the God-trick to work? A feminist philosopher of religion would be wise not to assume that criticism of the God-trick necessarily means anti-religion. The point of asking a woman or a man to reinvent herself or himself as other is to help to uncover the privileged male-bias in philosophy of religion, in what she or he was taught, and so in what has become familiar. Then, once the bias in the dominant approach to philosophical objectivity becomes apparent, what was familiar is made strange.[18] For this reason, as argued in chapter 2, feminist standpoint epistemologists offer legitimate criticisms of the supposed God-trick; the familiar seems correct because advocated by the powerful. In achieving only a weak objectivity, this trick excludes other forms of marginalized or nonprivileged religious belief.

Furthermore it is wise to refrain from associating feminist standpoint epistemology with the historical, social, and intellectual contexts of Marx's comments on religion. Any such historically specific association is open to grave distortions.[19] And the failure by one female philosopher of religion to take sufficient account of feminist standpoint epistemology on its own terms has already resulted in misrepresentation of feminist strong objectivity as anti-religion, diverging radically from my account in chapter 2 above.

So how should a feminist philosopher of religion approach questions of reason, embodiment, and belief? My proposal is to take a closer look at myth.

> Most ancient Greek myths are of Asian or unknown origin. This is true of those concerning Aphrodite, Demeter and Kore/Persephone. Their evolution should be understood as the result of migrations to different places where they were adapted to varying degrees, and the effect of historical developments. For myth is not a story independent of History, but rather expresses History in colourful accounts that illustrate the major trends of an era . . . As a result, (myths) retained a special relationship to space, time and the manifestation of the forms of incarnation. (Irigaray 1994, 101)

Myths offer material about incarnation. In them, embodiment has been configured in narrative form. Moreover myths offer the possibility of refiguring deities and their actions. Hence they can play a crucial role in the transformation of oppressive conditions and pernicious beliefs.

2 Rethinking Myth

My feminist critique of empirical realist forms of theism has suggested that the origin of religious belief can be understood in terms of noncontingent ideas, reason, and desire. As such, rational constructions of belief can be regulative of our world and so are better represented by symbols and myths than by contingent ideas and theories.[20] As narratives of human reality, myths serve both to limit our explainable knowledge and to make possible our multiple identities as complex reasoning, desiring, believing beings. As embodied men and women, we are decentered by our own conscious and unconscious myths of reality.[21]

Myth is different from constitutive reason which determines empirical knowledge. Unlike the determination of empiricial knowledge as contingent, myth does not create knowledge by either compiling empirical facts or manipulating the value of words. Instead myths are necessary in setting the limits of human knowledge, and so they serve a practical function. Any attempt to force myth into the role of constituting knowledge is dangerous: it ignores the distinction between contingent knowledge and necessary conditions for belief. The misconstrual of the function of myth results in the perversion and control of meaning.

> The mythopoetic energy cannot be converted [into activity constitutive of contingent knowledge and rational-empiricist explanation]. The efforts to record its activity will not cease; it is however essential to avoid a mystification in which this effort is granted the dignity of reason explaining the world of experience – assuming the word 'explain' maintains the same common usage as in the proposition 'Lightning is explained as an electrical discharge' and suchlike. (Kolakowski 1989, 130f)

Underlying the above warning to avoid the mystification of myth is the Kantian distinction between constitutive and regulative uses of reason. But in Kolakowski's terms, a certain rational activity is constitutive of our usable world, i.e. as manipulative of empirical material, while mythopoetic energy serves a regulative capacity in limiting meaningful belief.[22] Both empirical explanation and mythical meaning depend upon the regulative principle of reason to limit claims of knowledge and belief.

Kant's *Critique of Pure Reason* sets the limits to the use of human reason. And in Kant's transcendental idealist terms, there exists a crucial difference between the constructions of empirical knowledge and the application of (regulative) principles to relations of existence.

> For instance, I can determine *a priori*, that is, can construct, the degree of sensations of sunlight by combining some 200,000 illuminations of the moon. These first principles may therefore be called constitutive.
>
> . . .
>
> It stands quite otherwise with those principles which seek to bring the *existence* of appearances under rules *a priori*. For since existence cannot be constructed, the principles can apply only to the relations of existence, and can yield only *regulative* principles.
>
> . . .
>
> Reason is never in immediate relation to an object, but only to the understanding; and it is only through the understanding that it has its own (specific) empirical employment. It does not, therefore, *create* concepts (of objects) but only *orders* them, and gives them that unity which they can have only if they be employed in their widest possible application, that is, with a view to obtaining totality in the various series. . . . so reason unifies the manifold of concepts by means of ideas, positing

> a certain collective unity as the goal of the activities of the understanding . . .
>
> . . .
>
> [transcendental ideas] have an excellent, and indeed indispensably necessary, regulative employment, namely, that of directing the understanding towards a certain goal upon which the routes marked out by all its rules converge . . . this illusion (which need not, however, be allowed to deceive us) is indispensably necessary if we are to direct the understanding beyond every given experience. (Kant 1950 [1781,1787], 210-12, A180/B222-3; 533, A643-4/B671-2)

The above distinction means that transcendental ideas (when treated as regulative principles) do not constitute knowledge. But they can direct human understanding toward a practical goal without forgetting the illusion of claiming to know what is beyond every given experience. Interestingly other non-naive forms of empiricism could also employ Kantian regulative principles to deal with ideas which are necessary but inscrutable or, it can be said, to deal with ineffable knowledge.[23] So feminist standpoint epistemology, feminist poststructuralism, and Kantian transcendental idealism are not the only alternatives to the dominant form of empirical realism in philosophy of religion. But whichever post-Kantian alternative is chosen, there exists enough ground to treat myth as a regulative principle and not to equate it with constitutive knowledge of a supersensible reality.

Yet there remains danger in another extreme. Separating myth too sharply from reason could result in actually being deceived by the employment of regulative principles (as explained in the blocked quotation above). Self-reflexive and communal assessment of a myth's truth and justice, for others and ourselves, depends upon a distinctive form of rational scrutiny. Properly conceived in its constitutive and regulative roles, reason becomes a necessary counterbalance to myth created as a potentially illusory configuration.

When I speak of mythical configuration – rather than myth – further philosophical background is implied. Aristotle's notion of *muthos*, meaning emplotment, is brought together with Kant's notion of synthesis of the heterogeneous intuitions of experience. Both Aristotle and Kant are key figures in western philosophy's conceptualization of human reality as an ordered unity. They help to determine the role which configurations have had in mimesis, that is, in the representation of reality.[24] Configuration is the act of bringing separate and diverse characters and actions together to form a plot or story, and so a narrative unity. Importantly any myth can have various configurations. So the meaning of its symbols and actions can be imitated and performed in ever new ways.

Before outlining various forms of mimesis, it is necessary to have a straightforward, working definition of myth for a feminist philosophy of religion. My definition supports myth's use by feminists as a philosophical tool. And to work with myth in relation to philosophy, I agree minimally with the following:

> Myths are stories [which] are distinguished by a high degree of constancy in their narrative core and by an equally pronounced capacity for marginal variation. These two characteristics make myths transmissible by tradition: their constancy produces the attraction of recognizing them in artistic or ritual representation as well (as recital), and their variability produces the attraction of trying out new and personal means of presenting them. It is the relationship of 'theme and variations,' whose attractiveness for both composers and listeners is familiar from music. So myths are not like 'holy texts,' which cannot be altered by one iota. (Blumenberg 1985, 34)

I intend to explore the nature of myth (as above) which, unlike philosophical arguments but similar to music, is fluid. Its fluidity leaves myth open to new variations of sex/gender constructions, while retaining a core of symbolic meaning. Yet the above definition also raises certain questions for the feminist philosopher. Is the core constancy of myth something unconscious which re-emerges? Or is it some essential structure of meaning? An affirmative answer to either question could be problematic for feminist poststructuralists in particular. The poststructuralist critique of logocentrism seeks to undermine the metaphysical idea of an essential meaning or logic, whether unconscious or not. The question is: Does a core of constancy at the center of myth suggest a logocentrism or even a phallogocentrism?

Logocentrism, as the name given by poststructuralist critics to the western form of metaphysics, makes reason central. *Logos*, loosely construed, as rational discourse is taken to represent the singular, unified conceptual order; the presence or immediacy of things is centered on the dominance of the singular logic of identity which devalues and polarizes binary differences. And this center of logical identity could equally be identified with the phallus, hence phallogocentrism.[25] However, I will not take this reading of binary oppositions as decisively undermining the presence of mythical meaning. Notwithstanding the similarity of the core of mythical meaning with any possible (phal)logocentrism, I will not reject the role of myth in regulating dimensions of meaning; but I will return to this critical issue later.

The problem with myth, which necessitates specific forms of mimesis (to be articulated below), is that

> Insofar as a myth is a story which provides a common vision, feminists have to find new myths and stories in order to embody their goals and value judgements . . . Yet . . . myths also have a stabilizing, retarding function insofar as they sanction the existing social order and justify its power structure by providing communal identity and a rationale for societal and ecclesial institutions. (Schüssler Fiorenza 1975, 620)

So feminists have to find new configurations of old myths continually, in creating mimetic refigurations of mythical visions.

To qualify my nomination of myth as a feminist tool for the representation of reality, all philosophical defenses of rational belief are not rejected in favor of mythical reflections on belief. Nor is supposedly male reason to be given up for female desire. Instead the objective is to collapse any opposition between the rational subject and his own materially conditioned status, insofar as the latter has been projected onto the female other. In any case, this is a precarious division. Nevertheless this self-division has characterized modern rationality, and so philosophy of religion conceived as a rational enterprise.

It is helpful to trace the continuing presence of myth, in accompanying the history of western philosophy, as something different from reason, from philosophy itself as strictly conceived, and from fiction. The additional distinction, between myth and fiction, is revealing. As already suggested with reference to *Possessing the Secret of Joy*, fiction can serve an important role in constituting symbolic representations of, for instance, religious rituals. But generally myths are significantly different from novels and other forms of fiction:

> Mythical figures live many lives, die many deaths, and in this they differ from the characters we find in novels, who can never go beyond the single gesture. But in each of these lives and deaths all the others are present, and we can hear their echo. Only when we become aware of a sudden consistency amongst incompatibles can we say we have crossed the threshold of myth. (Calasso 1994, 22)

And yet a novel can be exploited as 'a myth-making form': for example, Mary Shelley's *Frankenstein* establishes a myth.[26] So to distinguish myth, no matter the context of its development, it has the distinctive characteristics of providing new vision on the past and for the future, by which the reader can become aware of consistency amongst empirically incompatible things. Ideally mythical configurations help us to discern otherwise unrecognized relations between empirically assumed opposites and, importantly, to be open to mimetic refigurations.

To continue with the case for converting myth and its symbols into a philosophical tool for feminists, the nature of myth is also unlike philosophy while similar to music. As stated earlier, myth, like music, has fluidity; by definition, it remains open to new variations while retaining a core of symbolic meaning. This comparison is implied in a major philosophical text by Ricoeur. In that text, his 'Interlude' ('L'interlude') on *Antigone* appears similar to a musical interlude, where the short study of variations in a mythical composition constitutes a self-contained piece presented between the parts of a sustained philosophical argument.[27]

However, Ricoeur's choice of using a myth about a tragic heroine reinforces the association of woman with nonphilosophy. An interlude on myth, as a break from a longer philosophical argument, affirms an ancient opposition between *logos*, and *muthos*. Man is placed on the side of *logos*; and woman with *muthos*.[28] In fact mythical configurations of Sophocles' fifth century BCE Greek tragedy *Antigone* by other modern philosophers have also employed myth to identify woman with familial duty, burial rites, and the abjection of physicality, e.g. burial of a corpse.[29] But again I suggest the possibility of refiguring the dominant meaning of such configurations.

A potentially more positive point for the feminist philosopher is that a contemporary continental philosopher of religion might agree to the existence of a core of narrative constancy in myth, as well as to myth's marginal variability.[30] Insofar as it invokes the spiritual powers of gods and goddesses, myth is irreducible to secular history. In this way, myth points to the inevitable limit of human institutions. But the question here is whether or not the sexed/gendered identities configured by myth are part of myth's marginal variability. To answer this, I will approach the configurations of masculinity and femininity in certain mythical narratives, as manifest in particular in women's actions and their implicit beliefs.

In order to elucidate the lived experiences of oppression in the lives of women and marginalized others, it has become apposite for feminists, in recent years, in philosophy to return to phenomenology. So despite poststructuralist critics, phenomenology can elucidate the lived experiences (*Erlebnis*, in German) which are not generally apparent in empirical accounts of immediate experience (*Erfahrung*). In particular, the phenomenological readings of myths can offer feminists tools for uncovering the general structures of meaning which constitute various dimensions of lived experiences, including religious, sexual, and familial. Poststructuralists have tended to criticize phenomenology for being irredeemably metaphysical. But given the concern of many feminists not to move away from concrete lived reality, it seems precipitate to rule out definitively a phenomenological approach to refiguring our visions of the world.

Caroline Walker Bynum has articulated a position on phenomenology which supports my use of myth.[31] She affirms that the phenomenology of symbols and myths can be valuable for studying gender in religion if two main points are maintained. For one thing, the polysemy of symbols, their multiple meanings, needs to be recognized. And then, as second-degree symbols, myths can weave the polysemy of primary symbols into narrative form. Thus understood, the open-endedness of symbol and myth would allow for the possibilities advocated here: that the configurations of patriarchy be refigured in terms of sexual difference. For another thing, the appropriation of the refigured meanings of myth should be made possible by phenomenology. This, then, would give myth a crucial role in, my terms, the transformation of sex/gender bias.

Granted these two points, a phenomenological reading can then discover (for us) the ways in which emotions evoke different dimensions of belief in signs, symbols, myths, and philosophy. Desires and emotions concerning the sacred give rise to these three different levels of language: the symbolic, the mythical, and the philosophical. This language of desire moves from the more concrete signs to the more abstract philosophy.

As already suggested, myth has been called nonphilosophy; at the same time, myth represents practical ideals and regulative principles in relation to philosophical texts. They serve to limit and preface what cannot be known or what is set outside of 'the economy of the same' (see next section). Myth represents impurity, sexual identity, and sexed/gendered characters, while philosophy represents purification, sex-neutral identity (which is nevertheless arguably male), and no gender-specific characters. In fact the following is true of Greek myths:

> myths . . . are themselves interpretations, descriptive and explanatory exegeses of beliefs and rites relative to defilement . . . [the] bond between defilement, purification and philosophy obliges us to be attentive to the spiritual potential of this theme. Because of its connection with philosophy, it cannot be a simple survival or a simple loss, but a matrix of meaning.
>
> . . . The sense of the testimony of the historians, orators, and dramatists is, therefore, completely missed when one gives only a sociological interpretation of it and sees it in only the resistance of the archaic rights of the family to the new law of the city . . . another kind of

> 'understanding' . . . bears on the unlimited potentiality for symbolization and transposition of the themes of defilement, purity, and purification. It is precisely the connection of defilement with words that define it which brings to light the primordially symbolic character of the representation of the pure and the impure. (Ricoeur 1967, 39)

Notice in the above passage the implied relation of philosophy to myth on the theme of purity/impurity. Such a relation has led philosophers of religion to study myths and their potential for symbolization of spiritually significant themes and issues. In particular, the significance in the myth of Antigone, where the spiritual but archaic rights of the family are opposed to the new law of the city, is referred to in the preceding quotation. Both Otto and Ricoeur, as phenomenologists of religion, have noted that the meaning of *deinon*, as used by Sophocles in *Antigone*, oscillates between the wondrous and the monstrous.[32] Strangeness of man/woman in this tragedy evokes ethical terror which, along with pity, constitutes the feelings associated with *katharsis* (purification); hence there is the connection between purity/impurity, as in purification/strangeness, *logos/muthos*, philosophy/myth.[33] Myth deals with impurity and purification which, in turn, gives rise to the purity of philosophical concepts. Without any great ceremony, phenomenology – even before poststructuralism – discovered that binary oppositions in western philosophy and its myths give greater value to the first term, in this case, purity and rational discourse. So philosophy, not myth, and male-neutral logic, not female desire, have the greater value in a true account of reality because of their emergence after purification.

A difference between phenomenology and poststructuralism rests in their reading of binary oppositions. In contrast with a hermeneutic phenomenologist like Ricoeur who seeks to restore meaning and identity to religious symbols, a feminist poststructuralist would necessarily seek to disrupt the fixed identity and hierarchy of gendered-value terms in dominant representations of belief. My suggestion is to rely to some extent upon the disruptive imitation proposed by feminist poststructuralism. Yet this reliance does not have to mean phenomenology needs to be rejected. Irigaray's own account of religious myths of reality is indebted to an unusual combination of philosophical approaches to the other in its ethical and religious dimensions, including the phenomenology of Levinas.

Thus there is a rich and varied background to Irigaray's transformation of the myths which have constituted the history of our sexual identity, our religious rites and forms of belief. And this background gives added weight to Irigaray's statement that

> The passage from one era to the next cannot be made simply by negating what already exists . . .
>
> . . . To consider the meaning of mythical representations of reality as merely incidental is concomitant to repressing and destroying certain cultural dimensions that relate to the economy of difference between the sexes. Such an approach also leads to a partial, reductive, and fruitless conception of History. (Irigaray 1993b, 24)

Following this, rather than calling for an end to history, to its myths of male sexual identity and representations of religious belief, I would call for their rethinking and so transformation. In an earlier work, Irigaray stresses the need to change the social order configured by myths, as well as transforming the technical study of them: 'The myths and stories, the sacred texts are analyzed, sometimes with nostalgia but rarely with a mind to change the social order . . . The techniques of reading, translating, and explaining take over the domain of the sacred, the religious, the mythical, but they fail to reveal a world that measures up to the material they are consuming or consummating' (Irigaray 1993c, 81). But care should be taken in reading this statement. Notice that it does not say anything about returning to the older stories and myths of matriarchy in order to oppose them to the texts of patriarchy.

3 Defining Mimesis

In the most basic and earliest terms, mimesis means imitation.[34] And Irigaray's distinctive use of mimesis has at least two stages. First, it consciously imitates the feminine role in a philosophical text conditioned by the *logos* in the masculine economy of 'the same.' Irigaray uses 'the same' (*le même*) to refer to the male subject who measures every other being against himself. According to this masculine economy, women are always 'the other of the same.' Second, in playing with mimesis, a disruptive imitation begins to take place. Mimesis takes on the role of miming in order to subvert 'the economy of the same' which has relied upon the feminine other for its own power to master and control. In her words,

> unless we limit ourselves naively – or perhaps strategically – to some kind of limited or marginal issue, it is indeed precisely philosophical discourse that we have to challenge, and *disrupt* . . .
>
> . . . [the] domination of the philosophical logos stems in large part from its power to *reduce all others to the economy of the Same.* The

> teleologically constructive project it takes on is always also a project of diversion, deflection, reduction of the other in the Same. And, in its greatest generality perhaps, from its power to *eradicate the difference between the sexes* in systems that are self-representative of a 'masculine subject'.
>
> . . . in order to pry out of them what they have borrowed that is feminine, from the feminine, to make them 'render up' and give back what they owe the feminine. This may be done in various ways, along various 'paths'.
>
> There is, in an initial phase, perhaps only one 'path', the one historically assigned to the feminine: that of *mimicry*. One must assume the feminine role deliberately. Which means already to convert a form of subordination into an affirmation, and thus to begin to thwart it . . .
>
> To play with mimesis is thus, for a woman, to try to recover the place of her exploitation by discourse, without allowing herself to be simply reduced to it. (Irigaray 1985b, 75–6)

To articulate the possibilities in configuring and refiguring mythical representations of reality, I have chosen to attempt to move beyond mimicry as affirmation in order to play with the traditional process of mimesis. Traditionally in philosophy since Aristotle, mimesis has been understood as the capacity to imitate or represent reality in narrative forms.[35] In turn, this tradition of mimesis has been read according to a threefold process.

Elsewhere I have followed Ricoeur in reading the three forms of mimesis as narrative prefiguration, configuration, and refiguration.[36] First, as prefiguration, mimesis represents the pre-understanding which is necessary for the narrative constitution of practical knowledge of the everyday world. For instance, prefiguration might include norms like consistency of healthy and rational behavior in responding properly to atmospheric conditions; this means a pre-understanding of the need to deal with changes in weather. Hence a prefigured form of narrative mimesis would guide action and give it coherence, allowing agents to carrying out everyday actions without being regularly undermined by natural phenomena; in this case, prefigured actions include the rational consistency of behavior in response to changing atmospheric conditions.

Second, configuration represents the synthesizing activity by which the knowledges of actions and characters are made the object, or the text, of a conscious and systematic unity as in the organized plot of a historical narrative. Examples of everyday configurations would include anything from (i) the synthesizing of the actions and characters in a natural and still miraculous event like a woman going through labor and giving birth to a healthy baby, to (ii) the synthesizing of the diverse actions and different characters which emerge after an unexpected, evil, and tragic event: for instance, the bombing of the Federal Building in Oklahoma City on 19 April 1995, as a result of which mothers mourned the death of toddlers at a playschool. But textual configurations can also be mythical; myth would emerge from synthesizing into a unity the significant actions and characters in a founding event, giving meaning to individuals in a community. The text of a myth is not strictly speaking the mimesis of an actual event, but it does give unity and meaning to historical events.

Third, refiguration represents the activity of the reader(s) who uses knowledge of prefiguring and configuring to go beyond the narrative unity of a configured text; this could mean to move beyond a dominant myth in order to recreate the world(s) of patriarchy. However, Irigaray employs mimesis in a further, unique feminist sense; her strategy of mimetic refiguration is not concerned with knowledge gained from an accurate configuration of historical and mythical reality, nor with an appropriate prefiguration of the world. Instead her two stages of mimesis as imitating and as miming represent a twofold refiguration. Ultimately Irigarary's refigurations aim to disrupt all prefigurations and to transform the gendered hierarchy of all dominant configurations by unearthing female desire and sexual difference.

The more traditional conception of the process of mimesis is restricted by mediation of already configured philosophical texts. The question is, can refigurations of sexual differences be brought about by the subject as traditionally conceived? Consider the following process:

> considered apart from reading, the world of the text remains a transcendence in immanence. Its ontological status remains in suspension – an excess in relation to structure, an anticipation in relation to reading. It is only in reading that the dynamism of configuration completes its course. And it is beyond reading, in effective action, instructed by the works handed down, that the configuration of the text is transformed into refiguration ... We might believe that the only mediation required between the pre-signification of $mimesis_1$ (i.e. prefiguration) and the over-signification of $mimesis_3$ is the one that is brought about by the narrative configuration itself through its internal dynamics. A more precise reflection on the notion of the world of the text and a more exact description of its status of transcendence within immanence have, however, convinced me that the passage from configuration to refigura-

> tion required the confrontation between two worlds. (Ricoeur 1988, 158–9)

Briefly this open-ended process of reading allows the possibility of disrupting biased configurations of sex/gender in myth. The reader's prefigured world could be changed by not only configuring its significant actions and characters into the meaningful world of a text, but by transcending this configured world into the new world opened up by a critical reading of the text. Ideally the configured text is the critical object of reading, but it may be necessary to move decisively beyond the mediated world, especially if that configured world projects an exclusive or biased identity. Effective action could transform the configuration of the text into refiguration of the subject's world.

In particular, in the case where a reader's prefigured world of patriarchy confronts a configured world of a male-biased text, a feminist philosopher of religion would seek a disruptive refiguring – to achieve effective action in transformative praxis of the male economy of the same. The dominant configuration of Adam and Eve is such a case.

However, the difficulty is that any confrontation between compatible, yet sex-biased, prefigured and configured worlds might simply confirm the status quo of injustice. A reading of a biased configuration of belief does not automatically generate its own energy – something which the fight against injustices would need. This means that to generate a disruptive refiguring of either the gender-differentiation of patriarchy or its gendered hierarchy of men over women is not a simple matter.

So the problem with the traditional form of threefold mimesis lies in the distinction between configuration and refiguration. Any configuration of sex/gender has to do with the immanent world of texts, while refiguration of sexual difference involves the subject further transcending this world of texts, that is, in transformative action and new, hopefully less biased refigurations. But from where does the impetus for the movement of transformation, i.e. for refiguring, come? Is the suffering of the marginalized or the desire for justice enough to begin the transformation of prefigured and configured worlds? And how is the desire for justice (of the marginalized) related to the recognition of justice (by the privileged)? There may be a problematic gap here between desire and cognition, the unconscious and the conscious.

The difficulty for feminists who intend to change old myths lies in moving forward beyond a privileged text to actual subjects. This would mean moving from the sex/gender structures of the patriarchal myth to the lived experiences of sexual difference. The danger for feminists is that the privileging of a configured text, as built upon the normative material of pre-signification, might merely reinforce the prefigured status quo of patriarchy and its injustices. In particular, I have been insisting that the feminist philosopher of religion needs to be able to express female desire in order to render visible sexual difference. But the oppression of patriarchy is not merely textual; it has to do linguistic, material, and social conditions of real subjects.

The potential for change in the traditional process of threefold mimesis rests upon the possibility that gender is not fixed by the text of any myth. If sex/gender roles are not prefigured as an invariant core of myth, then gender could emerge as a variable. The next step would be to discover sexual difference. The essential thing would be for the characters and actions of an event to be freely configured in the plot of a narrative text. Gender, then, could be read as not only a social and material factor, but also a textual and linguistic variable. Furthermore, if mimetically refigured, sexual identity could be disrupted by new categories and relations of sexual difference. In any case, this potential reading of sexual difference might offer an alternative to the problematic notion of gender, as constructed according to a fixed gender/sex opposition.

In this process, previously conceived gender relations could be challenged as strictly a male construct.[37] Gender relations could be questioned as fixed terms of male oppositional thinking. The new alternative to the static notion of gender/sex oppositions, as conceived by patriarchy, would be to conceive of subjects themselves, male and female, in process. This means complex, yet sexually specific, embodied beings whose subjectivity would be constituted by and constitutive of multiple figurations.

Importantly Irigaray's novel proposal for miming forces a new self-reflexive moment. Irigarayan miming would express sexual difference which would collapse the opposition of the privileged text/subject as a projection of the text. At the same time, it would break down the hierarchy of privileged male gender over devalued female sex. With the aid of Irigarayan miming, Ricoeur's own account of refiguration can be turned, in a more radical direction, against his acts of configuring.[38]

Kristeva also offers us distinctive strategies for refiguring the androcentric configurations of myth. Her analysis of a text focuses upon the gaps in its language. These gaps function as openings for disrupting static and biased images. I read these as openings for feminist miming: points at which the philosopher reflects back upon his own mimesis and questions the patriarchal prefiguring and configuring of women and men.

4 Sexual Identity in Religion

Sexual identity, as constituted by the symbols and myths of patriarchal religions, tends to deny difference. Seeking to disrupt both a patriarchal exclusion of the female other and a new entrenched matriarchal position, Irigaray aims to create an ethical order among women and men which would preserve sexual difference.[39] She calls for a new order in which both women and men remember their respective divine and sexual ancestries in myths, representing the difference of their sexual desires; but this does not mean two essentially different natures which solidify into entrenched oppositions. And her appeal to remember our distinctive ancestries is accompanied by her more immediate claim that our contemporary culture has forgotten our female ancestry, becoming 'unisex in our drives' and 'our mythology is neutral-male' (Irigaray 1994, 92). Fortunately, contrary to what has been thought, myths are not locked into univocal meanings or timeless configurations. Neither strictly patriarchal nor strictly matriarchal meanings have to dominate.

To illustrate her proposals, Irigaray insists that dominant interpretations of myths, concerning Antigone, Persephone, Eve, reflect their own stages of transformation; these are the stages which constitute the order of the present culture. In turn, this means that today our culture is only contingently ordered by patriarchal configurations of these myths. But the variety of possible ways to recount the destruction of female ancestry can be seen in the numerous configurations of the Antigone myth alone. Irigaray argues as follows:

> The destruction of female ancestry, especially its divine aspect, is recounted in a variety of ways in the Greek myths and tragedies . . . Antigone's uncle, the tyrant Creon, punishes by death her faith, her loyalty to her maternal ancestry and its laws, in order to safeguard his power in the polis.
>
> . . .
>
> In later versions or interpretations [of the destruction of female ancestry in myth], Kore/Persephone has become more or less responsible for her own fate, and is thus more like Eve the seductress, who leads man to his fall. It was nothing like that in the initial versions. But the story of Demeter and Kore/Persephone is so terrible and so exemplary that it is understandable that the patriarchal era wished to make the seductive woman bear the responsibility for its crimes. (Irigaray 1994, 100, 102)

In her work of the 1980s and '90s, Irigaray realizes the importance of love between us, as female and male. Ultimately the goal is a new ethical order of relationships between women and men. But divine love would originate with mother and child, with love between mother and daughter, not just between mother and son. So Irigaray concerns herself initially with the relationships of women-amongst-women so that women can be allowed to express love. The first step occurs with a revision of patriarchy's treatment of mothers and daughters.

> Patriarchy has constructed its heaven and hell upon this original sin. It has imposed silence upon the daughter. It has dissociated her body from her speech, and her pleasure from her language. It has dragged her down into the world of male drives, a world where she has become invisible and blind to herself, her mother, other women and even men, who perhaps want her that way. Patriarchy has thus destroyed the most precious site of love and its fertility . . . Hell appears to be a result of a culture that has annihilated happiness on earth by sending love, including divine love, into a time and place beyond our relationships here and now. (Irigaray 1994, 112)

In Irigaray's early writings the relation between mother and child, especially mother and daughter, is privileged. In contrast, as early as the 1970s, Kristeva warns that a new religion of a matrilinear form would not avoid violence or a new terrorism, if only reversing the form of sexism.[40] Kristeva cautions against creating a new belief in Woman which becomes entrenched, inhibiting explorations of ever-new identities.

The obvious dominant western myth stabilizing/retarding individual and communal identities of women, in relation to the divine, is the myth and cult of the Virgin Mary. Or in terms more amenable to Protestants, the myth of a first and second Eve represents the vehicle of sin and of salvation. Many women, including prominent feminists, have written on both Mary and Eve.[41] Despite or because of its popularity, this dominant myth has not been chosen as the central object of my critical refigurations. I do mention and question the Adamic myth as a founding myth of western culture. However, in order to maintain an open-ended framework for feminist philosophy of religion, I try not to privilege the dominant myths of Christianity or to debate the complex theological functions of Eve and Mary in Christian doctrine.

A founding myth refers to a narrative whose symbolism functions to give meaning to a culture and identity to a people. For example, the Adamic myth concerning the origin and end of evil can be described as a symbolic narrative which founds both the religious culture and sexual identity of men within patriarchy, while marginalizing women after Eve.[42] I will return to this marginalization of women and their desire. But, to repeat, myths are narratives which, although configuring into a meaningful unity the heterogeneous experiences of concrete men and women, always remain open to refiguring.

For another example of a founding myth, I take the Babylonian myth concerning the origin and end of evil, which is earlier than the Adamic myth. In this ancient narrative, the female goddess Tiamat represents a primordial chaos out of which order, the heavens, and the earth are created.[43] But this means that evil is associated with a primordial mother goddess whose chaos includes violence and a lack of identity, while the male god Marduk, who kills Tiamat, represents order and definition. Images from this Babylonian myth appear in the Hebrew scriptures. Significantly images of Tiamat include the vastness of marine waters and the power to either create or destroy.[44]

It appears that, in the earliest of mythical types constituting patriarchy, the primordial female figure represents the evil of excessive disorder and the dangers of female fluidity. The mythical killing of the primordial mother represents the symbolic act of matricide which founds the meaning of patriarchal history.[45] The myths of patriarchy go hand-in-hand with an androcentric bias. Human (male) identity as sameness is guaranteed by a divine maleness. In the Hebrew myth, a masculine and ideally paternal God, as well as a feminine other, bolsters masculine identity as powerful. In particular, evil is displaced upon woman, devaluing females. For Irigaray, an androcentric bias implies desire of the self-same.[46] And male desire of the self-same implies both male sexual identity as sameness and male gender as divinized in the ideal attributes of the God who reigns transcendent, supremely good, and so on. Together male self-sameness and masculine divinity repress female difference: she remains the mirror which makes possible male sameness as the other of the same.[47] She also remains the mediation of the divine.[48] Yet would western philosophers of religion agree that female desire remains both the pretext and excess in experiences of the divine as a God for and of male rationality?

Concerning the Adamic myth, contemporary philosophers of religion may admit that 'the story [of Eve's defilement] gives evidence of a very masculine resentment, which serves to justify the state of dependence in which all, or almost all, societies have kept women.'[49] But the Adamic myth remains dominant in western societies.[50] Or in more contemporary terms, it represents the west's androcentrism. Eve, in contradistinction from Adam, is weak as a tragic figure. The serpent also plays a significant role in the drama of temptation; but it represents the tragic and passive aspect of the subject who is tempted, without changing the anthropology. The serpent, then, signifies the quasi-externality of temptation projected onto the mediating object which seduces.[51] Thus while the man is associated with a good father-God and must learn to be the responsible figure, the woman is associated with an evil serpent, becoming the tragic figure who leads into temptation. And so according to patriarchal configurations of the fall, she becomes a figure of abjection[52] who must be excluded from sacred places. Ultimately, male autonomy appears dependent upon devaluing the female, her desires, and sexual difference.

At this stage, I turn to a question about the relationship of myth's language to desire and reason. Does sexual desire affect mythical language or does mythical language affect sexual desire? Recalling my brief discussion of language in chapter 3, I have come to favor the conception which gives language a mediating function; I assume a reciprocal conception of the relation between language and the meaning of reality. And in this case, the conception would be that myth's language affects, as well as is affected by, the religious meanings of desire; hence the sameness of meaning in language makes possible the formation of sexual identity by mediating desire.

With this conception in mind, it is Kristeva who offers the terms for analyzing desire in language. She discovers the place where desire disrupts the social-symbolic order of language; and this can be applied to a reading of the Adamic myth. Desire is crucial here in marking the place of abjection, i.e. the most propitious place for communication.[53] But notice that in following Kristeva, I have shifted the significance of desire at this point. Desire has a negative meaning for patriarchy; in the patriarchal configuration of Adam and Eve, it is a conscious inclination to deviate from a good rational intention. But then, with Kristeva's psycholinguistics, desire can be recognized as a potentially positive energy, however repressed in the unconscious, as an unnameable maternal trace.

The crucial term for Kristeva's analysis of desire in language is 'abjection.' The abject is neither subject nor object; but it is what has to be expelled for identity to be possible. It accompanies the very construction of the identity of the subject and the object. Moreover the place in language where the excluded maternal begins to break up the coherence of a configured text is in an abject space of desire.

The figure of woman appears in the abject spaces of the biblical text. These spaces are the gaps where the patriarchal text suffers ambiguity or incoherence.[54] For instance, the woman is represented ambiguously in biblical references to the Adamic myth as both defiling and purifying. Eve as defiled is – retrospective to the second Adam – dialectically related to

Mary, the Virgin Mother of the Son of God, who neither is defiled nor dies. The ambiguity in this abject space enables a splitting, whereby the figure of woman both threatens and conditions man's bond with the sacred.[55]

Although Kristeva enables recognition of this place of abjection, I would insist that discovery of the most propitious place for communication and change is possible only insofar as the formation of sexual identity is seen to be a mediated process; this implies that social and symbolic meanings would not directly or strictly construct our identities.[56] Instead our subjectivities, including sexual identity and nonidentity, would be formed through a self interpreted in the context of our symbolically mediated affective relationships.[57] However, my preferred conception of subjectivity as a mediated process may go beyond Kristeva's idea of a subject-in-process.[58] The hope would be that it remains possible to join certain postmodern feminists in celebrating the symbolic death of the unitary male subject.[59] This death would put the formerly excluded, desiring woman in a place of potential privilege: she represents something the unitary subject lacked but desired, now offering the possibility of discovering the place where reason and desire meet.

Concerning the male sexual identity of the Adamic myth, it appears to have been constituted both by Adam's difference from Eve and by Adam's relation to the sacred which involves the creation of the social-symbolic order of prohibitions and rites of purification. The interconnection of two points implicit in this situation is significant. First, Adam's differentiation as male from Eve as female *could*, if read diachronically, remain a difference in equality insofar as Eve is created out of the same original earthly creature (*ha'adham*; Genesis 2:7).[60] But, second, Adam's specifically human identity is determined with the distance created by the relationship or covenant with his creator God. When Adam's differentiation from Eve at Genesis 2:23 is read retrospectively in the light of the fall, then he is placed at the center of God's universe. But this centering also implies that Adam's identity as human is constituted by a hierarchy: the divine is privileged over the human, purity over impurity, immortality over mortality. Adam recognizes himself as impure, mortal, and human within the symbolic system of taboos and rites of purification. The systematic ordering of relations between subject and object constitutes both his distance from and his covenant with the sacred. However, woman as abject is excluded from this order, remaining a threat to man's bond with the sacred.

Read together, the two points reveal both an androcentric and a patriarchal bias in this configuration of the biblical story of Adam and Eve. Androcentric means that despite the possibility of difference in equality, the mythical configuration remains focused upon man and his relation to God. Patriarchal means that the ordering of the covenant imposes a hierarchy of power relations. The paternal term is always privileged; as the first term it is always assigned more value and power than any filial terms. And only masculine terms are meaningful; meaning breaks down with femininity.

This is evident in a selection of the exemplary personages in the great Old and New Testament narratives about the beginning and end of evil. According to the dominant configuration of belief, on the basis of biblical theology, the exemplary personages are patriarchal men. The dominant titles and figures in the Old Testament are fathers, kings, prophets, including Abraham, Moses, David, Isaiah, and the Messiah; then in the New Testament, Jesus is represented by the symbolism of the first and second Adam.[61] The mythical language concerning the first and second Adam brings together the privileged figures in the Old and New Testament narrative; at the same time, it assumes a patriarchal covenant ordered by laws of prohibition and purification.

5 Mimetic Refigurations

My contention is that mythical configurations of human and divine reality should be accompanied by their mimetic refigurations, and that the mimetic refigurations can enable us to recognize what content has been excluded from the formally rational constructions of religious beliefs. I mean by 'content,' besides empirical or intellectual intuition, material dimensions of reality such as concrete expressions of desire and love. In more general terms, the multiple aspects of human embodiment, of ethics and difference, still await discovery and expression.[62]

Building upon psycholinguistic readings of myth in their relation to philosophical texts, refigurations of mythical meaning can aim to disrupt the male configurations of rationality and patriarchy which have excluded women and sexual difference from philosophy of religion. Disruptive refigurations will offer new images from old myths of women in nature. And Irigaray's refigurations in particular reflect a highly original style of miming. Her mimings of already configured myths release the content and energy for a new reality and a new utopia. But the creation of a utopian vision by a disruptive miming must be approached cautiously.

Disruptive miming is necessary for the successful transformation of patriarchal myths and of theistic beliefs. In particular, this miming offers the possibility of disrupting the hierarchy which continues to be dominant in western philosophy of religion. But Irigaray's account of the hysteric describes both the necessity and the difficulty of mimetic refigurations:

> Hysteria: *it speaks* in the mode of a paralysed gestural faculty, of an impossible and also a forbidden speech . . . It speaks as *symptoms* of an 'it can't speak to or about itself' . . . And the drama of hysteria is that it is inserted schizotically between that gestural system, that desire paralysed and enclosed within its body, and a language that it has learned in the family, in school, in society, which is in no way continuous with – nor, certainly, a metaphor for – the 'movements' of its desire. Both mutism and mimicry are then left to hysteria. *Hysteria is silent and at the same time it mimes.* And – how could it be otherwise – miming/reproducing a language that is not its own, masculine language, it caricatures and deforms that language: it 'lies', it 'deceives', as women have always been reputed to do.
>
> The problem of 'speaking (as) woman' is precisely that of finding a possible continuity between that gestural expression or that speech of desire – which at present can only be identified in the form of symptoms and pathology – and a language, including a verbal language. (Irigaray 1991b, 138)

Usefully articulated in the above description of the hysteric's position is the difficulty of distinguishing expressions that adequately mime a new feminine or female symbolic from those that only imitate symptoms of the suppression of femininity. How do we understand the hysteric's miming in order to transform patriarchy?

Two stages, at least, can be distinguished in Irigaray's miming. The first stage consciously imitates the feminine role in a philosophical text conditioned by the masculine economy of the same. The second stage of mimesis becomes a disruptive imitation: it takes on the role of miming in order to subvert the economy which has relied upon the feminine for its power to master and control. It is the latter stage which I intend by mimetic refiguration.

What are the possibilities for women, especially for femininity, in mimetic refigurations? Is a new symbolic for women proposed, or is this to be a parody of the male symbolic? To broach these questions, I should point out that there is no agreement between Kristeva and Irigaray concerning men's and women's relations to femininity. The decisive issue is whether femininity can be represented in texts written by men as well as by women. Unlike Kristeva, Irigaray is explicit: sexual difference will reveal the sexually specific distinctiveness of women, of their language and identity. Yet Kristeva and Irigaray both confront the difficulty of distinguishing an authentic femininity from patriarchal constructions of femininity while living in our present world.[63]

To illustrate the way in which Kristeva attempts to refigure an old myth of femininity, I direct the reader to her writing on the myth and cult of the Virgin Mary. She produces a 'double writing,' splitting her written page in two in order to represent two sorts of maternal identities. On the one hand, there is a configuration of the patriarchal myth of the Virgin Mother; on the other hand, there is a woman's (Kristeva's) actual lived experiences of motherhood. Her double writing sets the mythical configuration of patriarchy against a mimetic refiguration of a woman's lived experience, in speaking of her own experience. Drucilla Cornell explains this double writing as follows:

> Kristeva's own 'Stabat Mater' (1977) can be understood to exemplify the 'double writing' . . . [which] I have interpreted . . . One side of the page analyzes the myth of the mother as it has played such an overwhelming role in religious traditions . . . but her concern is the way in which the mythology of the Mother obscures women's actual experience of maternity . . . On the other side of the page, she disrupts her own account and working-through of the significance of these myths with a poetic evocation of her own experience of pregnancy and birthing. Yet the myths are not simply denied, nor can they be, because even as they are critiqued as the distortion of women's experience and the 'instinctual' life of the mother, they retain a powerful hold over our imagination. We reimagine through these myths. But we also disrupt the images of our own refiguration. The status of these myths *as* myths is exposed as we also attempt to transfigure Woman as she is 'presented' in them. Double writing, in turn, indicates the limit of refiguration. As Kristeva rightly warns, the danger of belief in Woman is that we re-establish a 'new religion' which becomes its own edifice and does not allow for the continual exploration of new possibility, let alone the reaching out to the impossible. (Cornell 1991, 171–2)

In line with the above account, Kristeva confirms the difficulty with her own double writing on motherhood in 'Women's Time.' She explicitly warns that the double writing of feminism could become a new religion of entrenched identities.[64] Kristeva is aware that 'belief in Woman' could reverse sexism and anthropomorphism, resulting in mystification, not clarification. More precisely stated, feminists who promote a new religion on the basis of an ideal and essential Woman tend to turn their backs on actual social problems and repress sexual difference only to confirm the status quo of religious injustice.[65] To avoid these dangers, the alternative proposal here is to explore sexually specific and culturally differentiated mimetic refigurations of real beliefs and desires, especially of marginalized lives.

There can be no facile end to the present social-symbolic order, to philosophy, to history, or to the dominant religious myth of patriarchy. The inadequacies of merely proposing a new religion over and against the old are everywhere apparent. For example, Mary Daly replaces the Virgin Mary with a new female Christ-figure, creating a new form of power, and possibly of terror.[66] A mere reversal of power cannot confront the mythical configurations of a divine reality, especially patriarchal myths of our desires, loves, and fears, which remain part of our personal and corporate histories. Myths are not easily erased and histories are not wisely forgotten. The goal, in one sense, needs to be to refigure the present and future; but in another sense, the past needs to be dealt with: the past can be transfigured from a history of oppression into a history of remembering, especially remembering the suffering of innocent women and marginalized others.[67]

Notwithstanding these critical points concerning a new religion which essentializes woman, it is important to clarify the 'femininity' which both Kristeva and Irigaray recognized as repressed by the past. Here is a relevant critical comment:

> in referring to 'femininity', Irigaray and Kristeva do not speak of a transhistorical essence located in, for example, maternity or reproductive capacity. Rather, they refer to a femininity which is itself a product of the culture and language which represses it. Femininity is, precisely, that which is excluded from patriarchal representations and can only be glimpsed in their gaps and silences. For it to return, and to unsettle that which repressed it, a special process is required, because what is returning is not something always present in every individual woman. For Irigaray, this takes the form of a problematic mimicry of the position of the hysteric, who articulates publicly in her body postures the history forgotten by her society, including the history of 'low' culture. (Purkiss 1992, 448)

The critical point concerns Irigaray's problematic mimicry from the position of a hysteric.[68] Her mimicry is problematic in suggesting both the impossibility and the possibility of changing patriarchal exclusions of femininity. What are the criteria for distinguishing adequate expressions of the feminine or female symbolic? A minimum criterion is the exposure of sexual difference which avoids treating expressions of women's beliefs as unintelligible symptoms of the hysteric's desire, as determined by patriarchy.

At this stage, women (and men) can find the space and the ability to explore their multiple identities, given expression by freely configuring and refiguring myths. The goal of this exploration is significant: to discover a new utopian vision and, in Irigarayan terms, to think the difference for a peaceful revolution of our desires, of our sexual specificities, and of our beliefs concerning divinity. And for her part, Kristeva helps to identify the crucial space, or place, for the transformation of patriarchy.

According to Kristeva's psycholinguistics, the myth and cult of the Virgin Mary demonstrate that the maternal has remained an ambivalent, unnameable principle, since both outside of the paternal social-symbolic order and a condition of that order.[69] Precisely because of this ambivalence, the maternal principle offers a significant space for disrupting patriarchy, for a potential revelation of the sacred. As Kristeva explains,

> Let us call 'maternal' the ambivalent principle that is bound to the species, on the one hand, and on the other stems from an identity catastrophe that causes the Name to topple over into the unnameable that one imagines as femininity, nonlanguage, or body. . . . at the same time the most intense revelation of God, which occurs in mysticism, is given only to a person who assumes himself as 'maternal.' Augustine, Bernard of Clairvaux, Meister Eckhart, to mention but a few, played the part of the Father's virgin spouses, or even, like Bernard, received drops of virginal milk directly on their lips. (Kristeva 1986, 161-2)

Femininity, equated in the above with the body, remains nonlanguage in being grounded in the maternal principle. So this has an affinity with the position of the hysteric. However, for Kristeva, both men and women can experience, and so seek to give expression to, the maternal.

Bodily difference functions in the maternal principle prior to the nameable and so prior to the law of the father. The maternal is excluded at the point of the self's acquisition of language and so at the point of man's entry into the social contract; and arguably this is when sexual difference becomes repressed. This is the point of decisive separation from the mother; thereafter the maternal principle is applied to a space outside of the symbolic order of subject and object. Yet notice that as an ambivalent principle, the maternal still retains an attractive role, erupting into the social-symbolic order in moments of intense revelation of a divine love where abjection and the sacred come together. For example, this revelation comes in the ambiguous signs of the undefiled body of the virgin mother.

But note that with Kristeva's semiotic and its connection with femininity, she moves from an earlier, linguistic account of the semiotic to her interest in an idealization of the pre-oedipal mother.[70] The danger in this move is the equation of the semiotic with an idealized yet ultimately illusory feminine enclave. Kristeva herself warns against this danger in 'Women's Time.' Again it is the father of individual prehistory – the imaginary father or the Third Party – who must intervene within the semiotic to challenge this equation, moving the emergent subject, whether male or female, beyond the empty state of abjection.[71]

6 A Regulative Ideal: Reason and Desire

Myth can serve, positively, as an ideal by means of which practical reason regulates its use of its own concepts of deity for men and women, while granting that it knows nothing of the objective character of a supersensible realm.[72] In other words, for embodied beings, there is no possibility of a view-from-nowhere, no human knowledge of or from a realm not limited by the sensible, no absolutely correct representation of reality. As noted in Kant's *Religion within the Limits of Reason Alone*, 'if we limited our judgment to *regulative* principles . . . instead of aiming at *constitutive* principles of a knowledge of supersensible objects, insight into which, after all, is forever impossible for us, human wisdom would be better off in a great many ways' (Kant 1960 [1793], 65).

At the same time, feminist philosophers of religion who take seriously my argument concerning refiguration cannot rest content with the patriarchal myths which have served as the regulative principles accompanying philosophical texts. Instead women will (have to) play with mimesis in order to bring new life to mythical configurations of their own sex. Being recognized as guardians of nature, women seek to become divine; and in bringing nature to men, they return reason to desire in self-affection.

> Is not the 'first' stake in mimesis that of re-producing (from) nature? . . . As guardians of 'nature', are not women the ones who maintain, thus who make possible, the resource of mimesis for men?
>
> . . . A playful crossing, and an unsettling one, which would allow woman to rediscover the place of her 'self-affection'. Of her 'god', we might say. A god to which one can obviously not have recourse – unless its *duality* is granted. (Irigaray 1985b, 77–8)

Taking seriously the above, my overriding aim in this chapter has been to nominate myth and mimesis as philosophical tools for feminists who endeavor to rethink the patriarchal structures of philosophy and religion. Properly conceived, the tools of mythical configuration and mimetic refiguration can be applied to belief both self-reflexively and critically in order to disrupt entrenched positions. Such positions include the religious and sexual identity configured by patriarchy's myths. And these configured identities are especially difficult to dislodge as long as reason (the *logos*) is privileged as disembodied and as superior to desire, devotion, death; the latter realities are largely excluded from – or at the regulative limits of – philosophy, but portrayed in myth.

Philosophical defenses of religious belief should not merely be replaced by mythical reflections, nor reason by desire. But my proposal is to work at collapsing hierarchical divisions, especially those between the rational subject and his own materially conditioned status which has been projected onto the female or feminine other. By recognizing these divisions, a move is made toward changing the subject's own precarious position. The ultimate hope is that, in creating new versions of old myths or less biased versions of new myths, we can be connected with our own history as embodied beings and with each other as desiring, reasoning, intuiting, believing women and men. The next chapter attempts to illustrate this hope in disruptively miming mythical configurations of religious belief, in representing the actions, emotions, and rational passion evoked by particular women's beliefs.

Notes

1. Various examples illustrate the struggle by contemporary philosophers of religion to remain unaffected by human emotion, feelings, desire, or any bodily passions which are opposed to formal reasoning. For an empiricist defense of the agency of an incorporeal God, which relies upon the possibility that bodily entailment is not inherent in our reasoning at a strictly conceptual level, see Holtzer 1987, 189–209; cf. Mitchell 1973, 1–8. For an empirical argument about evil, knowledge of right and wrong, and of true and false belief, which in excluding emotions and feelings can seem callous toward the suffering of particular persons, see Swinburne 1987, 141–67. For the exclusion of feelings from a rational consideration of free will and the problem of hell, see Craig 1989, 186–7. For a traditional theist who follows Aquinas (while still being influenced by modern epistemology) in assuming that man's reason is valued first and foremost in a 'man' above carnal desire and inordinate passion, see Kretzmann 1988, 172–95. Finally, accepting that 'total devotion' should be given by 'man' to the God of Christian theism, Adams tries to understand rationally how this can be consistent with desire and love for other human

beings; see Adams 1986, 169–94; also, for the admission, however extraordinary, that passion is necessary in thinking about religious belief if human thought is to conform to its object, i.e. a supremely good God, see Adams 1993, 30–2.

2. A different, nonfoundational form of empiricism, which retains a realist account of empirical belief, could nevertheless be compatible with feminism. For elements of such an account, see Fricker 1994, 95–109.
3. A consequentialist approach to moral knowledge gained from 'abstracted' thinking about individual experience provides an instance of ends-justifies-means reasoning in Swinburne 1987, 150–61; cf. Lazreg 1990, 329; 1994, 45–62; chapter 1, section 2, above.
4. For criticism of a hegemonic reason, see Le Doeuff 1990, 1–13; for further criticism of the fallacious arguments of certain feminists who have assumed an exclusive conception of Enlightenment reason in criticizing it, see Green 1995, 10–26. Also, see my discussion of the dialectic of Enlightenment reason in part IV, section 2, below.
5. Swinburne 1991 (1979), 48–50, 72; Jantzen 1984; Holtzer 1987, 189–209.
6. Ibid. For a more introductory comment on the embodiment debate, see Corner 1991, 76–81, 87.
7. An example of a ramified belief is the doctrine of the atonement; see Franks Davis 1989, 248–50; cf. Swinburne 1989; Stump 1988, 61–91; Quinn 1993, 281–300.
8. Nevertheless Alston 1991 presents a serious case for perceptual experiences serving as grounds for knowledge of God.
9. But for someone who articulates the 'much more' which (he believes) ought to be recognized and defended in order to maintain reference to the Christian God, see Fodor 1995, 8–19, 287–9.
10. Concerning the danger of injustices due to assuming idealizations as different from appropriate use of abstractions, see O'Neill 1993, 303–23; 1996, 39–44, 62–4, 68–9, 110, 200.
11. Nicholson and Fraser 1990, 2–3, 26.
12. To develop a richer contrast between a feminist poststructuralist reading of human incarnation and an empirical realist account of the ramified beliefs in Christ's incarnation, consider both Irigaray 1991c, 164–90, and Swinburne 1986; 1989.
13. For the important distinction between the male imaginary (with its narcissism) and the philosophical imaginary, see part IV below.
14. Warner 1976, 34ff; cf. Gatens 1996, 53–5.
15. Daly 1986 (1973); Warner 1976, 19–24, 34–49; Kristeva 1986, 160–86; Ranke-Heinemann 1991, 27–46.
16. Cf. Gatens 1996, 53.
17. See note 1 of this chapter.
18. For use of the idea of making strange to describe the possible impact of feminist standpoint epistemology upon a woman student in philosophy of religion, see

Elliott 1994, 426–31. Employing similar metaphors in her significant discussions of justice, gender, and practical reasoning, O'Neill considers how, in received descriptions of social relations, issues of gender are 'passed over as if invisible,' and how 'familiarity' can mask contentious and unjust delimitations of typical problems; see O'Neill 1993, 316–17. In O'Neill's words,

> We beg questions if we assume that categories of thought that have been hospitable to male dominance and imperialism can be decisive for discerning or judging justice to those whose problems have been marginalized and whose agency and capacities have been formed, perhaps deformed, by unjust institutions. We cannot rely uncritically on the categories of established discourse, including the discourse of social scientists and the 'helping' professions, to pick out the significant problems. These categories are themselves matters for ethical concern and criticism. (316)

19. Newman 1994, 15–37. Newman's account of feminist standpoint epistemology deserves critical comment in the light of chapter 2 above. Her account exhibits a double lack of attention to (i) original feminist arguments and (ii) actual use of metaphor in a philosophical text. To prevent (i), this lack of attention to original argument resulting in the misrepresentation of a feminist epistemology, I propose avoiding hastily assumed equations with Marx (cf. Harding 1991; 1993). And to avoid (ii), this lack of attention to the actual use of a metaphor in a philosophical text resulting in specific historical inaccuracy, I suggest recognizing two things about Marx's philosophical writings.

For one thing, Marx's comments on religion paraphrase the account of religious belief originally presented by Feuerbach. When Newman writes, 'for Germany, criticism of religion has been largely completed' (Newman 1994, 20), this is Marx's view of Feuerbach's criticism of religion. Since Marx had not written much on religion at that time, it is highly contentious to assume that Marx himself had a specific 'theory of religion,' let alone assume that he had a theory of religion and sacrifice, affecting his social theory with anti-Semitism and, by association, making feminist standpoint epistemology racist; see Newman 1994, 19; cf. Hewitt 1995, 5–9, 176–7, 207.

For another thing, Bruno Bauer (1809–82) became an anti-Semite during his life; and Marx's 'On the Jewish Question' (1844) is a response to Bauer. But from these two points, it does not follow that Bauer's views can implicate Marx in anti-Semitism and, ultimately, implicate feminist standpoint epistemology in an anti-religious stance; cf. Newman 1994, 25.

Certainly all philosophers, but especially women seeking to legitimate a feminist philosophy of religion, need to beware of reading historical terms anachronistically. Otherwise the growth of feminist knowledge is threatened. Care has to be taken to avoid forcing the present meanings of terms back onto ethnically nonspecific metaphors. Newman's case against Marx is largely derived from his 'On the Jewish Question'; but she misreads Marx's metaphors, 'ritual sacrifice' and 'Jewry' (or possibly 'religion' itself as a metaphor). These metaphors describe the economic system of capitalism or the people who use money in a particular way in the nineteenth century; and it is almost impossible to find a nineteenth-century German not using metaphors that play on Gentile abuse of Jews. Marx applies these metaphors to everyone in civil society – both Christians and Jews. More important is that, in contrast with Bauer who is a confessed anti-Semite, Marx argues for the political emancipation of Jewry. Hence Newman's anachronistic misread results in unfairly and wrongly imposing anti-Semitic views on Marx; see Newman 1994, 25–6.

For more scholarly background on this question in Marx, see the 'Special Note A. Marx and the economic-Jew stereotype' in Draper 1977; cf. Marx 1992 (1974); Feuerbach 1989.

20. For the use of religious symbols and myths as regulative principles (despite his privileging of patriarchal figures), see Kant 1960 (1793), 54–65.
21. For further discussion, see Anderson 1996a, 112–30.
22. Anderson 1993b, 195–204.
23. Moore 1997, chapter 10.
24. Prendergast 1986, 1–27, 41–5, 216–21, 233–5; Ricoeur 1984, 52–7; 1988, 3–4, 262–4, 272–4, 326n12; Kearney 1996, 29–45.
25. Lechte 1994; cf. Derrida 1976.
26. See Clemit 1993, 139–74. Clemit argues that Mary Shelley exploits the novel as 'a myth-making form which is capable of critical scrutiny of political ideals' (154). But Clemit also demonstrates how Shelley's modern myth can be seen as both the source for a range of future images and the repository of literary and intellectual history (143, 154–5). In Clemit's words, 'she [Mary Shelley] recasts the Godwinian plot as a creation story, reworking both the Greek and Roman myth of Prometheus and the Judeao-Christian myth as mediated by *Paradise Lost*, and adding a critical commentary on Godwin's rational account of social origins in *Political Justice*' (155).
27. Ricoeur 1992, 241–9.
28. Ricoeur 1992, 241.
29. Hegel 1977, 276–7; 1991, 439; Kristeva 1982 (1980), 25–6, 83–9; Steiner 1984, 295; Nussbaum 1986, 51ff; Irigaray 1985a, 214–26; Ricoeur 1992; Anderson 1997.
30. For discussions concerning myth, see Anderson 1993b, 195–204; 1996a, 112–30.
31. Bynum 1986, 1–20, especially 2, 9–11, 15; cf. Ricoeur 1967.
32. Otto 1923, 25, 39-40; Ricoeur 1992, 245–7; cf. Kristeva 1991, 41–50, 65–77; chapter 3, section 3, above.
33. Kristeva 1982, 69–89; Nussbaum 1986, 52-7, 71-9; Ricoeur 1992, 244–8.
34. Kosman 1992, 51ff.
35. On mimesis as the representation of reality in western literature, see Auerbach 1968; Prendergast 1986. But on the subversive potential of mimesis (as 'poetic'), see Kristeva 1984 (1974), 57–61; cf. Aristotle 1965, 31–7.
36. Anderson 1993c, 125–7; 1996a, 112–30; cf. Ricoeur 1984, 52–7; 1988, 3–4, 158–9.

37. Braidotti 1994b, 52–67; also 1994a.
38. Ricoeur 1984, 4, 52–7; 1988, 11, 99–103, 159, 270, 326; cf. Anderson 1996a.
39. Irigaray 1994, 91–113.
40. Kristeva 1986, 205–8.
41. Daly 1986 (1973), 81–97; Schüssler Fiorenza 1975, 605–26; Warner 1976, 3–68; Kristeva 1986, 161–86; Maeckelberghe 1994, 8–42.
42. On founding myths and the mythical first man who represents the male ideal of unity-in-multiplicity, see Ricoeur 1967, 5, 244. If Ricoeur's phenomenology of religious symbols is accurate, then ancient myths configure the material content for ramified beliefs concerning original sin, evil, and sexual desire.
43. On the one hand, see Ricoeur 1967, 175–84 and, on the other hand, Daly 1987 (1978), 107–10.
44. Ricoeur 1967, 174, 177, 184, 198–206, 210. For a miming of the connection between women and marine waters, see Irigaray 1991c.
45. Irigaray 1991b, 36.
46. Irigaray 1985a, 32–4.
47. Irigaray 1993c, 111.
48. Irigaray 1993a, 116–29.
49. Ricoeur 1967, 254–5.
50. Ricoeur 1967, 260.
51. Ricoeur 1967, 256.
52. Kristeva 1982, 96, 127; Anderson, forthcoming.
53. Ibid.
54. To discover these spaces, see Ricoeur 1967, 28, 31, 37–8; Kristeva 1986, 234–63; Lechte 1990, 160, 177; Berry 1992, 250–64.
55. The ambiguity of women's blood identified with its defiling and purifying meanings also becomes a propitious place for communication; see Kristeva 1982, 96.
56. For a different reading of Irigaray, see Weir 1996, 90–111.
57. Nonidentity is another way to say that sexual difference has been repressed.
58. However, if the affective relationship and discourse between the subject and his or her analyst constitutes a mediation through identity of meaning in language, there exists the possibility of identity being a mediated process; see Kristeva 1986, 239–71; 1987a, 9, 26–7, 62–3.
59. Braidotti 1991, 1–2, 209–11.
60. The earthly creature is read as androgynous in Trible 1992 (1973), 74–8. Later rejecting androgyny which assumes sexuality, Trible recognizes the earthly creature in Genesis 2:7 as sexually undifferentiated; Trible 1978, 97–8, 141n17.
61. Ricoeur 1967, 6–7, 237–43; 1970, 38–40.
62. For a timely account of issues related to narratives of embodiment, see Gatens 1996, 49–55, 95–107.
63. The potential of Kristeva's semiotic, as the receptacle of pre-signifying maternal energies and female desires, to subvert the social-symbolic order of patriarchy will be seriously questioned in part IV, sections 3 and 5, especially.

64. Kristeva 1986, 161–86, also 188–213.
65. Kristeva 1986, 208–10.
66. For an account of Daly, see Suchocki 1994, 57–68.
67. For a politically engaged reading of Kristeva on transformation, see Cornell 1993, 1–11, 57–97, 106–11; also for a theological appropriation of Kristeva, see Chopp 1993, 38–45.
68. Irigaray 1985a, 53–5, 59–61, 71, 103; 1991b, 138; Cornell 1991, 147–52, 165–75; 1993, 107–11; Chisholm 1994, 267.
69. Kristeva 1986, 160–86. Cf. Warner 1976.
70. Kristeva 1984 (1974), 25-30; 1986, 161-86.
71. See chapter 3 above; cf. Kristeva 1986; 1995.
72. Kant 1960, 53, 55, 58, 63–5.

5

Figuring the Rationality of Religious Belief: Belief, Action, and Devotion

> *The* bhajniks *. . . have given of their impulses and energies to remake Mira, and through this have remade themselves – they have remade the world giving to it their stamp, and their hope for a better form of relationships.*
>
> Mukta 1994, 169

1 Figuring Belief: Reinventing Ourselves as Other

The purpose of the present chapter is to hold together and apply certain crucial conclusions from earlier chapters. The starting point is the epistemological – and arguably ethical – imperative implicit in Harding's feminist standpoint epistemology that we should 'reinvent ourselves as other.'[1] As seen in chapters 1 and 2, Harding distinguishes her feminist standpoint epistemology from the epistemological foundationalism of the naive empirical realist, as well as from the experiential foundationalism of the feminist empiricist. The latter form of foundationalism attempts to ground knowledge in women's experiences; this is in reaction to the former foundationalism with its unacknowledged sexism. But with her distinctive framework, Harding insists that

> what 'grounds' feminist standpoint theory is *not* women's experiences but the view from women's lives. . . . we can all learn about our own lives at the center of the social order if we start our thought from the perspective of lives at the margins . . .
>
> . . .

> I characterize as 'reinventing ourselves as other' the standpoint enterprise that produces agents of history and knowledge who use experience in their knowledge-seeking in a different way from that of proponents of [either the ahistorical foundationalism of 'the-view-from-nowhere' or the experiential foundationalism of the opposite extreme]. (Harding 1991, 269, 270)

Treating the heart of the standpoint enterprise as an imperative – to reinvent ourselves as other – the present chapter will look in two different directions, employing two feminist frameworks. Reinventing ourselves as other can be applied to specific beliefs which emerge, on the one hand, out of the repressed material of the female other's desire; and, on the other hand, from the lives of outsiders, even from a woman's own status on the margin. In addition to application of this ethical imperative, feminist poststructuralism aids application of the other imperative implicit in the preceding: to think from the perspective of lives at the margins.

However, before uniting the two feminist positions, and before applying the ethical and epistemological imperatives, a question arises for the philosopher of religion. The feminist standpoint epistemologists may seek to think as outsiders from within a common identity, but is this logically possible for a feminist philosopher of religion? The word 'religion' derives from the Latin *religio*, which in turn comes from *lego*, to bind. If religious belief binds different selves into one common, qualitative identity, it may be logically impossible to ground religious knowledge on either thinking from the perspective of lives at the margins or reinventing selves as other. If religion means a binding identity, it could presuppose that true belief is strictly built upon being an insider within a religious community of faith.

I would like to explore both the positive and negative potential in religious beliefs which as truth-claims bind people together, constituting a qualitative identity. Negatively, religious beliefs often constitute a common identity which would clash with the imperative which guides this chapter. Positively, religious beliefs have not always been strictly exclusive; they have aimed to include the radically other.

The initial proposal to reinvent ourselves as other might be taken to mean simply reading narrratives of religious devotion for knowledge of the other and the outsider; the aim would be to learn from examples of female devotion. But the danger in a straightforward reading is silencing the otherness of female devotion by forcing one's own privileged view onto the lives of others, hence erasing the distinctive reality of their foreignness. So to preserve the positive possibility of inclusion without ignoring the negative tendency of exclusion, the initial proposal must involve a more complicated process. And I propose a double task: (i) critically reading mythical configurations of belief, particularly of religious devotion as construed by patriarchy; and then (ii) disruptively miming these myths in order to uncover the desire of the other and to make possible the refigurations of female dissent and marginality. To ensure that this double task develops the positive potential of religious identity, this chapter follows a two-way or dialectical movement of getting at, on the one hand, the repressed desire of the female other and, on the other hand, the material conditions making up the lives of outsiders.

To begin the double task of critically reading religious beliefs, allow me to bring forward my earlier discussion of Kristeva and the idea of a post-patriarchal religion. Recall especially that patriarchal configurations of theistic belief have tended to eclipse female desire. In her more recent work, Kristeva insightfully illustrates the tension for patriarchal religion between inclusion and exclusion of the other. Most interesting is Kristeva's configuration of two different, potentially conflicting claims: first, that belief in a personal deity requires inclusion as 'the welcoming of a radical otherness, the acknowledging of a foreignness that one would at first tend to consider the most degraded;'[2] and second, that within a religious group, benevolence toward a foreigner depends upon a certain exclusion or erasure. This second claim means that the foreigner's acceptance by the religious group depends upon the erasure of the identity of the foreigner by the religious beliefs of that group. In other words, the marginalized other must accept the beliefs and dogmas of the center in order to be included in its religious identity.

Thus these two claims involve opposing factors of inclusion and exclusion; they expose a tension within religious identity. The examples which Kristeva takes from patriarchal texts each illustrate the ways in which the repressed material of female desire is recalled in encounters with a foreigner. In particular, Kristeva's narrative configuration of Jewish identity illustrates this tension in identity; but it also exemplifies the significance of my present concern to think from the life of a marginalized other, in this case, of a foreign woman. Similar to the foreigner who is excluded by external constraints, the sexually specific desire of the woman has to be erased (in the sense of being repressed) by the patriarchal configurations in order to acquire the religious identity of a monotheist. In chapter 3, I connected this repression of the strange with the feelings of an uncanny strangeness.[3]

Bringing together the preceding points, Kristeva's narrative configuration of Ruth from the Old Testament crystallizes a central experience of uncanny strangeness. I would read Ruth within this configuration as an outsider within.[4] In the following account, Kristeva illustrates the process of identity formation which constitutes monotheism:

> the [Jewish] alliance with God . . . nevertheless provides for, in its very essence, a primal inscription of foreignness [strangeness] . . . A foreign woman, Ruth the Moabite, crystallizes the tendency I have in mind.
>
> It was forbidden to marry a foreigner, particularly a Moabite, for the people of the land of Moab were especially hostile to the Jews at the time of the Exodus. Now it happened that in a period of distress in Judea a man named Elimelech left the country, settled in Moab, and his two sons married two Moabite princesses, Ruth and Orpah. After the men died Ruth and her mother-in-law Naomi returned to Judea, Ruth seemingly *desirous* to follow not only Naomi but also Naomi's God . . . Ruth . . . reminds us that divine revelation requires a disparity, the welcoming of a radical otherness, the acknowledging of a foreignness that one would at first tend to consider the most degraded.
>
> . . . It is true nevertheless that within a religious group, benevolence toward a foreigner depends on a precondition: acceptance of that group's dogmas signifies in fact that the foreigner as such has been absorbed and erased.
>
> . . .
>
> Let us then remain within the culture and endeavor . . . to recognize ourselves as strange in order better to appreciate the foreigners outside us instead of striving to bend them to the norms of our own repression. (Kristeva 1993a, 23–4, 28–9)

Inscribed in this narrative of Jewish identity is the shift from foreignness as otherness to a foreigner absorbed in the sameness of group identity. Remaining implicit in such religious identity is the inevitable tension between inclusion and exclusion of the strange. This tension results in the constant danger of eclipsing the other of female desire as well as the other who is the foreigner. There are, then, various possible readings of such religious identity, including that of patriarchy, which excludes female desire and marginalizes or erases (the history of) the nonprivileged other. Patriarchal monotheism stresses the significance of Ruth's child[5] who, in being adopted by Naomi, reinforces the paternal line of Jews to David. The dominant reading stresses Ruth's devotion as submission to the paternal line,

> So Boaz took Ruth and she became his wife; and he went in to her, and the Lord gave her conception, and she bore a son.
>
> . . .

> Then Naomi took the child . . . And the women of the neighborhood gave him a name, saying: 'A son has been born to Naomi!' They named him Obed; he was the father of Jesse, father of David. (Ruth [RSV] 4:13, 16, 17)

A superficial reading of the above lines about Ruth's role as devoted and passive wife and daughter-in-law illustrates precisely the danger of patriarchy for women. Reading these lines in terms of Ruth's devotion as a blindly steadfast love or a totally sacrificial steadfastness disallows any possibility of reading her devotion as the consequence of a conscious, rational act to remain faithful in fulfilling a chosen religious desire. Patriarchal configurations, however various in other ways, tend to eclipse precisely Ruth's rational act of devotion to her mother-in-law, Naomi, and to Naomi's God, although these can be mimetically refigured.[6] Kristeva has not adequately thought about what might be distinctive in Ruth's reasoning process and choice as a foreign woman to follow her mother-in-law. Arguably this is not a simple matter of following Levirate law.[7]

To be consistent with the epistemological and ethical imperatives guiding this chapter, I should reconsider Ruth's story from the point of view of the outsider within Jewish history, while following the chronology of the narrative. Rather than choosing to return to her own mother especially, since this is what Naomi insists she should do,[8] and rather than choosing to give priority to her own motherhood, Ruth first of all chooses devotion to Naomi, the woman who had been devoted to her, as her mother-in-law.[9] Besides forming this new relationship with the older woman whom Ruth respects, Ruth follows her own rational desire to be transformed by theistic devotion to Naomi's God and to those others united by devotion to the same God.[10] It is only later that Naomi encourages Ruth to seek out and lie with Boaz.[11] The point is that Ruth's own choices cry out for further understanding and/or miming.

In all this, it is Ruth from whom I (we) can learn to reinvent myself (ourselves) as other. She can be given epistemic privilege insofar as she remains the outsider within group identity. The critical question is: What can Ruth as the outsider within tell me about Jewish identity? In later sections of this chapter I will bring forward an argument concerning religious identity and sexual difference by configuring the religious devotion of two other (more privileged) female figures whose action can be refigured, even more radically than Ruth's devotion, as female dissent from patriarchy.[12]

As long as I stay with the patriarchal configuration of Ruth's devotion, a question mark concerning sexual difference is placed against the relationship between patriarchal readings of uncanny strangeness and female desire.[13] Depending upon the reading of the strangeness in Ruth's devotion, female desire remains repressed, even erased. There is, as well, a question concerning the monotheist exclusion of the marginalized other. Ruth as the female foreigner seems to be incorporated into patriarchy as the other of the same. The potentially decisive problem is that the outsider within, whether the figure of the female foreigner or the otherness of female desire, may be erased as an outcome of the religious identity of patriarchal monotheism; and this is true even if at some level patriarchy welcomes radical otherness. After all, the important line of Jewish identity virtually erases the mother–daughter genealogy leading to Ruth, the foreign woman; the privileged genealogy is the paternal line of Ruth's son Obed, who is father of Jesse, who is 'father of David', and David as father continues the Jewish line until the Messiah.

On a larger scale, the hierarchical structure of the patriarchal belief characteristic of Kristeva's configuration of monotheism needs to be further disrupted if a feminist philosophy of religion is to go ahead. By 'feminist,' I mean here a stance which would be against both sexed/gendered hierarchies, in which men as fathers are valued over women as mothers (or perhaps as dissenters), and gender-differentiation, whereby the privileged male is at the center of knowledge and belief. According to this stance, the feminist philosopher of religion would object that, when marginalized others are excluded from knowledge-construction, then the knowledge which is being justified tends to be the beliefs of those at the center; this renders claims to knowledge of reality partial and biased. The truth and authority of patriarchal knowledge is simply reinforced by the exclusive claims of traditional theism. I have already considered Kristeva's attempt to refigure patriarchy by disrupting the link between male authority and reality with the figure of the imaginary father; this third term ideally would mediate between the maternal and the paternal functions in the constitution of the subject's identity. But such refiguring could only be a beginning to the transformation of patriarchy in relation to the psychosexual dimension.

A virtue of Kristevan psycholinguistics is that the suggestive power of figures and myths remains in-process. The implication is that figurative language can invite the imagination to entertain novel possibilities beyond the repression and oppression of patriarchy; and the appropriate figures should prompt ever-new thinking about sexual difference by breaking down the separation of the psychosexual from the masculine social-symbolic dimensions. A danger in using the very same suggestive power of figures and myths is also undeniable.[14] To indicate this danger, it needs only to be said that Hitler traded in iconic figures woven into mythical configurations. But as has been learned especially from Irigaray, if not from Kristeva, the crucial difference from this dangerous use of icons is that the feminist poststructuralist does not trade in static figures or fixed configurations. Instead Irigaray, possibly more sucessfully than Kristeva, models her refiguring of religious and other cultural myths upon a psychoanalytic intervention which seeks a new ethical order preserving radical difference.[15]

In psychoanalysis, the analyst offers tentative configurations of the analysand's speech with the purpose of discovering the means to force the analysand out of repressive patterns of behavior and belief. By analogy, Irigaray's various mimings of cultural myths can be read to serve the purpose of moving women and men out of oppressive patterns of entrenched thinking and believing. In particular, I think it is instructive to acknowledge Irigaray's multiple readings of Antigone. No proposed configuration of Antigone is definitive. According to this model of mimetic figuration, there cannot be a fixed truth of woman or of women's beliefs. Instead the figuring of belief must continually move forward in anticipating the form that women's subjectivities, their desires and relationships might take in post-patriarchal religions.

2 Rational Passion and Female Desire: Yearning

Turning to develop further the link with feminist standpoint epistemology, the potentially discernible desire of outsiders within can be named 'yearning.' My understanding of yearning derives from two main sources which I use to illustrate the feminist standpoint enterprise.[16] These are, first, legends concerning Hindu women's *bhakti*, and second, bell hooks' African-American feminist perspective on marginality.

I will take the Hindu source first. *Bhakti* is essentially a religious life based upon forming relationships or associative bonds in devotion, and often songs (*bhajans*), to the Hindu gods or goddesses. This would be henotheism when *bhakti* is centered upon devotion to the one god Krishna, chosen out of many personal deities.[17] The major sustaining element of *bhakti*, in whatever form, is the ritual singing of congregational *bhajan*.[18] Yearning can be given expression in *bhakti* as follows:

> The many Hindu women who have not had spiritual gifts . . . nor [the] opportunities for spiritual development, nonetheless have agreed more times than not that *bhakti* is the crux of Hindu practice. Whether by reflecting on the stories about the goddesses, or participating in women's

> rituals . . . Hindu women have contributed strongly to the great stream of religious women who have turned their yearning for love and fruitfulness into [theistic devotion] . . .
>
> Usually the divinity they have worshiped has been more complicated or many-sided than the divinity worshiped by Westerners. It has been a divinity manifest in the capricious side of the goddesses and the gods, as well as in their acceptance and love. It has shone in the faces of Kali and Shiva, even when these destroyers have been smeared with blood or have been dancing their dances of destruction. Hinduism has taught women the centrality of sexuality to religious love, just as it has taught them that creativity and destruction are inseparably blended. (Carmody 1989 [1979], 64–5, also 52)[19]

The above account, taken from Denise Carmody's *Women and World Religions*, assumes that *bhakti* can be practiced as theistic devotion to a variety of possible personal deities. Kali is the dark, destructive identity of the female deity who has multiple identities in relation to a single male identity, Shiva. The point to grasp from this account is that the expression of the Hindu women's yearning is understood, paradoxically, as a rational passion; it is both active and passive. In earlier chapters, I have suggested that in modern western philosophy, rationality has been typically associated with male, mental activity, while desire has been associated with female, bodily passivity. But in the notion of yearning, the two are intimately connected. It could be said that the rational passion of yearning involves the active instinct to express desire either of or for the female other; hence this can serve to uncover sexual difference in expressions of love or devotion.

I have chosen to focus upon a specific case of Hindu yearning prefigured, configured, and refigured in the actual history, changing practices, and distinctive class or caste expressions of *bhakti*. This case exemplifies conflicting historical and, in my stipulated sense, mythical configurations of marginalized communities' yearning. For these configurations, I am indebted to and moved by the work of Parita Mukta who unearths the song of Mirabai and the common life of communities who sing her song. It is important to bear in mind that Mukta should not be confused with feminist poststructuralists such as Irigaray. Mukta is not informed by psycholinguistics or French philosophy. Instead her personally informed cultural and historical approach enables my practical application of feminist standpoint epistemology to questions of theistic belief from the perspectives of those Hindu women's lives remade by *bhakti*. Furthermore my particular interest in Mirabai is neither in a privileged goddess nor in a heroine of true belief, but in thinking from the life of a woman who practiced a specific religious devotion.

Since her life in sixteenth-century Rajasthan, North India, Mirabai has become a significant female figure in configurations of Indian religious and political dissent. Mira's act of dissent appears prima facie simple: she refuses marriage to a prince, the Sisodiya Rana of Chittor, and so she dissents from a princely life in favor of a life within a religious community (of *bhajniks*) which is also on the margins of her parents' life, that of the Rathors, of Merta.[20]

I turn to Mukta's historical and cultural study of Mirabai to enhance thinking from the perspective of lives at the margins. A decisive problem with the dominant configurations of rationality and belief is their representation of female action and emotion which excludes sexual difference. To confront this problem, I consider the configurations discovered by Mukta in which Mirabai's song of yearning is betrayed by both individuals and communities. In turn, Mukta's critical reading of modern patriarchal appropriations of female belief supports my claim that it is necessary to reinvent ourselves as other. If feminist philosophers are to understand and transform the ways in which patriarchal configurations have written and (re)written the beliefs of individual women and of whole communities, then they have to be able to rethink and remake their own selves and their own worlds.

Patriarchy always fails in its reading of the lives and beliefs of marginalized others, in this case, in reading the dissent of a female other. The dangers of western patriarchy for women emerge in (i) its individualist and empiricist appropriations of theistic devotion for the privileged male, (ii) its devaluation of the other of female desire, and (iii) its exclusion of the beliefs of marginalized peoples. Increasingly urgent is the need to rectify the betrayal of the voice of devoted women. Otherwise voices of yearning will be forgotten and an alternative memory of women's voices of dissent will be lost. True justice and knowledge can be achieved only when women's lives, past, present, and future, are taken back from their theft by patriarchy. In disruptively miming configurations of patriarchy, I not only seek to achieve truth, but to suggest the pressing goal of retrieving women's lives for a feminist philosophy of religion.

Second, in addition to a particular *bhakti* expression of yearning, there is the revitalizing work of bell hooks. hooks has inspired a unique epistemological, ethical, and spiritual commitment to get at the desire of the outsider within. Consider hooks' statement concerning the shared space and feeling of yearning:

> our desire for radical social change is intimately linked with desire to experience pleasure, erotic fulfillment, and a host of other passions. Then, on the flip side . . . many individuals with race, gender, and class privilege . . . are longing to see the kind of revolutionary change that will end domination and oppression even though their lives would be completely and utterly transformed. The shared space and feeling of 'yearning' opens up the possibility of common ground where all these differences might meet and engage one another. It seemed appropriate then to speak this yearning. (hooks 1990, 13)

In this statement, reason, desire, and religious belief can be found united in the space and feeling of yearning. And I stress that such yearning is the place of possibility, of common ground where all differences meet and engage one another.

A feminist philosopher of religion can discern this yearning in the devotional lives and beliefs of individual women and in marginalized communities. This discernment constitutes a preliminary step toward the larger project of disrupting the greatly valued disembodied reason of Adam in the dominant western myth of patriarchal rationality. In the light of the legitimate yearning of outsiders within, male-figured rationality appears to gain male identity by exclusion and so fails the test of adequacy to rationality's own principle of coherence. The precarious projection of the subject's own materially conditioned status onto the female other renders the rationality of this very same disembodied subject incoherent: that is, incoherent insofar as yearning breaks up the unity of its own rationality; evil as injustice and exclusion breaks up the goodness of its own reason. In the shared space of yearning, divinity emerges within the impurity of sexuality and from the embodied figures of the other's rationality. Henceforth my contention is that divinity need not be equated with the supposed purity of privileged male rationality.[21]

Actual expressions of yearning as a rational passion also support a recent argument for the existence of 'a woman of reason.'[22] With certain qualifications, this could suggest the existence of different figurings of reason which incorporate passion within philosophical and theological histories. For example, hooks' *Ain't I a Woman?* configures her own and other forgotten black women's rational passion as the ground for black racial, sexual, and spiritual liberation generally.[23] Consistent with earlier chapters, I do not argue for a separate rationality of privileged women only. Instead the symbolism for a woman of reason and passion represents alternative histories of differently figured reason.[24] Significant figures of this alternative tradition can be found within philosophical history as mythical or marginal expressions of yearning. Perennial myths keep alive the process of the configuring and refiguring of the rational passion of individuals and communities, challenging the idea that 'reason' and 'passion' are mutually exclusive terms.[25]

On a larger scale, it can be argued that a woman of reason is not necessarily a contradiction in terms; and neither is a female philosopher. Instead the woman of reason can be recognized as an existing, legitimate, and viable figure of human rationality. This apparently devalued figure of reason could be revalued for the rationality of belief and refigured for a feminist philosophy.

The rough parameters I gave for the terms of a feminist philosophy of religion in part I of this book can now be restated to support the preceding claims concerning yearning. Religious beliefs endorse particular actions and evoke particular emotions. Specific beliefs, actions, and emotions are, then, united in mythical configurations; in turn, these configurations remain implicit in specific forms of worship, for instance, in the ritual life of theistic devotion. Specific emotions are equally evoked in everyday experience by specific religious beliefs. But different from emotion, desire is part of the unconscious condition of all rational passion. In the form of an overpowering desire, passion is the opposite of active rationality; passion from the Latin *passio* is undergone, not freely initiated. Hence passion can be inactive in a similar sense to the repressed desires which constitute the other-projected, material condition of classically male rationality in western philosophy. Now yearning is the unusual blending of reason and passion, active rationality and passive desire.

In comparison, feeling is on a level with experienced emotion; but it is also an indication of deeper, unconscious desire. I have illustrated the significance of feelings for philosophy of religion with Otto's description of the nonrational factor of the divine in relation to the rational. Both feeling and emotion can express the nonrational factor of the divine, using the theistic language of a patriarchal social-symbolic order; but desire and passion accompany feeling and emotion as their unconscious condition; hence the latter are labelled as 'irrational' and frequently associated with the female other. Women generally remain associated with the male repression of desire; and those women within patriarchy who seek the means and power to express repressed desire find no other modes than hysteria.

If the parameters of my terms are fixed as such, how can they be used in this book both to describe and to transcend the social-symbolic order of patriarchy? My answer, which I am elaborating in this chapter, is that the essential key lies in miming dominant configurations; and note that this miming is distinctive in endeavoring to disrupt the male self-sameness of patriarchal theism which continues to dominate both the rationality and the myths of religious belief, at least in western societies. This answer does not imply that I stay strictly within the framework of feminist poststructuralism. Instead I contend that feminist standpoint epistemology, although being supplemented by certain tools from continental philosophy, especially psycholinguistics, remains crucial for the expression of new knowledges as found in dissenting voices and actions.

3 Reading Belief in Myths of Dissent

Myth and mimesis, in configuring and refiguring the rationality of religious belief, respectively, offer the possibility of expressing sexual difference rather than exclusive male self-sameness. The emergence of sexual difference in miming should be possible at the point where the psychosexual and the social-symbolic dimensions of our language and our lives meet. But what does this actually mean?

On one level, sexual difference is latent in myth, underlying the emotions evoked by, and the structure of feeling suggested by, its configurations of belief. The Indian legend of Mirabai and the Greek tragedy of Antigone have both been developed over time as myth. This legend and this tragedy both bear the distinguishing characteristic of myth's potential for multiple configurations of actions, characters, and emotions as founding events. As myth, they have each founded the meaning and identity of individuals and communities. Unlike philosophy and its disembodied subject, myth has an intimate connection with embodiment, with sexual and communal identities, and hence with spatial-temporal actions and emotions. Remember that 'myth is not a story independent of History, but rather expresses History in colourful accounts that illustrate the major trends of an era. . . . they retain a special relationship to space, time and the manifestation of the forms of incarnation' (Irigaray 1994, 101). But despite myth's representation of embodiment, any specifically female religious devotion – as with the devotion of marginalized others – can be devalued or erased by patriarchal myths of historical lives and actions. By 'devalued,' I mean that female devotion is not read as a conscious and rational stance to remain steadfast in love, but as a mere passive acceptance of a woman's position and condition. As argued in chapter 4, the dominant configurations of belief in western philosophy and religion tend to exclude female desire, forcing the erasure of sexual difference. And this tendency was also illustrated by Kristeva's configuration of Ruth. Remember that exclusion of female desire as other and erasure of actual women as outsiders are two different consequences.

These are not the same thing, so I employ both the terms of psycholinguistics and the imperatives of feminist standpoint epistemology. Female desire as other means not quite human. The marginalized woman as outsider means she is not quite normal, i.e. according to the norms of privileged, male humanity.[26]

To subvert patriarchy's dominant configurations of women, the problem is that

> Patriarchy has . . . imposed silence upon the daughter. It has dissociated her body from her speech, and her pleasure from her language. It has dragged her down into the world of male drives, a world where she has become invisible and blind to herself, her mother, other women and even men, who perhaps want her that way. Patriarchy has thus destroyed the most precious site of love and its fertility . . . Hell appears to be a result of a culture that has annihilated happiness on earth by sending love, including divine love, into a time and place beyond our relationships here and now. (Irigaray 1994, 112)

Patriarchy silences women by excluding their embodiment from the terms of its language. And this patriarchal language constitutes the social-symbolic order which erases women's relationships with each other and with men. So sexual and divine love between embodied subjects are rendered impossible within the social and temporal framework of patriarchy. However, in endeavoring to think from a nonwestern perspective, it should be possible to step outside, at least culturally, and glimpse, for the moment, the destructive impact of western patriarchy upon mythical configurations of theistic love and devotion. In particular, I have endeavored to discover the western patriarchy's impact upon the *bhakti* of Mira and Mira's people. The largely deleterious effect on women's relationships and beliefs will be seen below in Mahatma Gandhi's westernized configuration of Mira's life and devotion.

My aim in appropriating the feminist poststructuralist project of refiguring mimetically the male social-symbolic order of patriarchy is not to change particular configurations. Instead it is to propose an ongoing task to disrupt a whole social structure by transforming figures, myths, and the accompanying communal and individual injustices. The difficulty with the feminist poststructuralist project lies in trying to uncover the unconscious desire of, say, the woman-saint or the heroine of true justice who, within patriarchal structures, is like the hysteric silenced and paralyzed in gestural symptoms since determined by exclusively male language.

Consequently I am attempting to break out of this poststructuralist difficulty by considering actual, socially significant cases of yearning which have given expression and place to both female desire and outsiders within. In other words, I do not assume that women have no linguistic means to disrupt patriarchy; they can and have potentially expressed their yearning in dissenting voices and actions for a better life. Moreover as a rational passion, yearning can potentially incorporate women's differences in a multiplicity of expressions of religious beliefs. The new material of repressed desire begins to speak as a yearning in the process of reinventing ourselves as other. Such possibility and hope is expressed movingly in Mukta's description of the *bhajniks* who sing Mira's song. A particular Hindu form of religious community is constituted by the *bhajans* and *bhakti* of the female figure Mira.

> The *bhajniks*, through the voice of Mira, crystallize the humiliation faced by the people, and demonstrate a solidarity based around the experiencing of this. It is an affirmation of a community in open antagonism to the ruling one, and within which lie the seeds of a new social order. The community of Mirabai is essentially the community of *bhajniks* who, over the centuries, have provided a voice to the struggle for dignity, and hope of a better life. (Mukta 1994, 105)

The crucial thing in the above is the significance of the dissenting response of a marginalized community to its own humiliation. 'Dissent' means to refuse to consent, to cause dissension, to differ; it could also mean to defy. But this rough definition leaves open various questions about acts of dissent. Is dissent strictly an act of an individual at the center of a community, strictly a dissent from the norms of the privileged? Or can it be an action of the marginalized? Is dissent strictly a political act? Or can a religious action be recognized as dissent? I will read the dissent of Mirabai in terms of the yearning which unites a particular Indian people with a common morality and a devotional life as *bhajniks*. Here is a socially significant case of yearning as the space and structure of feeling which unite a religious community in hope for a better life. In particular, with the support of a religious community of *bhajniks*, Mira spends her life struggling against the powerful rule of the Sisodiyas in Rajasthan, yearning for love and liberty. Her dissent from a privileged marriage means that she voluntarily becomes an outsider or foreigner; and this has various profound, even violent implications. Mira is cut off from her mother's family, her former community, and her potentially privileged future as the wife of a prince.

Instead of a privileged life in devotion to a husband, Mira chooses a life of devotion to Krishna. This is not simply a life of humility but an identification with social oppression, i.e. with the marginalized castes, classes, and communities of North India. The basis of the community engendered by *bhakti* is a matter of belief, not a matter of kinship; the social prescriptions of birth, of caste status, or of sexually defined roles which typically form Indian familial and communal life do not apply. Belief, as the religious basis of *bhakti*, in turn engenders and nurtures the myth surrounding figures of dissent from social injustice.

Admittedly, feminist standpoint epistemologists do not typically employ myth, especially myth developed out of theistic devotion, to gain less biased knowledge. Their epistemological assumptions concerning language do not enhance reading myths of belief as binding structures of meaning. But my present use of myth as a story with a narrative core of meaning is, as demonstrated in the previous chapter, informed by both psycholinguistic and phenomenological readings of lived experience. I bring psycholinguistics and phenomenology, however different, together in my concern with symbolic expressions of meaning. To understand symbolic expressions of desire – of yearning in particular – it is helpful to consider phenomenological readings of belief: phenomenology uncovers the dialectical process by which structures of meaning are constituted.[27] By 'dialectical,' I mean the two-way movement between expressions of the individual in relation to communal conditions and communal conditions of reading in relation to the individual. This dialectical process of meaning-constitution was implicit in my account of the threefold form of mimesis: configuration represents the mediating moment constituted by and constitutive of the individual. The dialectical meanings of prefiguration and refiguration can be read in the individual/communal configuration of the myth's narrative.

A feminist standpoint epistemologist is not concerned with the sorts of textual concerns whereby meaning is mediated in the reading of a configuration. Instead, to constitute her starting point, the feminist standpoint epistemologist tends to rely upon the direct mediation of knowledge by way of the perspectives of the marginalized others who live alongside of the standpoint feminist. For example, knowledge is gained from the lives of those others such as racial and ethnic minorities who are encountered in their everyday world. Perhaps it could be said that their thinking attempts to move directly from the prefigured to the refigured by way of the other, but without the symbolic mediation by the configured text.

However, religious identity is distinctive in being constituted by and constitutive of its textual and symbolic configurations of traditional belief. In large part, it is the symbolic configurations of religious belief which render possible the handing down of beliefs from one generation to the next. The difficulty lies in interpreting beliefs, whether in myth or in miming. In comparison with phenomenological or poststructuralist frameworks of belief, the interpretative framework of the standpoint epistemologist appears relatively unencumbered by metacritical tools. There are no hermeneutical tools such as myth and mimesis for reading historical structures of experience. Hence the privileged American academic standpoint feminists try to think straightforwardly from the perspectives of the lives of their contemporary African-American, non-academic woman neighbor; that is, from what she might say without recourse to psycholinguistics, phenomenology, or hermeneutics. Yet metacritical tools can help the feminist philosopher of religion to avoid any entrenched essentializing of one religious identity or perspective against another, especially privileging of the fixed figure of a white, western Christian. The feminist poststructuralist offers certain tools for disrupting univocal configurations of rationality and belief.

So it is my contention that a feminist philosopher of religion will find it most beneficial to retain the two feminist positions in tension. This means using the tools of both feminist standpoint epistemology and feminist poststructuralism, notwithstanding their differences. In particular, poststructuralists take from phenomenological accounts of myth the descriptive method for elucidating the structures of repression and the history of oppression; these structures and history come together in narrative configurations. In turn, narrative configurations are constitutive of and constituted by religious identity. The re-enactment of myth and ritual as structures of feeling, in phenomenological terms, constitutes and is constituted by both religious and political spheres of communal and individual meanings. This dialectical process of meaning-constitution becomes crucial to specific forms of religious identity, determining whether sexual identity is accompanied by the eclipse or emergence of sexual difference.

For my argument to succeed, the imperatives of the feminist standpoint theorist to think from the lives of the marginalized others and to reinvent ourselves need to be compatible with the feminist poststructuralist refigurings of dominant configurations of belief. The mimetic refiguration of women's belief needs to succeed at disrupting the hierarchical structures of patriarchy. These structures are those which have marked the history of patriarchy both in the west and in western patriarchy's infiltration into configurations of eastern myths, especially infiltration by way of modern political philosophy. It is the hierarchy of privileged male values which must be dislodged if feminist philosophers of religion are to move beyond the perpetuation of deep cultural prejudices, sectarianism, or fanaticism in religious beliefs. Moreover my present refiguring of biased religious beliefs is supported by the ethically conceived and defended dissident speech.

'Dissident speech' is a phrase derived from Kristeva's discursive connection of political dissent and emancipatory refigurations.[28]

Without dissident speaking and concrete thinking from the beliefs of these other lives, beliefs constructed noncritically and nonreflexively remain biased toward the dominant perspective of privileged white males. Such bias tends to haunt even the beliefs of feminist empiricists; despite their feminist attempts to purge empiricism of its sexism, their epistemological framework lacks the tools for developing less partial knowledge of reality and avoiding cultural prejudices. In contrast, by seeking communal awareness of concrete differences of race, class, ethnicity, and sexuality, feminist standpoint theorists develop the epistemological tools of critical and self-reflexive thinking (although not, as seen above, specific hermeneutical or psycholinguistic tools which nonetheless will be retained here). Insofar as our epistemological enterprise aims at the generation of religious beliefs grounded in less partial truth and stronger objectivity, it is essential to learn to think from the lives of women and men of different races, classes, sexualities, and societies. And these are lives yearning for emancipation by way of rational dissent from dominant configurations at the center.

One important implication of the standpoint epistemological enterprise is that women as well as men of consciousness can be feminist. Men can achieve feminist objectivity, which is strong in its pursuit of how things really are, strong in truth and justice. This is true as long as feminist men, as well as women, learn to reinvent themselves as other – where otherness includes differences of sex, race, class, and ethnicity. If not, the logic and possibility of change to be brought about by standpoint epistemology are denied.

The interesting parallel to this becoming male feminists is the becoming of men *as* female in a particular form of Hindu devotion to Krishna.[29] But here the 'as' would seem to be in the sense of a comparison, with the force of 'like,' not 'same as.' This parallel between *bhajan*-singers and feminist standpoint epistemologists also brings out some of the difficulties for men who, like women, seek to become female or feminist, respectively. The fact is that, since before the sixteenth-century when Mira's *bhajans* expressed her theistic devotion, male Indian *bhajan*-singers have shown their love for the male deity Krishna by becoming his female lover through *bhajniks*.[30] This means in effect that the male *bhaktas* sing as and in the being of Mira.

One dimension of possibility in this becoming female is that

> When men of a society in which the male consciousness and male constructs are used as yardsticks for the whole of the human experience begin to sing in the *stri vachya* (feminine gender), then a radical shift

> occurs in the moral order. It requires a break from and a transcendence of the world as created and upheld by men. It requires the recreation of humanity in the female image. The world has to become strimacy, i.e. the world has to become female. This requires more, much more than an empathy with the female subject. Within the Mira *bhakti*, the process of becoming Mira and thereby entering the mind and heart of a woman comes out most strongly in the *bhajans* which evoke Mira's rejection of the Rana as husband . . .
>
> It can be argued that Mira herself becomes the Mira of the people, a specific figure with a complex structure of feeling, by being given this shape by those who have sung of her. (Mukta 1994, 87)[31]

Becoming Mira involves a dialectical process, giving a meaningful identity to a people by way of a unifying female figure. But becoming female, in this case, also has ethical, epistemological, and spiritual implications for men as well as women. These latter implications are especially significant for both the feminist standpoint epistemologist, who is concerned with reinventing ourselves as other, and the feminist poststructuralist, who is concerned with unearthing sexual difference.

Yet although sexual difference might be made manifest by recreating 'humanity in the female image,' there remains an arguable difference between men and women in becoming female. The point that might be made for contemporary feminists, who are worried about the sex/gender distinction as a cultural variable, is that the male *bhaktas* would have to retain a clearer distinction between the human and divine world while reinventing the female. I might then say that the arguable difference is between (women) becoming female *as* a woman and (men) becoming female *like* a woman; and the implication is that women become female as (generally) already embodied females, while men become female, as if embodied females, in order to gain access to the divine. The men would retain a distance from the specific bodily life-cycle of the female subject; if the woman's life-cycle (e.g. menstruation) adds to or distracts from the specificity of becoming divine, then the man's embodiment would have to remain at a distance from this specificity of divine/human incarnation. As a result, the woman in her *bhakti* would discover the specificity of the divine differently due to her human specificity, i.e. due to her femaleness or female humanity. In this sense, if becoming female constitutes the access to the divine, the female *bhakta* would still tend to have more direct access than the male *bhakta* to the divine.[32]

The significant point is that the devotional singer does not lose completely his or her sexual difference in miming myths. But the opposite would be true: in miming specific sex/gender relations, like that between the male deity Krishna and the *bhakta*, what is repressed about sexual difference can be uncovered. So those who mime Mira could reinvent themselves as other and yet recognize themselves upon self-reflection in their sexually specific embodiment. More could be said and written on the implications of this 'becoming female' for the contemporary debate over the sex/gender distinction.[33]

In myth, the distinctively divided devotion of religious women as different from men (even those men becoming female in Mira) are prominently represented by those women who dissent from religious beliefs at the center. Women within patriarchal structures always begin as marginalized by their sex in a way in which men do not; but those women who, before they act, are marginalized by caste, class, or race experience an additional split-consciousness as outsiders within patriarchy. This becomes more obvious as one rethinks the ironic and conflicting configurations of Mirabai, as well as the dominant configurations of the Greek tragic heroine Antigone. In the end, the communal criticism of knowledge-claims from the standpoint of the outsider and the self-reflexive criticism of religious belief, especially of privileged configurations, will challenge entrenched biases and prejudices against greater knowledge and better justice.

I have singled out Mirabai, the Indian saint, as a representative figure of dissent from class privilege. She gains knowledge by reinventing herself as other in devotion to both Krishna and to the common life at the margins. More generally, Antigone, the heroine of Greek and western philosophy, has served modern philosophers as the dissenting woman who is marginalized in her steadfast devotion to burial rites for her mother's son; this devotion is, however, ironic in religious terms in constituting a conflict of public versus private duties. Yet similar to the way in which myth emerges out of Antigone's tragedy of steadfast devotion, mythical configurations have followed from Mira's single act of dissent. The configurations of Mirabai vary in the degree to which the significance of the marginalized life of Mira is erased from the marginalized people's devotional songs (*bhajans*). Relying on Mukta's lucid description of Mira as a symbol,

> Mira exists as a potent symbol of spiritual strength . . .
>
> . . . Mira, the people's Mira, is neither a romantic heroine nor a deified goddess. The core of her life is nothing more and nothing less than her rejection of princely society, and her establishment of a life of affinity with pilgrims and wayfarers in her pursuit of a relationship with Krishna. Around this kernel have crystallized voices which have given birth to a powerful person of Mira in which she is more than herself.

> Mira's reality is the reality of a common creation. It is the intellectual and emotional domain of *bhakti* that has given this creation its own specific impetus and historical continuity. (Mukta 1994, 88)

Although initially configured as dissent from princely life and so a statement upon that life, Mira's act also has a highly significant impact on the lives of marginalized others. Her theistic devotion to Krishna definitely cuts across class and caste barriers. Mira, the *bhakti*-saint who dissents from a privileged life, becomes a voice for the oppressed; her song not only binds the *bhajniks* together but remakes them, just as she is remade in their singing.

However, unfortunately at decisive moments in the course of eastern and western histories, her belief, action, and devotion have been distorted by privileged men who have used the myth of Mira to support their own political beliefs. In modern times, this is most notably true of Gandhi's reading of Mira during the period 1958–83. In Mukta's words, Mira's song is betrayed. To understand the tragedy of this betrayal, it is important to elucidate the act of female dissent.[34] This act is built upon religious devotion to Krishna and to a common morality, and the condition of female marginality.[35] In order to elucidate this condition of marginality as constituted by the patriarchal structures of western philosophy, I turn briefly to philosophical configurations of Antigone, but will return to Gandhi's configuring of Mirabai's dissent.

4 Marginality and Dissent: Antigone and Mirabai

'Marginality' means the quality or condition of existing on the border, of being excluded from privilege, of being at the edge and not the center of reality. But, as with dissent, this rough definition leaves unanswered certain questions – this time – about the conditions of marginality. Is marginality strictly a condition in which someone might find herself or himself? Is it a social condition beyond one's control? Or can it be a voluntary condition as, for instance, the predictable consequence of a freely chosen act of dissent? In the former case, where marginality is an involuntary condition, once conscious of this condition as one's own, the double-bind is that neither dissent nor consent appears as an unambiguous alternative for the marginalized other.

By variously configuring the double-bind of female action, the myth of Antigone has given expression to historical perspectives on dissent in western philosophy, politics, and religion. The double-bind is that a woman, whose actions of religious devotion are already conditioned by her marginality, has two equally undesirable alternatives, whether consenting or dissenting. In contrast, privileged male action done for the sake of a religious duty can be configured philosophically – rationally – as allowing the possibility of dissent from a privileged position as patriarch, whether king, father, uncle, brother, or son with various consequences that may or may not result in marginality.

A more or less dominant reading assumes as uncontroversial that Antigone, the female figure in Sophocles' tragic narrative, 'acts in the service of spiritual powers' when she defies the edict of the king (Creon) in order to fulfill her familial duty as sister to give a proper burial to her dead brother (Polynices), even though he has become an enemy of the city and she will, consequently, be forced to face her own death alone with no friends or family to mourn her.[36]

But ironic and conflicting readings of Antigone exemplify the ambiguous senses of dissent and marginality suffered by women in western public and private life. In general, Antigone's act of dissent can be read, according to a patriarchal order, either as religious dissent from civil, public law or consent to familial, private duty. A mythical configuring of Antigone's act of dissent by patriarchal philosophy reflects both her standpoint as a marginal figure and the standpoint of the privileged in prefiguring sex/gender roles. But a refiguring of the very same action is made possible by both the marginal variability of myth and its narrative core of constancy.

In her mythical role, Antigone is in one sense a privileged figure and not marginal. As daughter of King Oedipus, Antigone clearly represents a member of an elite royal, ancient Greek family; and despite its incestuous nature, the family of Oedipus has the privileges of the ruling-class economic and social conditions of wealth.

Similarly Mirabai is born into a medieval Indian family of some privilege, and her story is privileged in being configured by, amongst others, the twentieth-century leader and philosopher of passive resistance, Gandhi.[37] However, although representing the lives of privileged women in ancient and medieval times, both Antigone and Mirabai, respectively, begin as involuntarily marginalized women. They are marginalized in the sense of being bound to their female roles and to their familial duties in the sphere of private life.

Then there are their respective acts of dissent. In addition to their marginality as female, both Antigone and Mirabai freely choose to dissent from the sense in which their lives are privileged and voluntarily suffer further marginalization. Notwithstanding the dissenting actions of Antigone and Mirabai, the significance of their respective beliefs has been further marginalized or silenced in order to serve the purposes of patriarchy.

Privileged men have contributed to forming and sustaining certain mythical configurations of their beliefs and the dissenting actions these endorsed. Notably these configurations represent feminine devotion mimetically as humility and submission to male authority. In other words, one dimension of the double-binds of female dissent is eliminated so that the woman's action can be read as the ideal of femininity in her devotion to the patriarchal family.

In particular, the modern German philosopher Hegel lauds the self-sacrifice of Antigone. According to what has become the dominant, patriarchal configuration, 'Antigone is the most beautiful description of femininity; she holds fast to the bond of the family against the [state's] law.'[38] The additional (non-Hegelian) double-bind in this configured act of feminine devotion suggests that once recognized as dissent from civil religion, female action can equally be read as dissent from private religious duty. Due to the public nature of an act of only momentary self-determination, Antigone fails to act religiously in any sustained, meaningful private or public sense. According to this line of reasoning, she dissents from both spheres of life and so ends doubly marginalized.

The tragic irony in religious devotion for women under the modern form of patriarchy can be most clearly seen in the progression in readings of marginality. This progression gradually undermines various acts of female dissent. The progression or, possibly more accurately stated, this regression is especially my concern insofar as female dissent slowly becomes read according to a male bias in modern philosophy and hence configured to conform with modern patriarchal structures. Again when either Antigone or Mirabai is configured according to modern political philosophy, a sharp distinction is drawn between public and private life, male and female action. And this distinction renders problematic accounts of female dissent.

The gradual distortion of female dissent is evident in the 'betrayal' of Mirabai's song by modern configurations of her devotion to a personal deity and a communal life. To begin with, '[Mira] chooses the path of emotional and political integrity and pays the price exacted. She lives a life of material and social hardship and recognizes that no true alternative can be evolved without going through these hardships, the necessary outcome of tearing asunder social and economic pivileges' (Mukta 1994, 161). Next, with this initial reading of her dissent, the song of Mira keeps alive the narrative of her rational and conscious act of dissent. I find insight into acts of dissent from this example of a Mira *bhajan*:

> Mirabai, you are my faithful devotee.
> Mirabai, please return home.

Mirabai, you know you are a princess, a Rathori princess
Rohidas is a Chamar by caste.
Mirabai, please return home.
Mirabai, the Rana will be wrathful
He will kill me. And he will revile you.
Mirabai, I ask you to return home.
Mirabai, your maternal home will be covered with shame.
The fortress of Chittor is covered with shame.
Mirabai, please return home.
Mirabai, you can hear people are slandering you
And they are slandering me.
Mira answers, my God will see to them all.
Mirabai, please return home.
Rohidas at the feet of Ramanand says,
Mirabai, remain true to your beloved.
(as cited in Mukta 1994, 110)

This *bhajan* tells of a rational process starting with reflection by Rohidas (Mira's guru from a lower caste) upon her conscious act of dissent from a royal life, moving to recognition of the possible punishment for this dissent, to realization of the even greater social consequences, and ultimately to a resolute acceptance of Mira's devotion to her beloved Krishna.[39] In addition, Mira's song is enriched by its identification with the people's morality and suffering. Her rationally chosen devotion to Krishna and to the people bound together in congregational singing has potential for the transformation of social and caste opposition.

Yet the further, deleterious consequences of patriarchy for readings of Mira's dissent emerge as follows:

> The song of Mira had lain latent within the lives of various subordinated groups in society – leather-workers, women, itinerant singers, etc. Acting as a force which provided strength and solace, which bound people together in a community of shared suffering, and which articulated a vision of better relationships, the song of Mira remained (and continues to remain) as a powerful hope seeking realization. These deeply-held visions and aspirations could have been actualized in the process of transformation of society during the struggle for national liberation. Instead the song was betrayed. (Mukta 1994, 182)

In order to relate this betrayal to my philosophical concern with female marginality and dissent, consider a particular line of questioning. When is dissent not read as dissent? When an assumption of marginality precedes the reading of the act, it might be read as self-sacrifice or passive resistance. If this is the case, dissent of the marginalized other makes no real difference for the life-conditions of the agent; thus read, the act would not be recognized as rejection of privileged norms. That is, even if it is meant as defiance, it fails (or, at least, seems to fail) in its impact on the center; there is no apparent movement from either margin to center or center to margin. Its significance is easily appropriated exclusively for reinforcing the privileged position at the center.

When might dissent be read as consent, as an equally unattractive alternative for the female agent? An act of dissent, whether similar to that of Mirabai or of Antigone, might be read as consent when a woman's marginality already determines the meaning of her act so that the difference between dissent from civil law or consent to familial duty becomes unclear. The double-bind of female action emerges in such a case, where a woman's choice seems to be undermined by two equally unpromising alternatives. There appears to be no significant difference between an act of dissent and an act of consent, since in either case the configuring of that action remains bound by her marginality under patriarchy.

Thus begins the tragedy of a powerful leader's reinterpretation of Mira's dissent. Instead of reading Mira's dissent as a rejection of patriarchal authority which aimed to transcend unequal social, economic, political, and religious relationships, Gandhi reinterprets her action. He consciously or unconsciously subverts the marginalized people's Mira by reading her dissent as consent to familial religious devotion. As Mukta explains,

> Gandhi is at odds . . . with the community of Mirabai, which had sought to negate through Mira imposed marital relationships, and which posed a challenge both to the institution of marriage and of widowhood. Gandhi's Mira, who sought 'devotion to one's husband' and who 'lovingly submitted to the punishment which the Rana inflicted on her' is far removed from the Mira who, through bitter struggle, established a life independent of the Sisodiya princely family, and who led a life of hardship which was nevertheless a transformative one. This [Gandhi's] Mira, instead of breaking the boundaries of established hegemonic relationships, in effect props up these relationships by refusing to overturn them. (Mukta 1994, 186)

An even stronger reading by Mukta supports the conclusion to my argument concerning patriarchal configurations of female dissent. Such configurations eclipse both the other of female desire and the actual yearning of the marginalized community:

> Mira's challenge and her subversion of the social order were contained by Gandhi, and her life and message were given a different twist by him.
>
> The people's Mira did not express a 'love' for the Rana. The people's Mira profoundly challenged the imposed marital relationship, and showed a transformative fearlessness in rejecting patriarchal prescriptions. This message of the people's Mira could have been invoked to generate the deepest stirrings of society in the course of the freedom movement, when the nature of a future society was an appropriate matter for debate. However, this aspect of Mira, which was of the utmost importance in placing value on the grave need to attain personal liberties, as against rigid community demands, was wiped out by Gandhi, and a message which could have been vital and powerful in changing fundamental social relations was distorted and made to serve patriarchal illusions of harmony within the domestic and political realm. (Mukta 1994, 188)

With such readings of the religious belief of women configured within patriarchy, I discern a double double-bind of attempted dissent. The patriarchal configuration of Mira's act, similar to Antigone's, indicates that female dissent is doubly plagued by dilemmas. As long as the condition of the female agent in ancient, medieval, and modern religions can be ignored as one of marginality, whether dissenting or consenting, then no real difference occurs for those at the center of public life. And yet in fact any public defiance of religious (civil) law takes the female agent outside the familial sphere of domesticity in which the act exhibits consent to private duty, in the case of Antigone and Mirabai either to bury one's kinsman or to devote one's life to Krishna, respectively. Why does the statement of this act as specifically female dissent fall on deaf ears?

The civil religion, rejected by those female agents who dissent, would be characterized by obedience to the king or princely order, to all edicts and laws. This is religious in the sense of obedience and reverence for patriarchal authority, especially when human (male) power could be interpreted as divinely ordained. The question is: When does reverence for civil religion allow, if it ever does, female defiance of the king or of any other figure of male authority?

The final result of these double-binds is that a woman's act of dissent, as intended at least, from patriarchy is to be doubly marginalized or distanced from public and private life. Returning to Antigone, if one reads her actions as motivated by spiritual powers, then the double double-bind seems to apply. Antigone is, first, marginalized as a woman who remains excluded from the public domain by the ancient *polis*, even when she initiates a political act of dissent; so she would have been marginalized in this sense whether she acted or not.[40] And, second, she is further marginalized from her family and religious community even as a consequence of her religiously motivated duty to bury her brother, since this involves 'unwomanly' public dissent from a civil religious duty to follow the king's edicts. Ironically this latter act represents both consent to familial duty and dissent from a female duty not to exceed the norms of a strictly private life; so even consenting, in one sense of the term, is doubly marginalized for such consent/dissent.[41]

5 Dominant Configurations of Religious Devotion

Recognizing that configuration is only the second stage of the threefold form of mimesis, I am ultimately more concerned with refiguration than configuration or prefiguration. Configuration is the object of feminist critique, but refiguration offers the possibility of transforming our vision of the world. With this in mind, let me state: first, the dominant Hegelian configuration of Antigone as representative of modern philosophy's account of religious devotion and female action; next, the sense in which Mirabai can be configured (as we ourselves might be) according to the same modern, patriarchal hierarchy of public/private, male/female oppositions; finally, the form of refiguring which aims to disrupt the sexed/gendered hierarchy implicit in the dominant patriarchal reading of female action silenced in philosophers' myths; I have also called this sort of refiguring a disruptive miming.

Hegel is well known in modern times for his ironic reading of Antigone. He configures the ironic exclusion of female action: the irony rests in a woman's public act which is excluded from public life and of her private act which is taken out of private life. This female character, the daughter of Oedipus, is also configured as the representative of private, religious life, as the 'equal opposite' of the male character who represents public, civil law. The distinctive Hegelian reading configures female and male characters as locked in inevitable conflict as (allegedly) equal opposites. This dominant Hegelian configuration of Antigone has influenced twentieth-century thought:

> the influence of commentary, particularly where it is of a philosophic or political tenor, also acts indirectly. Not very many general readers will

> have come across Hegel's Antigone interpretations at first hand. But the Hegelian reading of the play as a dialectical conflict of equal opposites has been widely disseminated in the climate of literary as well as that of theatrical presentation. (Steiner 1984, 295)

The crucial point is that this modern Hegelian reading of Antigone reflects the dominant configuration of her religious devotion in western philosophy and its re-enactment.

Consider this passage from Hegel's reading of the irony of female action for the religious life of the community:

> Since the community only gets an existence through its interference with the happiness of the Family, and by dissolving (individual) self-consciousness into the universal, it creates for itself in what it suppresses and what is at the same time essential to it an internal enemy – womankind in general. Womankind – the everlasting irony (in the life) of the community – changes by intrigue the universal end of the government into a *private* end, transforms its universal activity into a work of some particular individual, and perverts the universal property of the state into a possession and ornament for the Family . . . The community, however, can only maintain itself by suppressing this spirit of individualism. (Hegel 1977, 288)

For Hegel, Antigone embodies the fact that womankind is at once essential and threatening to the community. Hence woman is both praised and blamed for the very same action.

The contemporary political philosopher Seyla Benhabib sees the undermining of sexual difference by Hegel's ironic configuration of woman in the myth of Antigone. This is her modern feminist reading:

> 'Womankind – the everlasting irony (in the life) of the community – changes by intrigue the universal end of the government into a *private* end.' Spirit may fall into irony for a brief historical moment, but eventually the serious transparency of reason will discipline women and eliminate irony from public life. Already in Hegel's discussion of Antigone, that strain of restorationist thought, which will celebrate the revolution while condemning the revolutionaries for their actions, is present. Hegel's Antigone is one without a future; her tragedy is also the grave of utopian, revolutionary thinking about gender relations. Hegel, it turns out, is women's gravedigger, confining them to a grand but

> ultimately doomed phase of the dialectic, which 'befalls mind in its infancy'. (Benhabib 1992, 255–9)

From two contrasting standpoints – which nevertheless are male points of view – marginality can be strictly the consequence of dissent by those men, including Creon, who defy central norms from their privileged position. For my argument, it is important to stress the difference sex/gender and class make in the action of Creon in Sophocles' *Antigone*. Creon defies the tradition of burial laws but is not (at least, not immediately) marginalized. Hence in contrast with the civil religion of this privileged male (the king), I recognize the very different religious dissent of marginalized males who practice *bhakti*, becoming like a female saint as Krishna's lover. Without going into detailed contrasts, the present contention is that the differences between privileged male and marginalized action lead to the same question as those between male and female action. Can female or nonprivileged dissent from central patriarchal beliefs ever be recognized by the center and so effective at both the margins and center as dissent? This recognition is highly doubtful when, due to certain concrete differences, one's gender, sexuality, or status is from the outset conditioned as marginal.

Interestingly Gandhi appropriates Mira for his own purposes. His interpretations play upon the fact of her involuntary marginality as a woman and her private act of dissent as religious devotion. And this is devotion in the sense of submission to (not subversion of) patriarchal authority. But in this interpretation, Gandhi introduces more injustices, not liberation for women – at least, not for wives, not even his own.

> Mira . . . as interpreted by Gandhi, became a crucial lynchpin for him upon which turned his commitment and faith throughout the twists and turns of the momentous anti-colonial struggle. That this involved moulding and remoulding Mira into a cast completely at odds with the people's Mira, is a comment both on Gandhi's removal from the aspirations of the community of Mirabai, as well as his removal of her from the context within which she had been nurtured. (Mukta 1994, 183)

In Gandhi's own words,

> In Hinduism devotion of wife to her husband and her complete merger in him is the highest aim, never mind whether the husband is a fiend or an embodiment of love. If this be the correct conduct for a wife, may

> she in the teeth of opposition by her husband undertake national service? . . . I think there is a way out. Mirabai has shown the way. The wife has a perfect right to take her own course and meekly brave the consequences when she knows herself to be in the right and when her resistance is for nobler purpose. (Gandhi 1926, 511–12)[42]

The decisive problem with the above is that the so-called nobler purpose is judged by the patriarchal moralist himself: Gandhi. Carmody notes, although only parenthetically, that Gandhi's unilateral decisions concerning his own wife reflect some of his private injustice toward women.[43] For instance, he accepted low-caste duties for her. The pattern of his private injustices mirror his larger patriarchal reading of morality for women. As Mukta insists,

> Gandhi, in his firm intent to forge an 'ethical weapon' as against 'armed strength' with which to fight the colonial power, did all that he could to mould the precedents he held up as beings who suffered stoically and who won over the enemy through 'love'. In his eagerness to enjoin Mira into an evolution of a pure, ethical practice, Gandhi wiped out both the tensions and strengths which existed in the life of Mira, eradicated the deep subversion inherent in her message and made her into a very different being. (Mukta 1994, 185)

The unjust use of women by the patriarchal moralist dictates the meaning of 'love' for women.[44] Thus the following conclusion seems inevitable:

> Gandhi consistently sought to inculcate a moral being which would suffer tyranny cheerfully, a moral being which would not consume itself in hatred of the oppressor, and which would in fact serve as the instrument for the moral transformation of the oppressor. His depiction of Mira as someone who won over the Rana to her side through 'love' so that the Rana at last became her 'devotee' . . . flouts the message of the people's Mira, but is essential to him in propagating the 'truth' of his philosophy. (Mukta 1994, 187–8)

At this stage, it is easy to draw a parallel between the above patriarchal rereading of Mira and a patriarchal reading of the figure of Antigone. According to the latter, the female figure won over the king, Creon, to her side – albeit too late – through steadfast devotion to her familial, religious duty and so to her femininity. But this reading of Antigone as the ideal of femininity either ignores or implicitly rejects her true dissent as a woman from her familial role as wife, mother, etc. A double-bind inevitably haunts women as read according to the sexed/gendered hierarchy and gender differentiation of patriarchy. When the patriarchal constructions of modern political theory divide action into public and private spheres, women's religious duty is restricted to private life. So different from privileged men, women are simultaneously praised and blamed for fulfilling a religious duty involving action which leads them into public life. Such female action can never really be understood within the rational structures of patriarchy unless men can reject the formal divisions of modern political life. Only then can they be taught to think from the lives of marginalized others.

Notwithstanding the double-binds of women who attempt dissent from patriarchal norms, Irigaray provocatively refigures Antigone's public act of defiance as a 'digestion of the masculine': 'if Antigone gives proof of a bravery, a tenderness and an anger that free her energies and motivate her to resist that *outside* which the city represents for her, this is certainly because she had digested the masculine. At least partially at least for a moment' (Irigaray 1985a, 220).[45] According to this refiguring of the dominant configuration of female action, by taking on her brother's death – that is, not her husband's or a son's, but a public enemy's death – Antigone breaks down the (Hegelian) gendered opposition between private and public life. As a woman who digests the masculine, she does succeed at dissenting, at least, for a moment.

The patriarchal structures of modern political and moral philosophy, as found in both the west and the west's configurations of nonwestern women, discredit the female agent who acts publicly outside of familial religion for the very fact of acting in public. She is simultaneously blamed as the enemy of the community for the very religious action which has been praised as the ideal of femininity. This religious double-bind is added onto the more general marginality of women's condition; and this condition renders any female act of dissent ambiguous and hence unsuccessful under patriarchy. The marginality of the women's condition is not ultimately overcome by individual defiance. Dissent from duty when at the center of privilege may lead to marginality, but the converse is not necessarily the case, especially when configured by the privileged from their point of view.

A double double-bind of female dissent appears to constitute the potentially decisive challenge for the dominant configuration of religious devotion in modern philosophy. Dissent from religious duty when at the margin does not automatically lead to the center, nor does the choice of theistic devotion over familial duty necessarily lead to new forms of relationship. And yet the doubly marginalized woman comes to stand in a place of epistemic possibility for refiguring and reinventing (our)selves as other.

6 Rationality of Belief Mimed

The very process of reading myths creates a significant space for transcending both prefigurations of female belief and patriarchal configurations of religious devotion. This means transcending that which has eclipsed the desire of the female other and erased the lives of marginalized others. Like Hegel (especially as described by Benhabib), some philosophers may not accept or believe in utopian thinking about sex/gender relations. Yet I take support here from Ricoeur and Irigaray – however diverse in themselves – while joining with those feminist philosophers who urge the utopian moment in feminism. In the words of Cornell,

> we are trying to discover the possibility of the 'way out' from our current system of gender identity in which 'her' specificity opens up the unknown, in which sexual difference would not be re-appropriated. Through Irigaray's mimesis, we move within what has been prefigured so as to continally transfigure (refigure) it.[46] We not only affirm Woman, we continually re-metaphorize her through the 'as if'.
>
> The necessary utopian moment in feminism lies precisely in our opening up the possible through metaphoric transformation. (Cornell 1991, 169)

The key to this transformation is not allowing sexual difference to be reappropriated by the sexual identity of the dominant myth of rationality whereby her specificity is erased, excluded as the unknown. This use of metaphor and mimesis recalls Ricoeur's account of the way in which metaphor can rule the literal, as well as the way in which mimesis not only imitates by configuring but prefigures and refigures or transfigures action.[47] But Irigaray gives mimesis a unique and non-Ricoeurian sense. For her, miming does not simply mean a configuration of reality or a prefiguration of sexual identity. Instead her distinctive miming collapses these distinctions in a mimetic refiguring; this refiguring aims to disrupt traditional discourse, to transform sexual identity and reality of all sexed/gendered hierarchies. In this sense, miming takes the form of the feminine which disrupts as well as the masculine which is dissenting. Importantly Irigaray's miming is one way in which women can move within a sexed/gendered hierarchy and give its metaphors new meaning; it is certainly not a mere artistic imitation, neither mirroring the real in art nor copying the masculine/feminine as strictly defined by patriarchy.

In the case of Antigone's tragedy, myth develops out of the spectacle as a mimetic configuration of unmerited suffering which both provokes and purifies enduring human passions. Ricoeur connects the constancy of mythical narrative with a generic understanding of the human and, in particular, of the limitations pointed to by the tragic hero or heroine who suffers unjustly but with steadfast devotion.[48] It is the quality of steadfastness in this configuration which has led philosophers – including Hegel and Ricoeur – to represent Antigone's action as blind consent to familial, religious duty and not an act of informed political dissent. But I can still rename and so reclaim this steadfastness as distinctively female and conscious, and as rational devotion.

Concerning Antigone's steadfastness, at least one female philosopher insists over and against Hegel and, by implication, Ricoeur that Antigone's steadfast devotion to what is noble and just is not an unconscious intuition of religious duty or an unreflective position defined by her sex or gender. Instead her action is the result of a courageous political stance, consciously taken and held against the king's orders.[49] Does this mean both consent to familial, religious duty and dissent from Creon's civil religion? Or is it dissent from both and so from her own sex/gender? In returning to the question of a double-bind, let me consider further whether or not Irigaray can enable me to refigure religious dissent.

Irigaray's various readings of, and references to, Antigone bring out the double-binds of consent to, or dissent from, familial religion and dissent from, or consent to, civil religion, when miming women's marginality under patriarchy.[50] In particular, Irigaray disruptively mimes Hegel's configuration of Antigone. First, according to Irigaray, Antigone is the daughter who remains faithful to her mother, i.e. to her duty to the maternal blood tie. In this sense, Antigone consents to a religious duty to bury the dead maternal son and, at the same time, dissents from her patriarchal duty to follow her future husband and be a mother to his children. And yet this consent/dissent is not always read as such. It can also be read as consent to private devotion, i.e. of submission to the family, and so a dissenting act of self-sacrifice in burying an enemy of the *polis*. These different, double readings render Antigone's devotional act ambiguous, yet the dominant configuration construes her act as supporting patriarchy, as the ideal of femininity.

Second, this act can also be mimed as both female dissent from patriarchal religion and female dissent/consent to civil religion. Antigone dissents from patriarchal religion in acting publicly and dissents from civil religion in defying the king. But she also seems to consent to face her own death alone by acting publicly and defying her duty to remain in the private sphere. No one will mourn her, neither sister nor friend. Miming enhances these multiple possible readings.

Consider Irigaray's reading: '[Antigone] places this kinsman [i.e. her brother] back in *the womb of the earth* and thus reunites him with undying, elemental individuality. To do this is also to reassociate him with a – *religious* – community that controls the violent acts of singular matter and the base urges which, unleashed upon the dead man, might yet destroy him' (Irigaray 1985a, 215). In Hegelian terms, Antigone represents particularity based in nature or, in Irigarayan terms, undying, elemental individuality. But Irigaray's miming of Hegel's configuration of Antigone shows her buried alive in a cave; and symbolically the female figure is returned to the womb of the earth, like a goddess of the underworld. Despite any suggestions that Irigaray privileges Hegel's configuration, Irigaray's earliest miming of Antigone, as well as her various later references to this miming, represent a possible double reading of consent/dissent and dissent/consent.

Antigone consents to familial, religious duty to preserve her brother's individuality. Yet dissent is also seen in her religious action of duty to her brother's individuality which, in Hegel's words, 'perverts the universal property of the state into a possession and ornament for the Family' (Hegel 1977, 288). As a result of this public action, Antigone must be excluded from the city, from society. Moreover in Irigaray's words, 'she must be . . . deprived of freedom, air, light, love, marriage, children' (Irigaray 1991b, 199).

Irigaray equally refigures Antigone's sister, Ismene, who, while not dissenting, not publicly defying the king, suffers a fate which is not much better than that of Antigone. Ismene is 'shut up . . . in the palace, the house, with the other women, who are all thus deprived of their freedom of action for fear they may sap the courage of the most valiant warriors' (Irigaray 1985a, 218). The lives of both Ismene and Antigone are represented mythically as a 'living death'; this is to begin the refiguring of women's involuntary condition of marginality under patriarchy. Of course I need to be careful here to read concrete differences between lives of women, according to specificities of sexuality, status, class, religion, and race.

To disrupt Hegel's configuration of Antigone, Irigaray mimes the tie of woman and blood as constituting the double-bind of specifically religious action for women in patriarchal religion:

> Woman is the guardian of the blood . . . Powerless on earth, she remains the very ground in which manifest mind secretly sets its roots and draws

> its strength. And self-certainty – in masculinity, in community, in government – owes the truth of its word and of the oath that binds men together to that substance common to all, repressed, unconscious and dumb, washed in the waters of oblivion. This enables us to understand why femininity consists essentially in laying the dead man back in the womb of the earth, and giving him eternal life. For the bloodless one is the mediation that she knows in her being . . . [Woman] ensures the (memory) *Enrinnerung* of consciousness of self by forgetting herself. (Irigaray 1985a, 225)

Irigaray's refiguring is disruptive in identifying action in terms of sexual difference, as a miming of women's living death. In identification with her mother's dead son, Antigone forgets herself in order to preserve her brother's identity by returning him to the womb. Yet action done on behalf of the mother exposes unconscious, repressed female desire. For a moment at least, when female desire is metaphorically taken from the waters of oblivion, the miming of sexual difference is possible.

Finally, when I turn to certain lines of the translated text of Sophocles' *Antigone*, the significance of sex/gender for the double-bind of female action seems to be open to transformation. In Ricoeurian terms, this transformation would involve the refiguration of actual and possible worlds. Sexual identity could be refigured (even by Ricoeur) to include sexual difference as long as the significance of sex/gender appears to be part of the variability of myth and not part of the narrative core of constancy.[51]

For example, consider the words spoken by Antigone:

> how many griefs our father Oedipus handed down!
> . . .
> . . . our lives are pain – no private shame, no public disgrace, nothing I haven't seen. (Sophocles 1984, 59, lines 2, 6–7)

These lines could indicate that the marginality of the two sisters has been determined by their sexual identity under patriarchy as daughters of Oedipus, who himself figures dissent. No matter whether religious consenters or dissenters, the daughters both die silenced, suffering for the father's guilt. By contrast, these words could forecast Antigone's public act of dissent from the religious duties of this paternal line and her necessary act of consent to being guardian of the maternal blood tie, since symbolically the father's house is fallen.

For a further example, consider the difference which sex/gender makes for the religious action of Antigone according to the prefiguration spoken by Ismene:

> we must be sensible. Remember we are women, we're not born to contend with men. Then too, we're underlings, ruled by much stronger hands, so we must submit in this. (Sophocles 1984, 62, lines 74–5)

These lines could suggest that the assumed sex/gender role of women in a city-state of ancient Greece is represented by Ismene, Antigone's sister, who consents to the king's civil religion; she consents to playing her submissive role in the palace. Alternatively this prefiguration spoken by Ismene shows, by contrast with Antigone's dissent from her sex/gender role, that religious action by a woman under patriarchy suffers the consequences of both male action and female marginality. Women's actions can never be unambiguous if always haunted by a double-bind or even a double double-bind. The paradigmatic cases of Ismene and Antigone reveal that the female double bind is to either submit to the king's civil religion and be locked in the palace, or defy the king in order to fulfill a familial religious duty and be locked in a cave; either way, the woman is to suffer a living death.

If following Irigaray, it is possible to mime Ricoeur's own Hegelian configuration of Antigone as a conflict between equal opposites. In miming, Ricoeur's third form of mimesis can be turned back upon his own act of configuring Antigone's tragic action as a gendered conflict of equal opposites, of Antigone and Creon, female and male, margin and center. Ricoeur blames Antigone for her female lack of knowledge of a political distinction between friend and enemy when it comes to her brother; so she exhibits blind devotion to a familial, religious duty. But note that as a woman within this patriarchal configuration, she could not have had such knowledge of the *polis* in any case.

Notwithstanding this, I would take seriously the possibility of a metaphoric transformation.[52] Such a transformation would play upon the 'is' and 'is not' of a Ricoeurian account of metaphor in order to refigure the highly genderized prefiguration of Antigone as spoken by Creon in the dominant configuration. The following words of Creon leave no doubt concerning the genderized prefiguration of dissent and marginality:

> I am not the man, not now; she is the man if this victory goes to her and she goes free! (Sophocles 1984, 83, lines 541–2)

The curtailment of freedom is the punishment for a woman's attempt at dissent from her civil religious duty to remain in the private sphere and so, in dissenting publicly, to be 'the man.' With this strongly prefigured configuration, it appears that only the privileged man can remain free as a male to dissent from accepted religious practice and to choose as only one possible consequence the condition of marginality.

Consistent with this prefiguration, the popular Hegelian configuration of Creon and Antigone remains a highly genderized conflict between center and margin, man and woman. However, there is now significant ground for refiguring the double double-bind of female action endorsed by patriarchal belief. This would be to play upon the 'is' and 'is not' of sexed/gendered metaphors.

Critical reflection upon the difference gender makes for religious action has suggested that sex/gender can be read as part of the myth's marginal variability. It can also be agreed that Creon, as the privileged male dissenter, does not face either the double-binds of Antigone or the possibilities for breaking out of current systems of sexual identity, especially those systems reflected in the dominant configurations of male over female action. In contrast, Antigone's marginality as a woman allows us to try out the new possibilities in refiguring sexual difference. By reinventing ourselves as other, we might think from her perspective at the margins about the rationality of both feminine disrupting and masculine dissenting. Her act of devotion 'is' and 'is not' feminine. In digesting the masculine – for a moment – her dissent is recognized within patriarchal structures yet, at the same time, her dissent unearths the feminine. She speaks female desire in speaking her mother's grief. And, in this way, she begins the disruption of the patriarchal erasure of mother–daughter relations while also disrupting a sister–brother relation.

7 Preliminary Conclusion: Yearning Assessed

I would ask the reader to recall my readings of female desires, in figures of religious devotion, as a rational passion. There was Ruth's devotion to her mother-in-law Naomi and to the community bound together in devotion to Naomi's God. Ruth consciously gives up her own foreignness yet remains significant as a female foreigner within a community which has only a homogeneous religious identity. In this context, she both yearns to follow Naomi and seeks to be bound as the other to the spiritual community of Naomi's family in the transformation of formerly hostile individual, cultural, and national relations. I also presented the possible disruptive miming of Mirabai's *bhakti* to Krishna. Such miming intends the formation of new bonds across sex/gender, caste, clan, and family barriers.

In the preceding, myth has served to configure the difference which sex/gender, race, class, and caste make for dissent and marginality in religion. However, the constant danger for female dissent is that patriarchal configurations of belief will dominate, excluding sexual and other differences. Yearning appears, in response to domination, as the rational passion of religious belief. The vital reality of yearning can ideally give expression to sexual difference in the form of love between us, in equal relationships and in new bonds; this yearning is expressed, for instance, in the *bhajans* of Mirabai. And I turn to another context to support my use of yearning:

> Yearning . . . [similar to] the Marxian notion, . . . describes the central impulse or 'vital reality' of religion as a protest and longing for better conditions, for heart in a heartless world, the unquenchable yearning for a just world. [And yet] the 'vital reality' at the heart of religion became repressed and weakened through the historical process of [western] theology's accommodation to the prevailing power structures and political forces within which the [Christian] churches sought their institutional self-preservation. (Hewitt 1995, 207)

To uncover this repressed reality, communal criticism of knowledge-claims and self-reflexive assessment of belief about our world need to be constantly applied to expressions of desire. Not all yearning adequately expresses love and liberty for marginalized others or ourselves. But one rational test for adequacy in constructions of religious belief relies upon the expression of religious devotion and passion for love.

For example, the principle that at the heart of authentic *bhakti* should be the forming of love relationships can constitute a rational test for practical adequacy within a religious community. So if a response to the yearning for love and liberty as configured by dominant forms of belief and within the dominant culture's division between public and private is isolating, then it is also inadequate. Inadequacy in this example arises because men are associated with both public and private cultures while the actions of women are isolated in the private sphere of life. Hence instead of devotion to a morality and a song, which ideally bind individuals together, female devotion to an immutable deity in private isolation from the larger, public community ends in despair and thirst. Isolated devotion restricts expressions of yearning, which remain inadequate, since walled up within a private life of domesticity. In Mukta's words,

> A yearning after an imagined love within the walled existence of domesticity furthers the disenchantment and discontent – it does not fulfill. It can enlarge these walls slightly – it does not break them. Seeking comfort in a relationship which is permanent by nature of its very immutability provides strength in a harsh and emotionally lonely existence – but it transforms neither the self nor the Immutable. *Bhakti* provides sustenance to the soul to rise above drudgery. Holding the image of the Beloved close to one can stop the wells of the heart from drying up. But the rainbird continues to thirst. (Mukta 1994, 223)

Real hope and love need to be born amongst, in this case, the *bhajniks*, whose marginalized community is bound together. By remaking the figure of Mira in devotional singing, the *bhajniks* equally remake themselves or refigure their religious identity in their yearning for a better form of relationship. Similarly, bell hooks asserts that yearning should offer the place of possibility, of common ground where all differences meet and engage one another.[53]

The rational test of adequacy, applied to expressions of yearning, would equally reveal that the dominant configuration of Antigone dying, walled up in a cave, with no one to mourn her cannot be the end of her story. It is necessary either to reject her yearning as an inadequate or inappropriate response to her situation, or to mime her desire as a return to the womb, to the unrepresentable maternal body, to the *chora*, to the cave in longing to form a new relationship to the mother and the maternal line. Here Plato's analogy of acquiring knowledge as ascent from the cave is reversed. In miming the dominant configurations of Antigone and of western epistemology, Irigaray helps me to refigure the acquisition of knowledge as Antigone's descent into the cave. She reverses Plato's analogy of knowledge, suggesting that return to the cave is a return to the womb.[54] And with Antigone, the feminist philosopher is admonished to gain true knowledge by miming her dissent in order to uncover the buried maternal, female desire and the substantive rationality of women's beliefs.

Moreover taking the other, equally relevant view for the argument of this chapter, the process of refiguring religious belief can lead to a utopian vision only if the dialectical pattern is followed. And this dialectical pattern is illustrated by *bhajniks*; of special importance is that they remake themselves: 'The *bhajniks* . . . have given of their impulses and energies to remake Mira, and through this have remade themselves – they have remade the world giving to it their stamp, and their hope for a better form of relationships' (Mukta 1994, 169). In a sense, they both mime the female figure and her specific beliefs in multiple configurations and refigure mimetically their world in the process. Ricoeur's transformative praxis helps understanding of the three different moments of mimesis: prefiguration, configuration, and refiguration. But only the latter moment of refiguration can be transformed into disruptive miming and a utopian vision of concrete, future possibilities.

This chapter has attempted to preserve the suggestive power of myth and figurative language, without allowing the language to solidify in fixed images. The identity of female figures of religious devotion and rational passion needs to remain in-process in order for new images of nature and new figures of just relationships, of love between women and men, women and women, men and men, to be made possible. The practical ideal for religious belief would unite reason and desire in the shared space and feeling of yearning. Hence my rational defense of female action is to endorse a rational passion which maintains a bond of hope in sexual difference and female desire. At the same time as women take up the standpoint of the outsider within, they seek to express both their desire and their difference. The ultimate goal of such expressions is to generate the very best beliefs of a culture sensitive to concrete differences of sex/gender, race, class, ethnicity, without erasure of the strange.

Notes

1. Harding 1991, 270ff.
2. Kristeva 1993a, 23.
3. Chapter 3, section 3; cf. Kristeva 1991, 181–4; 1993a, 29–30.
4. For more about Ruth, see Bal 1987, 68–88; Kates and Reimer (eds) 1994.
5. To explain briefly the significance of this child, Naomi encourages Ruth to seduce and marry Boaz. Although an older man, Boaz is also a family relative of Naomi's husband. Ruth does what Naomi says, out of devotion to her and not, as some have suggested, to obey Levirate law. The Jewish law had to do with Ruth marrying her husband's closest kin, e.g. a brother; but her husband's brother(s) and close kin were dead. In marrying Boaz, Ruth does not directly fulfill the law, but she does produce a son in the line of David – an important fact for the advancement of patriarchy.
6. Kates and Reimer (eds) 1994, 87–90, 97–105, 111–24, 187–98, 347–68.
7. Aschkenasy 1994, 114, 120–4.
8. Ruth 1:8–9, 11, 15.
9. Ruth 1:10, 16.
10. Ruth 1:17.
11. Ruth 3:1–4.
12. For a highly relevant account of the great fear of a dissenting woman (*nashiz*), which is typical in a Muslim community (*umma*, or a mythically homogeneous group and a source of legitimate authority) as a fear of individualism as well as

the fear of women, see Mernissi 1996, 109–20. The source of such fear points to the real dangers in a disintegration of Muslim hierarchy and ordered unity: submission and surrender, not rebellion and dissent, are integral to Islam. Yet Mernissi demonstrates that Islamic memory contains various historical examples of dissenting women; in the past, generally only dissenting women of beauty, intelligence, and aristocracy were ever successful in subverting Muslim law. Today, Mernissi insists, 'Femininity as a symbol of surrender has to be resisted violently if women intend to change its meaning into energy, initiative and creative criticism' (120).

13. Kristeva 1991; 1993, 28–9.
14. For relevant criticism of the suppression of radical difference in Kristeva's psycholinguistic account of abjection and National Socialist discourse, see Wyschogrod 1990, 246–54.
15. Irigaray 1994. For criticisms of Kristeva, see Wsychogrod 1990, 246.
16. Harding 1993, 270. For another manifestation of women's yearning in philosophy, see Braidotti in Cavarero 1995, ix.
17. *Bhakti* might imply a form of mystical experience in relation to Krishna, but the implied conception of mysticism in *bhakti* would have to be closer to the variety which Jantzen demonstrates has been excluded from modern western philosophy of religion; see Jantzen 1994, 186–206. While the latter conception has described intense subjective experiences exclusively, *bhakti* is bound up with social relations and the pursuit of justice in a common life.
18. Zaehner's edition of the Hindus' sacred book, *The Bhagavad-Gita*, gives the meaning of *bhakti* as 'loving devotion' to Krishna and also defines it in relation to the root word *bhaj-* (1973, 181n). The list of the various meanings of *bhaj-* includes to share in, participate in; inhere in; belong to; enjoy, express sexual love: all of these are developed in various Hindu epics.
19. Cf. Mukta 1994, 223.
20. Mukta 1994, ix–x, 49–56. For further discussion concerning contemporary approaches to women and justice in developing countries, see Nussbaum and Glover (eds) 1995. This important and relevant collection of essays raises ethical and cross-cultural issues concerning women; and it focuses in its central case study upon the life of a contemporary woman in Rajasthan.
21. For support of this contention, see Kristeva 1982 (1980), 126–8.
22. Green 1995, 26–33, 149.
23. hooks 1981; hooks 1990, 12–13, 193–201.
24. Moreover hooks and Cornel West stress the importance in black histories of bonds between women and men for gaining knowledge of divine and human relationships, of passions and desires. A possible goal for spiritual bonding of women with men is to become, in their terms, a 'friend of mind;' see hooks 1990, 214.
25. Nussbaum 1986, 1–21; 1992, 261–90. For further philosophical argument concerning the passions and imaginings of philosophers, see Gatens 1996, especially vii–xvi, 31–45, 50–5, 127–35.

26. Battersby 1989, 193–210.
27. Ricoeur 1967; 1970; Bynum et al. (eds) 1986, 1–20.
28. Kristeva 1986, 292–300. For more on dissident speech, see Meyers 1994, 12–14, 59–61, 91–2, 95ff.
29. On men becoming (like) women by identifying with a woman's voice, e.g. Mirabai in Hindu *bhajans*, see Hawley 1986, 231–56. Note that generally my usage in this book assumes that *bhajan* refers to the devotional song or poetry, *bhakta* refers to a person who practices this devotion, *bhakti* refers to the devotional practice, and *bhajniks* refer to the groups of persons who are bound together by *bhakti*.
30. Hawley 1986, 231–6; Mutka 1994, 87.
31. Cf. Knott 1987, 111–28.
32. Hawley 1986, 236–43.
33. Gatens 1991a, 140–6.
34. Another twentieth-century political figure who has employed a myth to support his own beliefs is Nelson Mandela. Mandela uses Antigone as a western, mythical figure who represents, for him, the cause of his all-male freedom-fighters. This use is not illegitimate insofar as myths are open to multiple configurations. However, it is indicative of the shocking 'betrayal' by western patriarchy of women who are not recognized as significant agents because of the sexed/gendered biased beliefs concerning their roles or lack of roles in political and religious actions. The myth of Antigone could equally be mimed by a black woman who seeks to express the injustice in the total exclusion of her political role by black men who fight for freedom in South Africa. See Mandela 1994, 441–2.
35. Mukta 1994, 182–200.
36. Ricoeur 1992, 241–9, 256; cf. Sophocles 1984. For additional readings, see Hegel 1977, 266–89; Steiner 1984; Nussbaum 1986, 51ff. And for Irigaray's various refigurings of Antigone, see Irigaray 1985a, 214–26; 1991b, 199; 1993a, 116–29; 1993c, 114–23; 1994, 67–73, 85–6. On Irigaray's Antigone(s), see Muraro 1994, 327–31.
37. Cf. Mukta 1994, 183–8.
38. Hegel 1991, 439, also 206–8; 1977, 266–89; cf. Steiner 1984, 4, 19; Wood 1990, 245.
39. Mukta 1994, 105, 110–11.
40. Hegel, 1977, 276–7, 281–4; 1991, 206, 439.
41. Irigaray 1985a, 214–26.
42. Quoted in Mukta 1994, 189–90.
43. Carmody 1989 (1979), 60f.
44. For another reading of Gandhi which neatly incorporates him (and his view of love) into western patriarchal configurations of world religions, see Hick 1990, 123–5.
45. Cf. Irigaray 1985a, 221–6; Jagentowicz Mills 1987, 27.

46. For background on Cornell's understanding of *mimesis*, see Cornell 1991, 147–52.
47. Ricoeur 1977; 1984, 53; 1988, 4, 158–9.
48. Ricoeur relies on Nussbaum's account of deliberation, including the numerous Greek words used for deliberating in Antigone; see Ricoeur 1992, 244–5; cf. Nussbaum 1986, 51f. Bernard Knox also describes Antigone's steadfastness, with glowing terms of heroic individualism, in his 'Introduction to *Antigone*'; see Sophocles 1984, 53.
49. Jagentowicz Mills 1986, 141.
50. See note 36 above.
51. Remember the account of myth which I appropriated from Blumenberg (1985, 34) in chapter 4, section 2.
52. Cornell 1991, 169.
53. hooks 1990, 13.
54. Irigaray 1985a, 243–56, 310–11, 330, 339, 346–64.

IV
Conclusion

Final Critical Matters

the symbolic is the mode through which one makes present something which is not, is no longer or is not yet there. It is thus notably the medium of the future.

Le Doeuff 1991, 295

1 Reason and the Philosophical Imaginary

What would be the implications of agreeing with Le Doeuff that the symbolic is the medium of the future? For one thing, the symbolic would have both positive and negative potential. If the symbolic makes present a future in which women are submissive to men's images, as in the case of a wife of unquestioning compliance, then the potential is negative. But if the symbolic makes present a future in which women are free to question their own beliefs, to create philosophy in their own right, and not to be simply Swinburnians, Plantingians, Kantians, or even Irigarayans, then the potential is positive.[1]

For another thing, following Le Doeuff, the symbolic would include the specific images and myths which have been used by philosophers to express the limits and unity of reason. But the symbolic would not refer to the whole of the social-symbolic order which the feminist poststructuralist equates with patriarchal and male reason. Instead I would like to maintain a critical distinction between Le Doeuff's philosophical imaginary and Irigaray's male imaginary.[2] In the final analysis, only the philosophical imaginary would be the ground of possibility for a feminist philosophy of religion. Whereas the male imaginary conditions the masculine symbolic in which women are locked, 'fated to bang our heads against the wall,'[3] the philosophical imaginary creates the symbolic which can be questioned.

Concerning Le Doeuff's work on the philosophical imaginary, the following could be agreed:

> when Michèle Le Doeuff uses the term [imaginary], she distinguishes her [philosophical] notion sharply from Lacan's. It is not a psychological term describing the narcissistic and identificatory structure of two-person relations; rather, it is a rhetorical term which refers to the use of figures or imagery in philosophical and other texts. She sees it as a kind of 'thinking-in-images', the use of narrative, pictorial or analogical structures within knowledges. . . . it marks those places within philosophical texts where the discourse is unable to admit its founding assumptions and must cover them over. It signals thus a point of critical vulnerability within texts and arguments, a site for what remains otherwise unspeakable and yet necessary for a text to function. (Grosz 1989, xviii–xix; cf. Wright (ed.) 1992, 325–7, 433–4)[4]

Consistent with the above definition, my intention has been to query the nature of the philosophical imaginary in its employment of imagery which constitutes the credulity and coherence of reason, hence the unity of philosophy itself. In particular, I have questioned the rationality and myths of religious belief. But I have also taken seriously the psycholinguistic issue of repression by the myths of patriarchal belief. And yet throughout this book, I have held that the irrational imagined as female and symbolized variously as the feminine, the disorderly, the incoherent, and so on has had something to do with the nature of reason and hence of philosophy – and not necessarily with the nature of being female. Moreover I have proposed that, for philosophers, images of the female as irrational, or as a figure of nonreason, demand philosophy's scrutiny; otherwise there is dogmatism. I have attempted to scrutinize the philosophical use of images of the female in myths. In this way, I have raised the question of the symbolic in creating a privileged male future.

To an important degree, the argument in this book has been inspired by Le Doeuff's, and to a lesser degree, Lloyd's, musings on the philosophical imaginary. Gatens crystallizes this inspiration well in asserting that 'If the work of philosophers such as Genevieve Lloyd and Michèle Le Doeuff is to have the deserved effect, then philosophers will begin to accept responsibilities for the particular passions and imaginings that characterize their particular philosophies' (Gatens 1996, xii). With these responsibilities in mind, I would like to continue with the 'Final Critical Matters' here in part IV.

An early twentieth-century feminist assessment of philosophers' imaginings of women in myths reveals the symbolic as a medium for men's future as follows:

> To regard woman simply as a slave is a mistake; there were women among the slaves, to be sure, but there have always been free women – that is women of religious and social dignity. [But] they accepted man's sovereignty and did not feel menaced by a revolt that could make of him in turn the object. Woman thus seems to be the inessential who never goes back to being the essential, to be the absolute Other, without reciprocity. This conviction is dear to the male, and every creation myth has expressed it, among others the legend of *Genesis*. (Beauvoir 1989 [1949], 141)

Read in this way, women have allowed themselves to be symbolized in myth as the absolute Other, the inessential. Yet this now seems an extreme assessment. Although perhaps not privileged in the past history of western philosophy and of world religions, there are women who have resisted this symbolic representation.[5]

One of these resisting women, who could be read retrospectively as a certain sort of feminist, is Christine de Pizan (1365–1430). Pizan reread the Adamic myth, arguing a case for women's reason and their virtue.[6] She wrote a defense of woman and, specifically, the female body as created by God in Genesis:

> 'My lady, I recall that among other things, after he has discussed the impotence and weakness which cause the formation of a feminine body in the womb of the mother, he says that Nature is completely ashamed when she sees that she has formed such a body, as though it were something imperfect.'
>
> 'But, sweet friend, don't you see the overweening madness, the irrational blindness which prompt such observations? . . . There Adam slept, and God formed the body of woman from one of his ribs, signifying that she could stand at his side as a companion and never lie at his feet like a slave, and also that he should love her as his own flesh. . . . I don't know if you have already noted this: she was created in the image of God. How can any mouth dare to slander the vessel which bears such a noble imprint? . . . From what substance? Was it vile matter? No, it was the noblest substance which had ever been created: it was from the body of man from which God made woman.' (Pizan 1983, 23–4)[7]

Pizan also refigured the fate of the mythical female Circe whose configuration in patriarchal texts will be discussed in section 2 of this part. Rather than a witch, a whore, or simply a woman of bad behavior, Circe is figured by Pizan as a model of pioneering female behavior.[8]

Nevertheless the twentieth-century reading of women's compliance to images of the female as man's inessential other continues to plague philosophical accounts of women's relation to reason, as well as feminist accounts of patriarchal myths. As the argument goes,

> woman is defined exclusively in her relation to man. The asymmetry of the categories – male and female – is manifest in the unilateral form of sexual myths. We sometimes say 'the sex' to designate woman; she is the flesh, its delights and dangers. The truth that for woman man is sex and carnality has never been proclaimed because there is no one to proclaim it. Representation of the world, like the world itself, is the work of men; they describe it from their own point of view, which they confuse with absolute truth.
>
> It is always difficult to describe a myth . . . The myth is so various, so contradictory, that at first its unity is not discerned: Delilah and Judith, Aspasia and Lucretia, Pandora and Athena – woman is at once Eve and the Virgin Mary. She is an idol, a servant, the source of life, a power of darkness; she is the elemental silence of truth, she is artifice, gossip, and falsehood; she is healing presence and sorceress; she is man's prey, his downfall, she is everything that he is not and that he longs for, his negation and his *raison d'être*. (Beauvoir 1989, 143)

This situation has certainly characterized those modern approaches to philosophy in which conflicting images from myths have been employed to represent the impossible nature of woman as the inessential other. These mythical images have indirectly and ambivalently defined the rationality of belief as male, by way of the exclusion of the incoherent female. And these are also precisely the images which have been the object of my criticism and refiguration.

The persistent negative, philosophical reading of woman in myth forces a critical question. Can the symbolic, in its conception of reason by way of the exclusion of woman as the other, ever be disrupted sufficiently in order to create a new vision of the future for both female and male beliefs? I have contended that the images, myths, and dominant configurations of the subject and its other are not invariable and historically fixed. However, a feminist philosopher of religion would probably want to confront the further question: Are religious images of a personal deity merely narcissistic projections of sexual desires? And if so, should growth in knowledge of reality mean that autonomous (and non-psychotic) subjects, communities, and nations no longer have a need for images of a personal deity – say – of a protective or all-powerful father-figure?

In response to such questions, a feminist philosopher could assert that authentically conceived and strongly objective theistic beliefs of women would not come from psychological need alone, nor from epistemological ignorance but, significantly, from a rational passion for justice.[9] After all, feminism is a movement for social change; and justice implies emancipation from (the injustices of) oppression. Moreover I have linked justice with strategies for rationally constructed, religious expressions of liberty and love by women and all marginalized others. My additional assertion, that yearning identifies a rational passion for justice and a vital reality of religious belief, might seem to move the proposed feminist philosophy of religion decisively beyond anything resembling the contemporary, analytical definition and function of reason in philosophical justifications of religious belief.[10] My aim has been supplementation and revision at the level of presuppositions. And often this has meant elucidating the myths and images which are indications of these presuppositions. So allow me to complete the defense of my critical proposal for the rationality of religious belief.

Reason, in its substantive form of yearning, represents the human potential for justice and freedom or liberty. These potentials are Enlightenment ideals; in Kantian terms, they are regulative ideals. However, the feminist gloss on these ideals is that, today, human potential must clearly include the specificities of bodily life, whether that be the distinctiveness of women's desires or substantive expressions of love in relationships. A rational world would, then, be a humane world in which oppression and repression, social and individual injustices, could be overcome. In this way, reason as a tool of freedom is not simply preoccupied with rationality as measured by principles of logical coherence or evidential consistency, of simplicity and credulity. Nor does reason function strictly as the formal rationality in tests for the coherence and truth of the classical theistic attributes of omniscience, omnipotence, omnibenevolence, and impassibility. Instead rationality becomes relevant as it functions in both action and passion, especially in devotion to principles of liberty and love. Yet has my proposal for a feminist philosophy of religion moved me totally beyond the concerns and arguments of contemporary representatives of analytical philosophy of religion? Have I gone beyond empirical realist defenses of theism in seeking to account for this rational passion for justice in myth, mimesis, theistic devotion, female dissent? It is worth considering whether or not this proposal has taken us beyond critical discussion of, for instance, Swinburne's case for the coherence of classical Christian theism.

Instead of antagonism or rejection, my proposal encourages a rethinking of the fundamental presuppositions in contemporary philosophy of religion. I encourage especially the rethinking of the presuppositions concerning reason, desire, the origin of belief, and the situatedness of our most objective claims to true knowledge of reality. But I contend that feminist revisions have not taken us completely beyond Enlightenment philosophy as conceived after Kant.[11] In support of this contention, I note that Enlightenment philosophers have given accounts of a rational passion. Kant writes about a human desire for the infinite and about his awe of the starry heavens above and the moral law within him.[12] Equally Augustine's description of a yearning for the God in whose image he is made remains important for Enlightenment philosophers as a rational form of passion.[13] Augustine's account of a triune God seems a projection of his own nature which, since created in the image of his God, yearns for a threefold deity. The principle underlying this account is that man yearns toward the original pattern in which he is formed.[14] In addition, Otto's twentieth-century account of the holy as both morally and sexually terrifying/fascinating supports the expression of religious belief as a yearning for justice and love. Otto describes the holy as an a priori category which is nonrational, not irrational, since relating to the rational yet existing prior to experience.[15] Otto also identifies the yearning to behold justice in human form and the devotional response to such majestic justice and love in the teachings of Krishna.[16] But the problem for a feminist philosopher of religion with all of these supporting examples is that, whether expressed by Augustine, Kant, or Otto, the responses to yearning reveal strongly patriarchal images and myths of belief. In particular, they give privilege to belief in the love of the Son and the Father.[17] In the end, this gives the patriarchal myths of Christian theism a superior status above all other forms of belief.

Not only are my arguments concerning yearning relevant to philosophy of religion, but my proposal for a feminist approach to the rationality of belief remains concerned with concepts implicit in analytical philosophers' rational justification of theistic belief. These include the epistemic duty to legitimate theistic belief, as well as the necessity to distinguish rational belief from psychological need. The crucial difference between the traditional male theist or atheist and the feminist philosopher, as conceived in this book, is the revised feminist conception of rationality. Not only is it necessary to insist upon refiguring the symbolic, which defines rationality by way of excluding the female imagined as irrational, but also to re-establish a more substantive or, in Kantian terms, practical account of reason for the philosophy of religion. This has led to taking into account both the questions of sexual difference and the biases which render objectivity weak.

I have made an explicit choice to find support for the rationality of belief in certain readings of Kant's writings. Kant supports this project insofar as his account of religion within the limits of reason argues strongly against both the naive claims of empirical realists and the blind faith of religious enthusiasts.[18] The distinctive move toward a feminist philosophy occurs in turning to disrupt the patriarchal structure of classical theism, including any patriarchal images used by Kant to define Enlightenment reason. My intention has been to reassert in the spirit if not the arguments of Kant that, on the one hand, rationality and reality do not correspond perfectly due to the limitations of human reason; on the other hand, blind faith in subjective enthusiasm needs to be tempered by the critical truth of reason. What remains open to critical scrutiny in Kant himself are some of his most fundamental presuppositions concerning the limits and purity of reason. And these presuppositions become evident in the philosophical imagery which continues to be at work in his attempt to account for the unity of philosophy (philosophical truth) and the coherence of pure reason.

For instance, as already discussed, Kant employs the imagery of an island surrounded by a sea of illusion. Kant is not alone in doing this. He finds this sea imagery in Bacon; and it reappears in Hegel and other post-Kantians who use imagery in which an island is the land of truth. The territory beyond truth is the stormy ocean or that sea. Even Quine, as quoted in my Preface, finds it useful in this century to imagine the philosopher as a mariner in a ship on the open sea. The objectionable tendency with the Kantian account is that it takes the sea to evoke images of female emotion or turbulent desire, while the island of pure understanding remains the territory of male reason. But this could be forcing sexist metaphors onto philosophical texts. So how do I read the following?

> the land of truth [is] . . . surrounded by a wide and stormy ocean, the native home of illusion, where many a fog bank and many a swiftly melting iceberg give the deceptive appearance of farther shores, deluding the adventurous seafarer ever anew with empty hopes, and engaging him (*sic*) in enterprises which he can never abandon and yet is unable to carry to completion. Before we venture on this sea, to explore it in all directions and to obtain assurance whether there be any ground for such hopes, it will be well to begin by casting a glance upon the map of the land which we are about to leave . . . enquire (for instance) by what title we . . . consider ourselves as secured against all opposing claims. (Kant 1950, 257)

For the sake of argument, the stormy ocean in this section could symbolize the philosopher's encounter with uncertainty and contradictions, associated with female desire as untruth. But even with this possibility, the larger picture of Kant's Enlightenment account of practical reason could still disturb a sexist view of truth. Rationality is not strictly formal or theoretical in the corpus of Kant's work. Hence reason also serves an important, substantive role as a tool of freedom which must always be open to criticism by any free citizen.[19] And so Neurath's ship is perhaps closer to Kant's construction of practical reason: both serve to sustain and to constrain our thinking as much as they must be constantly worked on and, in the process of moving forward, reconstructed.[20]

In order to get at possible assumptions concerning sexual difference in Kant's use of images to account for reason as both practical and theoretical, allow me a digression in order to consider some additional post-Kantian readings of the sea imagery. After Kant, the dialectic which characterizes Enlightenment accounts of reason is perceived in the early twentieth century by two German philosophers who portray in myth the Enlightenment philosopher's journey upon stormy seas. These two German philosophers are representatives of the early Frankfurt School: Max Horkheimer (1895–1973) and Theodor Adorno (1903–69).

2 Enlightenment Rationality and Patriarchy

Informed by the post-Kantian accounts of Hegel, Marx, and Freud, Horkheimer and Adorno recognize the paradoxical nature of reason as conceived by the male philosophers who sowed the seeds of the Enlightenment. Amongst these philosophers is Bacon, whose ideal of the unity of scientific method and imagery of the land of truth are taken up by Kant.[21]

It is significant here that Horkheimer and Adorno illustrate the paradox of reason with a configuration of rational action and myth. Once more, it is evident that issues of gender or sexual difference are latent in the philosophers' use of myth. Horkheimer and Adorno retell the story of the character, life-journey, and actions of Odysseus as derived from Homer's *Odyssey* (from the eighth century BCE).[22] Reading Odysseus's ancient journey on the stormy ocean retrospectively makes it possible for Horkheimer and Adorno to treat Homer's *Odyssey* as a particular prelude to Kant's modern account of the native home of illusion. Reflecting back upon ancient philosophy in this way, modern philosophers have created a philosophical history in which reason is opposed to myth, rational man to nature and woman. So, for example, the rationality of Odysseus's beliefs are threatened by mythical powers; and these powers are represented in female figures, notably in Penelope, Circe, and the Sirens.

Horkheimer and Adorno argue that the paradox of the Enlightenment dialectic arises because reason is treated as both instrumental and substantive. Instrumental reason assumes that the end justifies the means; such ends-means calculation is generally apparent in the empirical rationality of modern science and technology. Substantive reason, in contrast, is rationality grounded in freedom, seeking justice and more than formal equality. Potentially it could seek equality in love between sexually specific beings. For Horkheimer and Adorno, the source of the devaluation of substantive reason lies largely in the drive by science and scientific man to dominate nature. Yet the particular Enlightenment emphasis upon instrumental reason is also driven by the desire to find freedom from the unpredictable power of nature, especially as represented in myth. But since this is not reason in its substantive form, the use of freedom from nature is ironic; in aiming to be purely theoretical, reason has transformed human freedom precisely into its opposite – denial of its own nature.

As the hero of Homer's *Odyssey*, Odysseus is configured by Horkheimer and Adorno as the modern male subject whose self-consciousness unfolds in an ironic journey of apparent self-preservation and liberation from the mythical powers of nature. This liberation, which from a feminist perspective is highly doubtful, appears to be achieved through the exercise of Odysseus's subject-centered, calculating reason, whereby the ends justify the means. But this strictly male victory of self-preservation is won at a cost. The victorious domination and control of nature by scientific rationality rests upon a paradox in that the subject-centered reasoning is achieved by man who is also in nature. The implication here is that he must equally dominate and control nature in himself.[23] I have already shown that this implication is also mimed by the feminist poststructuralists.

The impossible position of the disembodied epistemological subject was exposed in a critique of its weak objectivity. (Note that this epistemological position is taken by the empirical realist who does not recognize any transcendental idealist framework, since from a transcendental perspective the empirical subject would appear embodied.) Paradoxically this Enlightenment subject's impossible position is a supposedly disembodied position originally conceived by naive empiricist philosophers keen to use scientific method to render the objectivity of true belief possible. Yet this objective position is impossible not only because the subject has failed to take into account the fact that he, too, is fully embodied in nature, but because he has failed to recognize the partiality of belief which remains an unavoidable aspect of his being embodied. To cite Irigaray again,

> The discourse of the subject has been altered but finds itself even more disturbed by [the Copernican] revolution than the language of the [premodern] world which preceded it. Given that the scientist, now, wants to be in front of the world: naming the world, making its laws, its axioms. Manipulating nature, exploiting it, but forgetting that he too is in nature. (Irigaray 1993a, 125)

If persuaded by the argument that having been defined by the exclusion of images of desire as female, reason has projected its own material conditions onto the other, then it could be further argued that the roots of the allegedly contemporary crisis of reason lie in (the paradox of) the Enlightenment subject himself. This is more or less the argument made evident in Horkheimer and Adorno's development of the Odysseus configuration.

For one thing, Odysseus's rationality is configured in resistance to sexual desire, in not succumbing either to the enchanting song of the Sirens' promise of pleasure or to the deception of the seductive goddess Circe. In particular, Circe configures female ambiguity as both corrupter and helper.[24] The Sirens are woman-headed birds perched over the rocks of Scylla and Charybdis; these birds are known especially for their allegedly irresistible song – a song which would enchant sailors so that they would lose control of their boats and be dashed to pieces on the rocks. Circe is an ambiguously seductive goddess whom Odysseus encounters in his travels; and importantly she is also the female figure who unites reason and sexual desire. Ultimately Odysseus's successful resistance of enchantment, sexual desire, and so female nature condemns him to a particular contradiction of self-denial: the denial of a mythical (ir)rationality for a supposedly civilized rationality means denying his own embodied nature. In addition, this struggle to deny nature in himself is also to represent man's renunciation of femininity and the female other.

For another thing, Odysseus's domination of women appears to be embedded in the so-called civilization of his reason. This is further represented by his treatment of Circe as the prostitute. Circe configures an older form of rational life which existed prior to patriarchy. From the perspective of modern, civilized reason, Circe represents the realm of promiscuous, unordered sexuality in which nature is still undivided from reason and so undifferentiated. The Horkheimer–Adorno interpretation is both post-Kantian and post-Freudian: Circe represents the repressed desire which rational, modern man has projected onto the female other in his attempt to dominate nature. Without this female figure as the other, it would be impossible to establish the decisive separation of reason from desire and man from nature; this separation is essential to instrumental rationality.

Yet in the Horkheimer–Adorno configuration of the *Odyssey*, Circe has the virtually unacknowledged capacity to transform man by reconciling him with the very nature that has been denied. Presumably Odysseus's denial is built upon the (false) fear of every Enlightenment man of being transformed (back) into an animal. Ironically for the Enlightenment man, this anti-Enlightenment transformation offers the possibility and not the destruction of man's reconciliation with nature and woman in peace and harmony.[25]

Sadly in this configuration of Odysseus's subject-centered mastery of nature, the fate of Circe mirrors the fate of women in modern patriarchy. According to the central images of patriarchy, woman is either seductive whore or submissive wife (married as a virgin). And in the end, Odysseus's rejection of Circe, as the whore, for his blindly compliant wife, Penelope, seals woman's fate: man stands opposed to harmony with nature and hence with female desire. According to Horkheimer and Adorno, Circe represents the 'pure lie that posits the subjection instead of the redemption of nature'; and this implies the subjection of woman under male authority.[26] After his travels, Odysseus returns home to Penelope and resumes his domestic role within the patriarchal order; he reasserts his control over the household and over ordered sexuality.[27]

It is important to reflect critically upon the Enlightenment configuration of the patriarchal control over the household and sexuality found in Horkheimer and Adorno's *Dialectic of Enlightenment*. A cogent feminist argument has been put forward concerning the missing half of the story in which a specifically modern form of patriarchy is established by Enlightenment philosophers, most notably by Locke and other social contract theorists. The contemporary feminist philosopher Carole Pateman produces the other half of this story. In Pateman's revisionary account of modern liberal theorizing, the social contract as a deeply patriarchal construction is accompanied by the sexual contract:

> The most famous and influential political story of modern times is found in the writings of the social contract theorists . . .
>
> The original contract is a sexual-social pact, but the story of the sexual contract has been repressed . . . The story of the sexual contract is also about the genesis of political right, and explains why exercise of the right is legitimate – but this story is about political right as *patriarchal right* or sex-right, the power that men exercise over women. The missing

> half of the story tells how a specifically modern form of patriarchy is established . . .
>
> The social contract is a story of freedom; the sexual contract is a story of subjection. The original contract constitutes both freedom and domination. Men's freedom and women's subjection are created through the original contract – and the character of civil freedom cannot be understood without the missing half of the story that reveals how men's patriarchal right over women is established through contract. Civil freedom is not universal. Civil freedom is a masculine attribute and depends upon patriarchal right. The sons overturn paternal rule not merely to gain their liberty but to secure women for themselves . . . The original pact is a sexual as well as a social contract: it is sexual in the sense of patriarchal – that is, the contract establishes men's political right over women – and also sexual in the sense of establishing orderly access by men to women's bodies. (Pateman 1988, 1–2)[28]

This feminist argument is significant here for two main reasons. First, the untold story of the sexual contract highlights the difficulty encountered in the previous chapter concerning the dominant configurations of religious belief. The religious devotion of both Antigone and Mirabai are configured by dominant men (and dominant women) in order to support civil freedom as masculine; the ideal devotion of femininity is, then, restricted to the private sphere of family and read as submission to patriarchal beliefs.

Second, the story of the specifically modern form of political right raises a question concerning patriarchy as a universal assumption. My argument is against a distinctively modern form of patriarchy, against the concealment of the specificities of women's reason, desire, and belief. But this is not to suggest that patriarchy determines the lives of all women and every religious belief in the very same way. Instead the implication is that eliminating the diverse, distorting effects of patriarchy for the advancement of feminist philosophy of religion is no simple matter. For me, the crucial thing is to recognize the structures of patriarchy at work in the rational justifications of theistic belief.

So let me scrutinize the figures in Horkheimer and Adorno's account of the *Odyssey*. The figure of Penelope portrays a definite contrast with that of Circe. As read by patriarchal man, Penelope is the epitome of the good and faithful wife; she maintains Odysseus's home all the time he is away, remaining loyal to him always, never seeking out another partner to fill her lonely days and nights.[29] Thus the different roles of wife and whore configure the division of labour for women in patriarchal societies. As the embodiment of promiscuous sexuality, Circe must still submit to the control of male authority; as the embodiment of ordered sexuality, Penelope submits to her husband's control in remaining faithful to him, despite his absences and his promiscuity.[30] With regard to the female figures in the *Odyssey*, the following could be claimed:

> Scarcely does she know herself, scarcely does she begin to glimpse nostalgia for herself – her *odyssey*. To be able to tell her tears from those of Ulysses. Not because they were weeping the same loving tears, but because she took part in his quest for love for himself. Which does not come to the same thing. That might happen if woman also went in quest of 'her own' love. Successfully accomplishing her journey. (Irigaray 1993a, 71)

In turn, distorting social structures emerge under patriarchy as man tries to deny nature and so substantive reason; these structures create injustices for women and marginalized others.

To combat distorting structures, Horkheimer insists upon the use of substantive reason as the tool of freedom. Now a feminist philosophy of religion might combat the injustices of social structures by affirming the content and reality of a yearning for justice. In this light, I would refigure the truth-claims of patriarchal religions, however indirectly, exposing the aspirations of innumerable human beings who face suffering and injustice. The refiguration of truth, both hidden and repressed, awaits the prior task of miming.

Irigaray offers a twofold strategy for miming the patriarchal configurations of reason and love. It is necessary, first, to mime in the sense of an imitation and, second, to mime in the sense of a refiguration of reason and love as two possible paths to the divine. The background to this strategy is crystallized in the following quotation:

> he takes her light to illuminate his path. Without regard for what shines and glistens between them. Whether he wills it or not, knows it or not, he uses this divine light to illuminate reason or the invisibility of the 'god'.
>
> In the meantime he will have taken from the beloved woman this visibility that she offers him, which strengthens him, and will have sent her back to darkness. He will have stolen her gaze. And her song.[31] (Irigaray 1993a, 210)

The above passage exposes woman's role in patriarchal paths to the divine; in order to subvert woman's subordination, the patriarchal configuration of male and female roles in love-making have to be refigured.

3 Reason's 'Crisis' and the Female Symbolic

Various continental philosophers have made a case for a crisis of reason in which men have been caught: the patriarchal theft of woman's gaze no longer illuminates man's reason. According to Irigaray, men need to return to woman both her visibility and her song in order to rediscover the divine light of reason between two subjects. And identifying this crisis of reason may ironically put women in a place of intellectual privilege. If this is so, the privilege implied will have to do with the female symbolic and the new future which the female and male symbolic together can create.[32] Again the danger to avoid is a reversal of the sexism; sexism can lead to creation of a different, exclusive future in which privileged women alone, not men, determine the symbolic.

Nevertheless giving women a place of intellectual privilege could involve recognizing what the feminist philosopher not only gives to other women but offers to men as well. The difficulty is to find an adequate way to recognize authentic expressions of religious belief compatible with the desires of women and men; the specificities of these desires have been repressed by the myths of patriarchy. But Irigaray finds the means, in following the hysteric, to mime male language.

In the course of this book, both Le Doeuff and Irigaray have helped to raise the question of reason's adequacy to its own principles. Rationality has been found inadequate insofar as it is equated with masculinity and the male subject, while femininity is in turn equated with irrationality; and so the female other has been excluded from the justification of belief. As argued in parts II and III, in order to achieve his autonomy as rational, the male subject projects fundamental aspects of his own physicality onto the female other.

The ironic implication of the above argument is that the female other comes to stand in a place of potential privilege. Perennially, in symbol and myth, like those of Eve and the Virgin Mary, or Circe and Penelope, the female other configures the material of desire and bodily life, from birth to death, which has been excluded from the content of justified true belief.[33] Recognition of this material content as having been excluded, devalued, or repressed renders questionable the privileged male preoccupation with justification of belief. So it has been important to query reason's adequacy in justifying belief with tests of rational coherence or evidential consistency.

One immediate consequence of my inquiry concerning reason is that the rational construction of belief took on greater significance as an epistemological task than it has had in modern philosophy. And the new task of rational construction emerged as prior to belief's logical and empirical justifications. In addition, my contention has been that the epistemological framework by which beliefs are rationally constructed makes all the difference. In its modern empiricist form, epistemology has determined both the previously covert construction and overt justification of partial and biased belief. Allegedly male beliefs have been constructed by projecting all material aspects, all limiting and constraining conditions onto the female other and/or onto the other race, class, or caste. Feminist philosophy of religion thus has a crucial opportunity to supplement the epistemological framework of religious belief whose construction has been biased according to hierarchies of sex, gender, race, ethnicity, and class.

A brief account of Simone de Beauvoir reveals that an early feminist version of this argument about male belief was already anticipated in 1949. And of course, Beauvoir greatly influenced the generation of feminists of which Irigaray is a significant, if critical, representative. It seems appropriate, then, before completing my argument, that the author of a classic feminist philosophical text of this century – *The Second Sex* (1949) – should be consulted. It would be wise to consult Beauvoir concerning authentic expressions of religious belief apparently compatible with the desires of women and men, which have been repressed by the myths of patriarchy. Influencing not only Irigaray but more positively Le Doeuff, yet clearly of a different wave of feminism from both, Beauvoir proposes nothing like Irigaray's miming of language or Le Doeuff's thinking-in-images. Yet she elucidates the situation of women and nonreason as imagined traditionally by (male) philosophers.

Beauvoir does not deny that there are women, i.e. that women exist. Yet neither does she define women by their biological nature. The problem, for her, is that women have allowed themselves to be defined as the inessential other, the immanent not transcendent, *en-soi* not *pour-soi*, object not subject, determined not free. Famously, Beauvoir asserts that 'one is not born rather one becomes a woman' (Beauvoir 1989, 303).

Beauvoir's view of a woman's becoming is deeply committed to the existentialism of Jean-Paul Sartre. As indicated earlier, Le Doeuff suggests that Beauvoir suffers from the Héloïse complex. In particular, Beauvoir holds fast to Sartre's central tenet that the subject is condemned to an absolute freedom and so a total responsibility for his or her life. Together these two – freedom and responsibility – are so burdensome that self-denial (*la mauvaise foi*) is inevitable. In this light, woman as the inessential other finds it easy – or deceptively natural – to deny her true freedom by simply being man's other.

Of central interest is that Beauvoir's account of women's situation gives me the reading of patriarchy often assumed by feminists in the last half of the twentieth century. That is, man as the transcendent subject (the master) posits himself as essential and free, while woman as the immanent object (the slave) accepts her role as inessential.[34] This relationship between man and woman as, respectively, absolute subject and absolute other is then internalized by women; hence there results both the sexed/gendered hierarchy and the gender-differentiation of patriarchy. Beauvoir's greatest hope is that woman will one day cease to see herself in the eyes of the master and come to recognize her freedom and so responsibility to define her own self. However, one crucial problem with this hope is Beauvoir's reliance on Sartre's now decisively criticized account of the transcendent subject. For Sartre, the subject, in overcoming his initial state of *en-soi* (in-itself), becomes *pour-soi* (for-self); but the *en-soi* becomes truly free (*pour-soi*) only by creating himself in opposition to another, immanent in-itself. Yet no one person can ever be this Sartrean totally free, transcendent ego unconstrained by material, social, cultural, personal conditions. And it is difficult to imagine that a woman willingly consents to being the free subject's inessential other (*en-soi*) – any more than a slave accepts enslavement.

Notwithstanding the existential inaccuracy of Sartre's account of the subject, Beauvoir accurately describes the oppositional thinking of modern political philosophy. This is the thinking which renders men and women opposites, yet which continues to function in dominant configurations of women in myth. This thinking recalls the account of the ever-popular Hegelian configuration of Antigone. With this account, I stress again that not only is thinking in polarized opposites artificial and unhelpful, but also men and women are not – as claimed by modern political philosophers – equal opposites; implicit in such thinking is a distorting, however covert, hierarchy of sexed/gendered relations.

Beauvoir's Sartrean – and Hegelian[35] – account of the subject's transcendence appears unbelievable; and her account of the history of women in philosophy seems equally misleading. As suggested already with reference to the medieval author Pizan, it is simply wrong to take Beauvoir literally when she writes, '[women] have no past, no history, no religion of their own' (Beauvoir 1989, xix). And yet I might agree that the canonized, written history of philosophy has excluded women, both as philosophers and as figures of reason.

So where does one turn for authentic expressions of theistic belief which do not exclude female desire? Where turn for the symbolic with positive potential for the future of women and for the rationality of their religious beliefs? For the psycholinguist Kristeva, the problem of excluding expressions of female desire begins with the learning of language. Remember that for Kristeva, learning a language – which is constitutive of the social-symbolic order of patriarchy – is equivalent to matricide. Hence mourning, in the wake of the symbolic murder of the child's mother, appears to be a normal stage in the learning of language and so the formation of a separate identity. In contrast, melancholia marks a certain crisis in symbolic mediation.[36] The implication is that there seems no way to bring desire of and for the female, murdered with the mother, back to life, unless a crisis allows the semiotic to emerge in art or religion or the madness of melancholia. But even then, is the melancholic artist or poet any more than a product of patriarchy?

Kristeva herself concludes that the failure of the symbolic mediation between the psychosexual and the social-symbolic orders of a subject's development results in psychosis and so, I might say, in crisis. Melancholia is evidence of a psychosis or illness of the patient who fails to achieve autonomy and meaning, and so fails to face reality. However, I might still conclude that this moment of crisis, whether or not read as an illness, offers the (only) potential opening in psycholinguistics for a critique of power relations; in turn, this critique would constitute the grounds for a transformation of the social-symbolic order of patriarchy. But am I, then, proposing a female symbolic to replace the male symbolic of patriarchy, the latter defined psycholinguistically as constituting the patriarchal language of the present symbolic order? If possible, although now doubtful, this sounds suspiciously like a proposal to reverse the very oppositional thinking which the arguments in previous chapters have struggled to transcend.

Instead I would like to emphasize my choice in taking insight from the feminist poststructuralist readings of patriarchal beliefs, myths, and the buried maternal, but not staying within the realm of psycholinguistics. The aim has been to rethink the nature and function of the distinctively philosophical imaginary. The notion of yearning has been introduced to bring out what has been identified as strongly objective indications of female desire, as in the rational passion for justice expressed by specific, marginalized African-American women and men or Indian *bhaktas*.[37] In Horkheimer's terms, what is encouraged is the search, in different religions, for the records of actual and mythical men and women who have left indications of the significant suffering for love and liberty.

Admittedly an additional tool was needed to recognize female desire. Miming was used to try to subvert patriarchal records of theistic devotion. Yet how, precisely, to 'mime' has never been easy to state unambiguously. As a hermeneutical tool, miming is not a simple mechanism. But at the very least, by introducing this tool as a means of refiguring, I have resisted any straightforward reproduction of static or fixed, positive images of female figures. The task of transforming patriarchal justifications of theistic belief is necessarily far more difficult and fluid than those philosophers schooled in strictly formal reasoning might anticipate. And acknowledging this fact remains in itself extremely significant. I asserted, and hopefully it was accepted, that fixed and static, literary or historical, configurations are not a safe way to propose a sound alternative to patriarchy; the constant danger with static figures is a new form of sexism.

In order for records to be discovered, and for accounts to be heard, of women's yearning, I have read female resistance in acts which can be configured as devotion and refigured as dissent. Before it is possible to disrupt the social-symbolic order of patriarchy, women have no choice but to take on patriarchal symbols and language in order to be understood as dissenting from within dominant accounts of reality. This is to be understood in the peculiar sense illustrated with readings of Antigone and of Mirabai, of women who publicly dissent and so take on a masculine function, for a moment at least. At the same time, the specificity of female desires and new forms of love-relationships have to be discovered and imagined, respectively. Initially, this must be done with distinctively female/feminine actions which nevertheless challenge sexed/gendered hierarchies in order that they might be dislodged. One of my definite, feminist aims is to find new figures – for the symbolic – of reason and belief for the future of women and men. Yet is this future a result of a coming together of the masculine and the feminine? Or will it result from a subversion of the masculine by the feminine? Both or neither?

On the one hand, in Kristevan terms, the imaginary father of individual prehistory makes possible the transition from narcissism to *agape* only as a conglomerate of both maternal and paternal functions; Kristeva identifies the conglomeration as the Third Party who is conceived before the child's awareness of sexed roles. In other words, an identifiable yet imaginary father is often a projection of the maternal role onto a third term, who gives unmerited love and protection. On the other hand, the alternative aim of subversion has been illustrated in Irigarayan terms with Antigone, in that for one moment Antigone digests the masculine.[38] There remains the ever-present possibility of imagining a conscious act of female dissent in which a woman takes on a previously conceived masculine role in acting publicly, but also – more significantly – acting to transform familial and communal relationships.

4 Belief and the Existence of a Personal Deity

Even if the miming of female dissent and the images of a maternal father constitute the symbolic as medium of a new future for men and women, a philosophical issue remains for theism. Can belief in the existence of a personal deity be rationally justified for men and women? Tests for the coherence of the concept of the theistic God alone have been rejected; an empiricist search for evidence from the directly perceived world has been rejected; in addition, neither the cumulative argument for the existence of God, which would unite the two previous sorts of justification, nor the proof that theistic belief is properly basic have been accepted as sound in themselves. In the end, such empirical realist justifications of religious belief have been shown to be blindly biased, since lacking any tools for critical, self-reflexive thinking upon their own embodied standpoint.

Besides trying to expose the function of belief in a patriarchal deity with male-neutral attributes, it might be argued (by some feminist theologians) that if sex matters, there should exist the possibility of rationally constructed belief in a sexed deity with specifically female attributes, e.g. of desire and love between sexually specific beings. To appropriate, very loosely, Le Doeuff's definitions, if 'the symbolic is the mode through which one makes present something which is not . . .,' then a personal deity might be the symbol *par excellence* of 'something which is not' present – female subjectivity – but 'which one makes present' and is anticipated as 'not yet there' (Le Doeuff 1991, 295). However, note that in defining the symbolic, Le Doeuff is definitely not discussing the existence of a god or goddess – let alone a distinctive form of female subjectivity.

Yet I also proposed that the symbolic as 'the medium of the future', in the terms of Le Doeuff, has both positive and negative potential. Again moving beyond Le Doeuff, could the symbol of a goddess instead of, or in addition to, a god for men, be the way to make present sexual difference? More importantly, can the symbolic in the form of a personal deity serve as the ideal of the potential within a man or a woman?

Irigaray's poststructuralist approach to the imaginary has offered feminist philosophers provocative writings on divinity and sexual difference. But another of my aims in this final part has been to distinguish carefully the distinctively philosophical imaginary from the male imaginary of Lacanian psycholinguistics. Does Irigaray's approach to the imaginary intend to criticize only the male imaginary? Or does she expose the unspeakable dimensions of the philosophical imaginary? Choosing one of these alternatives as a response may not be adequate. The male imaginary names the structure by which the privileged subject is constituted as male within a patriarchal, social-symbolic order; and the role of the imaginary, in psycholinguistics, is constituted by the stages of separation, language-acquisition, and identification imposed upon an infant by this social-symbolic order. Irigaray has developed a critique of the male imaginary in her miming of Freud and Lacan, as well as miming other figures in the history of western philosophy. And I submit that in her miming of Plato and Nietzsche in particular, she could also have something distinctive to say about the philosophical imaginary (as distinct from narcissistic projections of ideal male attributes); I will come back to this in section 6 of this part.

So Irigaray has endeavored to uncover sexual difference by disrupting patriarchal myths, and this has potential implications for the feminist standpoint epistemologist's call to reinvent ourselves as other. Following Irigaray, I was led, first, to elucidate dominant mythical configurations of religious belief, and female actions and desires; and, second, to propose the possible refiguration of male configured beliefs while, at the same time, miming our own beliefs and myths. This second step has served as a response to the imperative, to reinvent ourselves as other.

On one level, I may have confronted the narcissistic and identificatory structure of two-person relationships between philosophy mentor and philosophy student, God and man, man and mythical women. This confrontation exposed the privileged relations of the male imaginary – relations which need to be transformed. Yet on another level, I have suggested that the philosophical imaginary cannot be reduced to this male imaginary and reductively opposed to an alternative female imaginary. In exploring the philosophical imaginary, there has been no attempt to justify the empirical existence of female goddesses or to justify a metaphysical trinity of the feminine divine in place of male gods and the male imaginary. Instead imagery of actual and mythical women, who act rationally out of devotion to a duty or a deity, have served as sites of transformation: the imagery of myth and symbol in philosophical arguments exposes points of both vulnerability and possibility in accounts of rationality and belief. By refiguring the symbolic to form a future for reasoning, desiring, acting, believing women and men, I have tried to think on the level of the philosophical imaginary.

Thus my thinking has not been strictly about the narcissistic structure of two-person relations. But as a consequence, the feminist philosopher of religion is still left with the query: To what sort of deity is one rationally justified in giving devotion? Or what sort of belief, if any, can be constructed concerning a personal deity? And ultimately these questions might move us away from the philosophical to the psychological structure of personal relationships, between personal deity and devotee, goddess and woman, etc. Yet a reduction to the psychological is strenuously resisted.

Once more following Kant, especially in the light of Horkheimer, it is possible to agree that according to the philosophical terms set out in previous chapters, the existence of a god or goddess could mean an ideal existence in the sense of the projection of a goal for which one strives. This ideal cannot be pointed to, not like one could point to a chair to know it exists before trying to sit in it. Instead this ideal is known to exist in a practical sense as it functions in thinking and living. For example, Mirabai becomes a regulative ideal, in Kantian terms, as a practical symbol of spiritual strength, for the thinking and living of a community, in devotion to a personal deity.

But to be consistent with this regulative sense of 'exist,' the fictional sense would have to be rejected. If theistic belief is accepted as a viable practical ideal, then it could not be equated with what is pejoratively called a mere fiction. A fiction, if like a fairytale or perhaps a good novel which has been made up, could not serve like a practical ideal or regulative principle of reason, in limiting and guiding claims to knowledge. In contrast, it is possible to agree that the divine does often exist in a mythical sense; this is not to imply the sense of a nonliteral account which is claimed by modern science to be empirically false, but is to suggest a configuration which serves to constitute a group's meaningful identity. In this light, myth is comprised of both a narrative core of constancy and a marginal variability, allowing for constantly different interpretations. The mythical sense of 'exist' is not necessarily incompatible with the practical ideal sense – the mythical and the practical would be good counterbalances for each other.

This last point is again supported by the example of Mirabai. In her rejection of the hegemony of a princely life for a more just, spiritual life, she serves as both a practical ideal and a mythical figure. She gives a community of people both a potent symbol, as an ideal for which they can strive in thinking and living, and a potential identity, founded upon her dissent from the material, emotional, and spiritual injustices of her former, privileged life. Thus configurations of Mirabai take on the quality of myth, as the voices of the *bhakti* constitute a reality and a story which are more than that of the actual, individual Mira; the founding event of her dissent remains (only) the core of the story, constituting the identity of the community, united in devotion to a personal deity (Krishna) and to a common life, characterized by a morality of more just relationships.

Yet in what further sense can anyone say that the feminine or female divine exists? Most obviously, it should not be forgotten that 'exist' could mean a real or an empirical existence. For example, it could be meant in the sense of the simple assertion that the chair, which I am sitting on while writing this book, exists; or on a larger scale, that the earth exists. Yet due to the serious nature and significant function played by a deity who exists ideally and/or mythically, it is not likely I should accept any trivial or any naive empirical realist sense of existence. The necessary meaning of myth appears in sharp contrast with the contingent knowledge concerning empirical material; so, too, the practical function of the existence of an ideal remains in contrast with the theoretical account of existing evidence or facts. Finally, there are two remaining senses in which a deity could exist. Do I accept these as well? Yes and no.

First, concerning the sense of existence as an illusory idea, it is wise to keep open the possibility that I might suffer under an illusion. But it does not follow that all accounts of a deity or theistic devotion are illusory. For instance, as found with the notion of yearning, there are illusory forms of yearning which result in despair or a thirst. Especially illusory is the isolating form of yearning which remains cut off from community, communal criticism, and strongly objective, self-reflexive thinking. Second, and lastly, the historical sense of 'exist' is ambiguous (not surprisingly). Again, to be consistent with those senses of exist accepted above, it is necessary to avoid a naive empiricist sense of historical, e.g. of a 'brute fact' or an accumulation of facts proving the existence of a god. But it is helpful to be able to account for a specific conception which endures for a time due to its function as a regulative principle, but also possibly due to ignorance and need. This historical dimension of what exists could change, in serving an explanatory or limiting purpose for a period of time until, for instance, something inexplicable is explained or some temporary structure of male discourse is discarded. Admittedly not all of the preceding senses of 'exist' overlap neatly. Yet my contention is to value the very possibility of using multiple meanings for 'exist' in order to construct belief in non-oppressive ideals and possibly deities, female or male.

5 The Problem of a Universal Assumption: Patriarchy

So far I have left any critique of patriarchy implicit. My intention has not been to expose a universal structure called 'patriarchy' which could be identified as the source of all and every woman's oppression by men – past, present, and future. As Butler rightly cautions,

> The very notion of 'patriarchy' has threatened to become a universalizing concept that overrides or reduces distinct articulations of gender asymmetry in different cultural contexts. As feminism has sought to become integrally related to struggles against racial and colonialist oppression, it has become increasingly important to resist the colonizing epistemological strategy that would subordinate different configurations of domination under the rubric of a transcultural notion of patriarchy . . . The feminist recourse to an imaginary past needs to be cautious not to promote a politically problematic reification of women's experience in the course of debunking the self-reifying claims of masculinist power. (Butler 1990, 35)

Instead of promoting a reification of women's experience, I have turned to feminist standpoint epistemology to aid thinking from the lives of women who differ from a highly specific western standpoint of privilege. My suggestion is that a common patriarchal structure characterizes the very specific forms of theistic arguments, concepts, and the content of theistic concepts in the privileged western debates in philosophy of religion; and these debates presuppose the liberal male model of public life as the arena for justifying beliefs. A few incredibly precise (often to the point of being impossible to ascribe to real life) arguments and concepts have come to dominate analytical philosophy of religion in the twentieth century, at least in privileged Anglo-American circles; and these have been undeniably patriarchal. So with no intention of assuming a common cross-cultural women's experience, I have nevertheless attempted to expose the ways in which these specific patriarchal configurations of religious belief have also infiltrated western political and religious appropriations of theistic devotion, as in Gandhi's configuration of Indian *bhakti*.

Perhaps certain theists and others would not want to read Gandhi as a patriarchal moralist of a western political persuasion. Yet I have been persuaded by the injustice and falsehoods in Gandhi's use of Indian women. In particular, there are the dangerous distortions in Gandhi's own reading of the dissent of Mirabai. He rereads her uniquely *bhakti* creation of new forms of love-relations in western terms of the private/public, female/male dichotomies of modern political philosophy; hence he eliminates the tensions and the possibilities of nonpatriarchal configurations of Mira's song for women in North India as well as beyond.

Elsewhere Gandhi also employs patriarchal images of Jesus's nonviolent love, e.g. the son of a god, the god-man, and the incarnate *logos*, in order to legitimate his passive resistance in terms compatible with western patriarchal readings of religious morality.[39] Western philosophers of religion in turn confirm this compatibility in their accounts of Gandhi; not surprisingly, they represent Gandhi as a world-religious figure who supports their own patriarchal images of the divine.[40]

And I have to admit that there is no easy way to completely avoid configurations of female dissent, love, and desire according to patriarchal structures of belief and myth. Even after a mythical configuration of patriarchy is clearly elucidated, miming is necessary but difficult. Kristeva, for example, has appeared to be caught up in a potentially endless struggle to extricate female desire, femininity, and the buried material from the symbolic order of patriarchy. She cannot offer any absolutely certain way out of the diverse forms and images of patriarchy. Although her writings expose the complexities of the task of transformation, she reveals the double-bind for women within patriarchy. The subject whose life is meaningful, apparently rational, lives a life structured by the symbolic, as the Law of the Father. To reject this paternal law for the semiotic relation to the maternal, as in the poetry of the melancholic subject, is to accept irrationality and non-meaning.[41] The double-bind is that neither of these alternatives of apparent rationality or irrationality is attractive for a feminist philosophy. In other words,

> subversion [of the paternal law], when it appears [in Kristeva], emerges from beneath the surface of culture only inevitably to return there. Although the semiotic is a possibility of language that escapes the paternal law, it remains inevitably within or, indeed, beneath the territory of that law. Hence, poetic language and the pleasures of maternity constitute the logical displacements of the paternal law, temporary subversions which finally submit to that against which they initially rebel . . . Pleasure beyond the paternal law can be imagined only together with its inevitable impossibility. (Butler 1990, 87–8)

Stated in more philosophical terms, a problem emerges concerning the very existence or ontological status of Kristeva's semiotic as potentially subversive. 'Semiotic' refers to heterogeneous pre-signifying biological and social energies. But how do I know these energies exist? And if they exist, how do I recognize them if, and when, they are subversive of patriarchy? Kristeva's semiotic is defined as the pre-symbolic which exists prior to cognition, while patriarchy constitutes the social-symbolic order which is necessary for recognition of the pre-symbolic. Once expressed according to the symbolic, the pre-symbolic would seem to lose its subversive potential.

Now the argument for the existence of the semiotic as the pre-symbolic, and for its manifestation as poetic language which must break into the symbolic, looks circular. If poetic language depends upon the semiotic for its existence, it cannot then be evidence on the level of language for the existence of a subversive, maternal semiotic. Or if female desire must first be repressed in order for patriarchal language to exist, and if I can only find meaning in language which is expressed, then to attribute meaning to desire before it is expressed in language is impossible. Either the semiotic (including maternal energies and female desires) exists at the same time as its linguistic expression, or the linguistic expression exists prior to the semiotic. If the former, the semiotic must be equated with the symbolic and so not a pre-signifying, subversive multiplicity of energies. If the latter, then the semiotic is constituted by language; and if that language is patriarchy, then female desire – even as that which is repressed – is a construction of patriarchy.

Can this vicious circularity be avoided? Ideally the philosophical imaginary, if it exists as I have suggested, could remain independent of the circular relation of semiotic and symbolic. It would, then, have to be neither strictly semiotic nor strictly symbolic, since independent of the alternative, of psychosexual or social-symbolic, of female or male, two-way relations. In order to discover the distinctively philosophical communication which could transcend this dichotomous thinking, I will turn to a miming of philosophical texts. In particular, critical engagement with Irigaray's miming of Nietzsche's attack on the liberal humanist discourse of 'man' and 'God,' with its normative Christian conception of the self, comes in here.[42] Not only does Irigaray struggle to free the female other from her estrangement but, as the marine lover, she sees new possibilities for the subjectivity of Nietzsche's male philosopher. Irigaray implies that traditional male language needs to be mimed or mimicked by someone like the hysteric who, in order to express her desire, has to 'speak' with gestures or in new forms of expression. Similarly the woman who is excluded from reason, from philosophy, from religious belief, has to mime her rational passion, her desire for wisdom, her longing for love between women and women, women and men, between mothers and daughters, sisters and brothers. This miming gives expression to love in relationships debarred by patriarchy's love between men and their own loved objects only. Miming ideally brings out these other relationships and their differences so that love is not merely an expression of the self-same subject.

Irigaray's disruption of the male imaginary reveals the ways in which cultural formations have held women back from, in her terms, the movement of becoming. Women have not been allowed to speak, reason, or express their sexual difference in other than male terms. Instead women are described in terms of their slavery, exile, degradation, fall, submission, or even their living death. And, at least for me, the paradigmatic examples of such descriptions remain Irigaray's miming of Antigone and her sister, Ismene. Both women suffer a living death.

Antigone is the figure of the entombed woman, buried alive, deprived of air, food, and freedom. Similarly Ismene is locked in the palace for fear of her effect on men.[43] According to the exclusively male imaginary, identity as unity and continuity depends upon attaching death to femininity; the male subject preserves himself from loss of identity by projecting death onto the female other.[44] Hence the woman is fragmented, in bits, castrated, separated – as a figure of death.

Yet the problem of fragmentation also points to a possibility. Although death ordinarily appears the opposite of life, of wholeness, of identity, it is arguably the condition of life. For example, for the Buddhist, death can be the equivalent of achieving Nirvana: the release from earthly existence as the condition of life's enlightenment, bliss, or fulfillment. Insofar as death allows for such a new state, it is creative, not destructive. And for a more elaborate example, Irigaray attempts to speak a woman's experience of living death. She speaks 'this flesh that is never spoken' and, through the refiguration of woman's flesh and blood in a new language, inaugurates a new era.

> Beyond the circularity of discourse, of the nothing that is in and of being. When the copula no longer veils the abyssal burial of the other in a gift of language which is neuter only in that it forgets the difference from which it draws its strength and energy. With a neuter, abstract *there is* giving way to or making space for a 'we are' or 'we become', 'we live here' together.
>
> This creation would be . . . by means of the opening of a *sensible transcendental* that comes into being through us, of which *we would* be the mediators and bridges. Not only in mourning for the dead God of Nietzsche, not waiting passively for the god to come, but by conjuring him up among us, within us, as resurrection and transfiguration of blood, of flesh, through a language . . . that is ours. (Irigaray 1993a, 129)

The sensible transcendental, if realizable, would not separate the sensible world of flesh from the conditions of its possibility.

In her miming of the unspeakable in Nietzsche's philosophy of unbound subjectivity, Irigaray has the figure of woman speak, in the form of lament, about a living death. The woman is 'dwelling in death without ever dying' (Irigaray 1991c, 28; cf. Nietzsche 1954).[45] And it is a miming of death, as an example of the refiguration of rational belief, which I would like to present as a final word on women reason, and the imaginary. Irigaray's hermeneutical involvement with Nietzsche's text does not produce a narrative moving in a Hegelian fashion to ever greater self-consciousness, but a romance ballad telling of a yearning for release from self-estrangement. Admittedly Irigaray's marine lover will be disappointed because Nietzsche's philosophy does not go quite far enough to achieve her goal of an ethics of sexual difference; but I believe it is useful to gain inspiration and direction from the marine lover for the rebuilding task of a feminist philosophy of religion.

6 Death and Woman: Destructive and Creative

Death is one dimension of lived experience, promised for discussion, which has not been directly confronted in previous chapters. Antigone, the figure who is walled up in her tomb, returned symbolically to her mother's womb, remains isolated, cut off, suffering a living death. I have failed so far to mime this configuration of women's lived experience of death in order to rebuild rationally the symbolic for her belief in the future.

To answer the question concerning the feminist philosopher's place of privilege, I use Irigaray as a foil, responding with her marine lover's miming of Nietzsche. In her narrative of yearning for love between two subjects, Irigaray's marine lover goes beyond Hegel's dialectic. Remember Hegel's description of the initial situation in which the master and slave live: it is death in life. As already noted, the highly distinctive twentieth-century French receptions of Hegel's master and slave dialectic influenced Beauvoir directly and Irigaray indirectly; so when reading Irigaray's lament of woman's living death, it is helpful to bear in mind how she moves beyond Beauvoir's account of woman's enslavement in (her own) complicity to the male subject's self-definition.[46] To quote once more from Butler's important work on the French reception of Hegel,

> The dissolution of their antagonism paves the way for an embodied pursuit of freedom, a desire to live in the fullest sense. 'Life' in this mediated sense is not merely physical enduring – that was seen as a posture of death in life in the case of the (slave). The desire to live in the full sense is rendered synonymous with the desire to become the whole of life. Desire is thus always an implicit struggle against the easier routes of death; domination and enslavement are metaphors for death *in life*, the presence of contradictions, that keep one from wanting life enough. (Butler 1987a, 55)

Irigaray's idea of a living death recalls the above, Hegelian account of desire and death; yet she certainly uses Lacan's post-Hegelian discourse on subjectivity. Even if a woman wants to become fully herself, her voice has been silenced in a living death by the Law of the Father which structures the discourse of patriarchy. A woman's desire can only cry out silently from her position of nonspeaking being: she longs to speak the unspeakable. As such, woman represents a figure of the night. In Freudian terms, she is the dark continent. In Irigarayan terms, she has been a slave to the daylight of the male imaginary.

Yet different from this strictly male imaginary, the philosopical imaginary seeks to discover a point of critical vulnerability within texts and arguments. As a feminist philosopher, I have been interested in this imaginary as a site for what remains otherwise unspoken and yet necessary for a philosophical text to function. But can I find 'spoken' in Irigaray's miming the unacknowledged points of the philosophical imaginary? Consider the following:

> A ground rises up, a montage of shapes disintegrates. The horror of the abyss, attributed to woman. Loss of identity – death.
>
> . . . There is always *more of* death, than the one already identified. And the/a woman who withholds herself from the identifiable, therefore threatens – with death. A residue left over by the set up of representation: she lives in death.
>
> She does not die from it. Except as a subject. This life in death sustains the death that is the life of the spirit, a death that gives (back) life by dint of the fact that the other (male or female), who buttresses it, is not really dead. Only as subject; that which the subject of discourse uses for nourishment. (Irigaray 1991c, 91)

In the above passage, Irigaray is miming the figure of woman found in Nietzsche. But my insistent question is: Does this miming manage to elucidate a philosophical imaginary which is neither exclusively male or female? If so, does this elucidation reveal a possible task for a feminist philosopher of religion? The task could be simply to uncover the figure of woman in philosophical texts in order to dislodge the exclusively male symbolic which has made woman a slave. But the burden of this task would be to mime the figure of woman *philosophically*, and not to imitate only, so that a new future can be created in which woman no longer has to say 'yes' to male phantasies.[47]

The impetus for creating this new future in the symbolic would not come exclusively from the female philosopher. The male philosopher's true embodied self has also been concealed by a male imaginary. Although male phantasies have made man the only god while she is a slave to his phantasies, in this scenario both men and women fail to express their true desires and their fully embodied rationality. They fail to see this because man and woman have been mutually dissimulating. Until woman speaks, 'she' remains complicit in this concealment:

> But I want to interpret your midnight dreams, and unmask that phenomenon: your night. And make you admit that I dwell in it as your most fearsome adversity. So that you can finally realize what your greatest ressentiment is. And so that with you I can fight to make the earth my own, and stop allowing myself to be a slave to your nature. And so that you finally stop wanting to be the only god. (Irigaray 1991c, 25; cf. Nietzsche 1954)

In using the marine lover's lament as a foil, I take the liberty of substituting the woman's voice in the text with that of Héloïse speaking. As faithful student and lover, Héloïse, metaphorically speaking, can be imagined as always saying 'yes' to Abelard. Her devotion, unlike that of Antigone or Mirabai, is to Abelard, not to a spiritual duty or a personal deity; she does not dissent, but says 'yes.'[48] The lamentation of the marine lover brings to my mind such a woman. In the letters which Héloïse writes to Abelard, there is evidence of her faithfulness, and his silence; of her complicity, and his dissimulation; of her admiration, and his reputation as a philosopher, and later as a monk. But in Irigaray's miming, from the waters beyond the tomb where the woman is walled up, submerged in a living death, a voice is speaking to the male philosopher. It is even possible that this voice speaks to Abelard:

> But your innocence also wills that you should never speak to her, to the one whom you give everything and whom you entrust for present and future with the redoubling of your affirmation. And all she may say to you is: yes.
>
> From this 'yes' of her flesh that is always given and proffered to suit your eternity, you draw your infinite reserves of veils and sails, of wings and flight . . . Of sublimation and dissimulation. For this flesh that is never spoken – either by you or by her – remains a ready source of credulity for your fantasies. (Irigaray 1991c, 33)

The above miming of veils and sails, of wings and flight, could be read in the terms of Le Doeuff's account of the Héloïse complex. The metaphors are suggestive of, on the one hand, the veiling of Héloïse and, on the other hand, the setting sail of Abélard onto the stormy seas of controversy and illusion. The depiction is easily of the male philosopher who needs his creativity to be admired in conquering the seas of scandalous storms; his reputation is only preserved by dissimulation; his credulity rests squarely upon the silent support of her beliefs. Furthermore, her deflowering is lost only once with no possibility of a love between the two sexes, no becoming of a divine reality between them. Continuing Irigaray's miming,

> It is because she never says anything but 'yes' to your all that you are able to go off so far, so high, soaring up in your dream life. Spreading her out, folding her up, securing her, letting her flap freely, according to your fortune, or to the weather you're having, the wind that's blowing for you, the rain or storm of the moment. Once she is deflowered, you can draw infinitely upon her for your weaving, your painting, your writing, your music too . . . For the beauty you create. (Irigaray 1991c, 33)[49]

Again the imagery of a journey on a turbulent sea assumes that 'she' conditions and makes possible 'your' freedom. The role of the female figure in this picture recalls not only Nietzsche, but Hegel's dialectic where initially the slave makes possible the master's disembodied freedom. What appears new in Irigaray's miming of the philosopher's life becomes the disruption of the female voice of support, of living death. Death contains a destructive potential, even the potential to disrupt patriarchy; to destroy the exclusive privileging of male sexual identity, his imaginary, his symbolic and his reality. Perhaps woman can celebrate the imaginary in the philosophical sense of using imagery and narratives to imitate and disrupt the unspeakable in the text.

The philosophical imaginary is broken open by the symbolic death of the male subject; this death opens onto female becoming. This symbolic death can put woman in a place of potential, intellectual privilege.[50] As learned from Hegel's dialectic, both domination and enslavement are modalities of death in life.[51] Previously man's fear of death has been projected onto woman. But once the master sees death in domination, he will come to recognize his own fragility, facing the disruption of his former privilege.[52] However, until her refusal of enslavement, she remains the object, the one predicated as the other, outside of his objectivity; she is the matter on which he grounds his subjectivity so that it can be seen. In Irigaray's words,

Predicatable insofar as she is an 'object in general', the/a woman remains external to the objective. From this outside position she grounds its economy – by being castrated, she threatens castration. Glimpsing that she may sub-tend the logic of predication without its functioning having anything properly to do with her, leads to the fear that she may intervene and upset everything: the death of the subject would be nothing less. A ground rises up, a montage of shapes disintegrates. The horror of the abyss, attributed to woman. Loss of identity – death.

. . .

She grounds predication without strictly speaking being marked by it: she is not determined through the application of such or such a quality. She sub-sists 'within herself' beneath discourse. As that which has also been called prime matter.

Out of the storehouse of matter all forms are born. She brings them into the world, she 'produces'. From between her lips comes every figure: a warm glowing heat comes out of that self-embrace and becomes 'visible'. But once, one single time and one instant only: beauty. Afterward, or by default and repetition, there are veils. Unless there be a divine reality. (Irigaray 1991c, 91, 92)

The above text offers a good illustration of Irigaray's use of psycholinguistics. 'She' represents the role of woman in our discourse. And as object in general, she constitutes the unconscious condition of autonomous-male discourse which, if left unquestioned, becomes dogmatism, undermining what philosophy is by definition. As long as man is subject and she is an object without specificity, her otherness appears to render his subject position possible. In Freudian terms, he appears secure in his identity, while she is symbolically castrated. Once she threatens to become as a woman and so to disrupt his male economy of desire and drives, then he becomes fearful of his own death. Her difference – sexual difference – has been repressed in the constitution of man's predication; he uses her to ground his language. Irigaray provocatively contends that this situation of exclusion and (potential) dogmatism will disappear if and when a divine reality is allowed to visibly condition the love between man and woman. Ideally this would be in the mediation of a sensible transcendental.

In chapter 5, I illustrated the possibility that over and against male privilege, the woman can be read as acting to digest the masculine. She can refuse her subordinate role as submissive wife, mother, lover. She can consciously choose dissent. She can choose death, and against what is thought to be rational, new life. What would this mean for Abelard? for the male philosopher of religion? for sexual love? for life drives? for death?

A specifically female dissent from tradition could discover a divine reality in a new form of love between mothers and daughters, women and men, and all the other relationships which have been excluded by patriarchy. Instead of equating *eros* with fragmentation and loss of identity, it can be seen positively in the coming together of two subjects in their own renewal. Ironically death drives and *eros* may not be as destructive as the life drives which continue the subordination of women serving a function within patriarchy as mothers without their own desire:

> the negative side of death drives is fairly apparent. What has been emphasized very little, even blindly contested, is the destruction at work in life drives themselves, in so far as they do not respect the other, and in particular the other of sexual difference . . .
>
> Urged by *eros*, man immerses himself in chaos because he refuses to make love with an other, to be two making love, to experience sexual attraction with tenderness and respect. Male sexuality has once again annihilated human individuation . . .
>
> . . .
>
> It is accepted that *eros* destroys identity, not that it fulfils it.
>
> . . .
>
> And instead of contributing to individuation, or to the creation or re-creation of human forms, eroticism contributes to the destruction or loss of identity through fusion . . . and so is not likely to have a positive future here on earth.
>
> This notion of love has led women to forget themselves, to submit childishly or slavishly to male sexuality, and to console themselves, through motherhood, for their fall and exile from themselves. Motherhood – promoted by spiritual leaders as the only worthwhile destiny for women – most often means perpetuating a patriarchal line of descent . . . To women, more secretly, motherhood represents the only remedy for the abandonment or for the fall inflicted in love by male instincts, as well as a way for them to renew their ties to their mothers and other women. (Irigaray 1994, 97, 98, 99)

The above argument sounds negative: life drives have meant slavish submission to male sexuality. Yet the positive implication is that subversion of female submission will motivate a search in *eros* for the renewal of desire and reason.[53] What does this imply for women and philosophy of religion? This suggests the role for feminist philosophers in overcoming women's separation from men. Instead of allowing myths and symbols in religion to offer women comfort and consolation in childish meekness and motherhood, it becomes necessary to refigure women's autonomous acts of dissent and devotion in the context of ever-evolving relationships. The subversion of male power does not occur by escaping into a separate female existence or into an isolated longing.

Real hope begins by confronting the identification of reason as a strictly disembodied faculty, while resisting the rejection of reason and all past philosophy with it. An overly formal concept of reason sharply contrasted with desire is too technical and 'thin' for its role in assessing the profound nature of religious belief. But desire is not adequately uncovered and understood when unrelated to the critical capacity of reason. Philosophical analyses of and feminist concerns with a combination of reason and desire, as expressed in the yearning for truth, need to come to the top of the agenda in contemporary philosophy of religion.

I urge the feminist philosopher of religion to commence with the subversion of the biased and partial, theistic beliefs supporting the status quo of patriarchy. By imitating the relation of woman and man to reason and desire, to divine light and love, the feminist philosopher may be able to discover the points at which man has taken woman's light to illuminate his reason and his 'god,' with no concern for the love shining between them. Under patriarchy, the two – male and female lovers – are not equal. He takes strength from her love, sending her back to darkness. Yet in stealing her light and her song, he cannot retain reason and belief for long without loss of his own identity. He is threatened by the disembodiment of his own dangerously atomized and formalized self. Despite philosophy's past exclusion of the female other, the symbolic remains the potential to make present the embodiment which is not, or not yet, there between men and women.

Notes

1. Le Doeuff 1991, 59–60, 162–5, 295–6.
2. Remember that the male imaginary names the structure by which the privileged subject is constituted as male within a patriarchal, social-symbolic order. The importance of the imaginary in psycholinguistics lies in its image-structure (i.e. the separation, language, and identification imposed upon an infant) by which sexual identity is constituted.
3. Cornell 1991, 91.
4. However, for equally relevant arguments concerning the importance of sexual imaginary or imaginaries for women's conceptions of themselves sexually and socially as persons, see Cornell 1995a, 4–20, 80–3, 103–6; Gatens 1996, vii–xvi, 125–6, 140–1. While Cornell relies upon Kant for her conceptions of personhood and practical reason, Gatens relies upon Spinoza for a monistic

account of the mind and body; further work could be fruitfully done on the difference between these two feminist philosophers in their understanding of persons as sexed beings. Despite their different subtexts, both authors seek a philosophical conception of the imaginary as a domain or context in which a positive sense of sexual difference can be discovered; this discovery of sexual difference would become transformative of who we are. Cornell explains her Kantian-influenced, psychoanalytic position as follows:

> the freedom to struggle to become a person is a chance or opportunity which depends on a prior set of conditions that I refer to as minimum conditions of individuation . . . each one of us must have the chance to take on this struggle in his or her own unique way. It is under my definition a project that demands the space for the renewal of the imagination and the concomitant re-imagining of who one is and who one seeks to become. Hence, my insistence on the imaginary domain as crucial to the very possibility of freedom. (Cornell 1995a, 5)

5. Lerner 1993, 247–73, 281; Green 1995, 7, 26ff.
6. Pizan 1983 (1405); cf. Lerner 1993, 49–50; 143–6; 192–5; Green 1995, 27–43. For other readings of the creation myths and, in particular, the two different stories in Genesis, see Trible 1992 (1979), 74–83; Bal 1987, 104–30.
7. Compare this passage from Pizan with Beauvoir 1989 (1949), 141.
8. Pizan 1983, 69–70.
9. This would also be true of the theistic beliefs of those men who are feminists, at least according to the feminist standpoint and feminist poststructuralist terms stipulated in previous chapters.
10. Swinburne 1981, 33–103; Plantinga and Wolterstorff (eds) 1983; Audi and Wainwright (eds) 1986; Abraham and Holtzer (eds) 1987; Alston 1991; Plantinga 1992, 436–41; Audi 1993, 70–89.
11. For a highly significant application of Kant's practical philosophy to questions of women's lives and justice, see O'Neill 1993; 1995; 1996. For some feminist criticisms of Kant's formalism, see Code 1995.
12. Kant 1956 (1788), 166.
13. For a critical account of Augustine's total devotion (including all of his reason and passion) for his God, see Adams 1986, 169–94. Although aware of the potential problem with Augustine's all-encompassing love for the Christian God excluding other human loves, Adams does not raise the question of homoeroticism.
14. Augustine 1963, VIII, X.
15. Otto 1923, 136–41, 175–8.
16. Otto 1923, 186–8.
17. Otto 1923, 142, 178; Augustine 1959; 1961, 250–2, 270, 278; Kant 1960 (1793), 36–9, 42–7, 54ff.
18. Kant 1950 (1787); 1960. Cf. Kunneman and Vries (eds) 1993, 211–56; Anderson 1993c.
19. Kant 1950, 593, A738/B766; cf. Cornell 1995a, 11–20.

20. Kant's own imagery of a modest building (a 'dwelling house' but not a tower that would reach to the heavens), building materials, and builders for the construction of practical reason might also be considered; see O'Neill 1996, 60–4; cf. Kant 1950, 573–4 A707/B735.
21. Kant 1950, 4, Bii, 19–20, Bxii, 257 B294–295/A236; Bacon 1974; Horkheimer and Adorno 1972, 1–17, 42.
22. Horkheimer and Adorno 1972, 32–6, 43–80.
23. Horkheimer and Adorno 1972, 33–4, 54–8.
24. Horkheimer and Adorno 1972, 32–4, 69–70.
25. Horkheimer and Adorno 1972, 70–4.
26. Horkheimer and Adorno 1972, 72.
27. For a highly provocative account of Penelope's generally unacknowledged subversion of this order in her act of weaving and unweaving, which saves her from a remarriage, see Cavarero 1995, 11–14, 16–19, 28–30.
28. For more discussion of the self-contradictions created by patriarchy for male sexuality, see Horowitz and Kaufman 1987, 81–102.
29. For an alternative, subversive reading of Penelope, again see Cavarero 1995, 4, 11–30.
30. Homer 1980, 6–7, 9–11, 261–2, 277–85, 290.
31. Recall the account of Mirabai's song and its betrayal in chapter 5 above; cf. Irigaray 1992, 7, 61, 70ff.
32. Whitford 1991a, 97–110; 1994, 379–400; Schwab 1994, 351–78.
33. For examples which support this claim, see Beauvoir 1989, 139–98; Cavarero 1995.
34. This account of the master and the slave, man and woman, has been influenced by a particular twentieth-century French reading of Hegel's dialectic; cf. Beauvoir 1989, 64–5, 162, 435–6, 612–13; Descombes 1980, 9–57; Butler 1987a, 92–9, 138–56.
35. Chanter separates sharply the Sartrean and Hegelian influences upon Beauvoir's thought. Yet it could be argued that Kojève's Marxist reading of Hegel – and especially his master–slave dialectic – had a decisive influence upon Sartre's thinking, just as it also did upon numerous other intellectuals in Paris between 1933 and 1968; cf. Merleau-Ponty 1964a, 109–10. Beauvoir could have acquired her views in part from the general dissemination of Hegelian ideas within her intellectual milieu; and if Le Doeuff's Héloïse complex is correct, the influences upon Beauvoir cannot be easily separated from Sartre's; cf. Merleau-Ponty 1964a, 109–10; Beauvoir 1968 (1965), 43; Kojève 1980; Descombes 1980, 9–57; Roth 1988; Anderson 1993c, 4, 6–9; Chanter 1995, 55–67.
36. Kristeva 1986, 147–52; 1989 (1987), 13–14, 43–4, 228.
37. hooks 1990; Mukta 1994.
38. Irigaray 1985a, 220.
39. Gandhi 1957 (1940), 136; 1959, 9–10.

40. Hick 1990, 106–25. On Hick's patriarchal images of the divine, see Anderson 1992, 15–21.
41. Kristeva 1989, 33–44.
42. Johnson claims that in *Marine Lover of Friedrich Nietzsche* (Irigaray 1991c),

> Irigaray's feminine self speaks as one seeking to cut herself loose from all imposed, normative conceptions of the self. And this new femininity-in-process sees a powerful ally in Nietzsche's attack on the will-to-power covertly expressed through the liberal humanist discourse on 'Man' . . .
>
> Irigaray gets swept up in this longing for reconciliation (for release from painful estrangement from the loved object); a longing expressed by her as a lament for Nietzsche's estrangement from his own essential possibilities. The desired union could have been realized, had Nietzsche only proven himself adequate to those essential potentialities discovered by his marine lover. (Johnson 1996, 27–8)

43. Irigaray 1985a, 218; 1993a, 117, 118–20.
44. Irigaray 1985a, 215.
45. For a miming of death, woman and the incarnation of Christ, see Irigaray 1991c, 164–90.
46. Beauvoir 1989, 64–5, 162–3.
47. The ground for maintaining both a philosophical form of miming and a psychoanalytic undertaking of mimesis is given in Irigaray 1985b, 74–7. Arguably her miming of Nietzsche is an example of the former.
48. Abelard and Héloïse 1974, 109–56.
49. Compare this passage with the images surrounding the 'I' (woman)'s search for identity in relation to the 'you' (man) in Irigaray 1992.
50. Anderson, forthcoming.
51. Chapter 2, section 4, above; cf. Hegel 1977.
52. Irigaray 1991c, 93.
53. For a woman's (I's) voyage in search of her identity in love in relation to 'you,' again see Irigaray 1992.

Summary

The ultimate goal of this book is to give its readers a feminist argument concerning the contemporary approach to philosophy of religion. It is hoped that the argument, however complex, for the transformation of sex/gender-biased beliefs has been eagerly followed and that the reader has been able to learn to work with the philosophical tools and new frameworks offered for supplementing philosophy of religion. The next stage is for the reader herself or himself to think through the argument against empirical realist forms of theism and the proposal for a feminist philosophy of religion in order to develop her or his own thinking on these matters. Future debates on women, rationality, and religious belief should continue to be lively. The categories presented here are not meant to be definitive, but are meant to stimulate the growth of feminist knowledges. More new thinking from women philosophers of religion is eagerly awaited. In the final sections of part IV, I have attempted both to elucidate the actual functioning of the symbolic, the philosophical imaginary, and patriarchal myths, and to guide women and men toward becoming philosophers who reason, desire, and believe passionately in non-oppressive ideals.

In addition to the philosophical matters in parts I and IV, each of the five main chapters in this book contains its own argument. But a more general argument holds together the four parts. To conclude, allow me to restate the salient points of the particular and general arguments.

In chapter 1, the contention that, currently, philosophers are facing a 'crisis' of rationality was presented and assessed. This provided a starting point for the chapter's main argument: that the functioning of rationality in contemporary analytical philosophies of religion, especially in naive empirical realist forms of theism or atheism, must be rethought, even transformed. Instead of privileging the empirical and logical justifications of theistic belief, the very construction of belief as rational was found to need prior critical thought and new philosophical tools. The chapter ended with a proposal to retain rationality – despite the crisis – with the support of Kant's limitations on theoretical reason's function, while also proposing to refigure both the patriarchal images (including Kant's) and the underlying myths of reason which have dominated western philosophy of religion.

Chapter 2 took up an important section of the argument from chapter 1, concerning the feminist epistemological frameworks. In the earlier chapter, these feminist frameworks of belief served in elucidating different approaches to the crisis of philosophical reason. Then the second chapter developed its argument by focusing upon one of the frameworks: feminist standpoint epistemology. Essentially the feminist standpoint argument is that Enlightenment accounts of objectivity, especially the empiricist variety, have been too weak, since blindly biased to sex/gender, race, class, and ethnicity. Now the philosopher of religion who seeks to maintain the rationality of belief, out of a sense of epistemic duty, should be compelled by the recognition of these built-in empiricist biases to new strategies for stronger objectivity. I found that feminist standpoint epistemology was lacking in one crucial respect: it lacked the material content for the specificities of religious belief. This feminist framework has no means to discover and defend women's sexually specific and distinctive expressions of desire, devotion, or death. Nonetheless it is precisely these latter expressions of lived experiences, however devalued, which constitute a crucial dimension of the content for distinctively religious truth-claims.

Chapter 3 took seriously this particular lack of material content, seeking to uncover the specificities of women's lived experiences which have been missing from belief, especially religious belief. My argument is that the feminist poststructuralist helps to uncover the sought-after material content of female desire for feminist epistemology. Despite its prima-facie anti-epistemological stance, feminist poststructuralism does not necessarily privilege desire over reason, irrationality over rationality. Rather it offers feminist epistemologists the psycholinguistic tools to begin to unearth what has been buried by patriarchal structures of belief and myth. I also admit that the methods of psycholinguistics are not, in philosophical terms, completely successful. And yet feminist poststructuralists can set philosophy of religion in an appropriate, new direction for uniting desire and reason, even rediscovering them united in myth.

Chapter 4 adopted this new direction. My argument returned to criticize the impossible position of the disembodied, epistemological subject by exposing the contradictory nature of its formally rational, religious beliefs In turn, this argument offers a possible rethinking of myth. I have tried to demonstrate that reason and desire are brought together in mythical configurations of religious belief. My argument continues to show the necessity for feminists in defining different forms of mimesis. These forms, then, would serve as tools for disrupting dominant and fixed configurations of exclusive religious beliefs.

Chapter 5 reached the full complexity of my argument with the actual figuring of belief. I endeavored to weave together several images and their various interpretations. Multiple configurations and refigurations of female dissent were employed in order to demonstrate the often buried or misconstrued rationality in women's expressions of religious belief, action and devotion. The key term, 'yearning,' identified the distinctive passion of the woman of reason.

Part IV reiterated certain earlier points while still confronting some unacknowledged points of critical weakness. Both Beauvoir and the early Frankfurt School pair Horkheimer and Adorno were used to illustrate crucial dimensions of my argument about women, reason, and philosophy. The restatement of and critical amendments to the book's main arguments in part IV affirmed the continuing importance for feminist philosophy of the Enlightenment ideals of justice, liberty, and love.

Although insisting upon a critical distinction between the male and the philosophical imaginaries, I asserted the deep significance in a refiguring of woman and death. It becomes possible to see how the symbolic is the mode through which we can make present the specificities of female and male desires without giving up reason. The symbolic provides the images for a vision of the future. In imagining death, it reveals death's intimate connection with yearning for love between fully embodied men and women. So the philosophical imaginary responds to a lack of desire in accounts of religious belief by making death, in particular, present. And death's relation to desire of and for the other directs us to the necessary, material content in philosophical constructions of belief, forcing both women and men to confront concrete cases of injustices in life. The limits of empirical knowledge of death do not put an end to seeking new content for beliefs. Rather empirical limits indirectly demonstrate the necessity of practical ideals. Only nonconstitutive ideals in a Kantian sense serve to regulate our knowledge. At the same time, these ideals transcend the formal limits of the empirical world by making possible a rational passion which is practical, and not theoretical like the formally impossible. This utopian vision, binding women and men together in new beliefs about life and death, becomes the necessary condition for thinking the differences of sex/gender, race, class, and ethnicity.

Bibliography

Abelard, Peter and Héloïse. 1974. *The Letters of Abelard and Héloïse*, trans. and introduced by Betty Radice. Harmondsworth: Penguin.

Abraham, William J. and Holtzer, Steven W. (eds) 1987. *The Rationality of Religious Belief: Essays in Honour of Basil Mitchell.* Oxford: Clarendon Press.

Adams (see McCord Adams).

Adams, Robert Merrihew. 1986. 'The Problem of Total Devotion', in Audi and Wainwright (eds) 1986. *Rationality, Religious Belief and Moral Commitment*, 169–194.

Adams, Robert Merrihew. 1993. 'Truth and Subjectivity', in Stump. ed. *Reasoned Faith*, 15–41.

Alcoff, Linda and Potter, Elizabeth (eds). 1993. *Feminist Epistemologies.* London: Routledge.

Alston, William P. 1976. 'Two Types of Foundationalism', *Journal of Philosophy*, 73, 165–85.

Alston, William P. 1987. 'Religious Experience as a Ground of Religious Belief', in Joseph Runzo and Craig Ihara (eds), *Religious Experience and Religious Belief.* New York: University Press of America, 31–52.

Alston, William P. 1991. *Perceiving God: The Epistemology of Religious Experience.* Ithaca, NY: Cornell University Press.

Alston, William P. 1993. *The Reliability of Sense Perception.* Ithaca, NY: Cornell University Press.

Anderson, Pamela. 1992. 'Ricoeur and Hick on Evil: Post-Kantian Myth?', *Contemporary Philosophy*, XIV: 6 (November/December), 15–21.

Anderson, Pamela. 1993a. 'After Theology: End or Transformation?', *Literature and Theology: An International Journal of Theory, Criticism and Culture*, 7:1 (March), 78–86.

Anderson, Pamela. 1993b. 'Narrative Identity and the Mythico-poetic Imagination', in David Klemm and William Schweiker (eds), *Meanings in Texts and Actions: Questioning Paul Ricoeur.* Charlottesville, VA: University of Virginia Press, 195–204.

Anderson, Pamela Sue. 1993c. *Ricoeur and Kant: Philosophy of the Will.* Atlanta, GA: Scholars Press.

Anderson, Pamela. 1996a. 'Myth, Mimesis and Multiple Identities: Feminist Tools for Transforming Theology', *Literature and Theology: An International Journal of Theory, Criticism and Culture,* 10: 2 (June), 112–30.

Anderson, Pamela Sue. 1996b. 'Wrestling with Strangers: Julia Kristeva and Paul Ricoeur on the Other', in Alison E. Jasper and Alastair G. Hunter (eds), *Talking It Over: Perspectives on Women and Religion.* Glasgow, Scotland: Trinity St Mungo Press, 129–49.

Anderson, Pamela Sue. 1997. 'Rereading Myth in Philosophy: Hegel, Ricoeur and Irigaray Reading *Antigone*', in Morny Joy (ed.), *Paul Ricoeur and Narrative: Context and Contestation.* Calgary, Alberta, Canada: University of Calgary Press, 51–68.

Anderson, Pamela Sue. Forthcoming. '"Abjection . . . the Most Propitious Place for Communication"': Celebrating the Death of the Unitary Subject', in Kathleen O'Grady, Ann Gilroy and Janet Gray (eds), *Bodies, Lives, Voices: Gender in Theology.* Sheffield: Sheffield Academic Press.

Anscombe, Elizabeth. 1979. 'What Is It to Believe Someone?', in C. F. Delaney (ed.), *Rationality and Religious Belief.* Notre Dame, IN: University of Notre Dame Press.

Aquinas, Thomas. 1981. *Summa Theologia,* trans. Fathers of the English Dominican Province. Westminster, MD: Christian Classics.

Aquinas, Thomas. 1989. *The Literal Exposition on Job: A Scriptural Commentary Concerning Providence,* trans. Anthony Damico and Martin Yaffe. The American Academy of Religion: Classics in Religious Studies. Atlantic, GA: Scholars Press.

Aristotle. 1965. 'On the Art of Poetry', in *Classical Literary Criticism,* trans. T. S. Dorsch. Harmondsworth: Penguin, 31–75.

Aristotle. 1984 (1912–52). *The Complete Works of Aristotle.* The Revised Oxford Translation, ed. Jonathan Barnes. Princeton, NJ: Princeton University Press.

Armstrong, Karen. 1993. *A History of God.* London: Mandarin.

Aschkenasy, Nehama. 1994. 'Language as Female Empowerment in Ruth', in Kates and Reimer (eds), *Reading Ruth,* 111–24.

Assiter, Alison. 1996. *Enlightened Women: Modernist Feminism in a Postmodern Age.* London: Routledge.

Audi, Robert. 1993. 'The Dimensions of Faith and the Demands of Reason', in Stump (ed.), *Reasoned Faith*, 70–89.

Audi, Robert and Wainwright, William J. (eds). 1986. *Rationality, Religious Belief and Moral Commitment: New Essays in the Philosophy of Religion*. Ithaca, NY: Cornell University Press.

Auerbach, Erich. 1968. *Mimesis: The Representation of Reality in Western Literature*, trans. Willard R. Trask. Princeton, NJ: Princeton University Press.

Augustine. 1959. *Treatises on Marriage and Other Subjects*, ed. R. J. Deferrai. New York: Fathers of the Church.

Augustine. 1961. *The Confessions*, trans. R. S. Pine-Coffin. Harmondsworth: Penguin.

Augustine. 1963. *The Trinity*, trans. S. McKenna. Washington, DC: The Catholic University of America Press.

Augustine. 1972. *The City of God*, trans. Henry Bettenson. Harmondsworth: Penguin.

Bacon, Francis. 1974 (1660). *The New Atlantis*. Oxford: Oxford University Press.

Bal, Mieke. 1987. *Lethal Love: Feminist Literary Readings of Biblical Love Stories*. Bloomington, IN: Indiana University Press.

Barbour, Ian. 1974. *Myths, Models and Paradigms*. London: SCM Press.

Barthes, Roland. 1993 (1972). *Mythologies*, trans. Annette Lavers. London: Vintage Books.

Bartky, Sandra Lee. 1990. *Femininity and Domination: Studies in the Phenomenology of Oppression*. London: Routledge.

Barwell, Ismay. 1994. 'Towards a Defence of Objectivity', in Lennon and Whitford (eds), *Knowing the Difference*, 79–94.

Battersby, Christine. 1989. *Gender and Genius: Towards a Feminist Aesthetics*. London: The Women's Press.

Battersby, Christine. 1992. 'Philosophy: The Recalcitrant Discipline', *Women: A Cultural Review*, 3: 2 (Autumn), 121–32.

Beauvoir, Simone de. 1968 (1965). *Force of Circumstance*, trans. Richard Howard. Harmondsworth: Penguin.

Beauvoir, Simone de. 1989 (1949). *The Second Sex*, trans. H. M. Parshley, introduced by Deirdre Bair. New York: Vintage Books.

Benhabib, Seyla. 1992. *Situating the Self: Gender, Community and Postmodernism in Contemporary Ethics*. London: Routledge.

Benhabib, Seyla. 1995. 'Feminism and Postmodernism: An Uneasy Alliance' and 'Subjectivity, Historiography, and Politics: Reflections on the "Feminism/Postmodernism Exchange"', in *Feminist Contentions: A Philosophical Exchange*, introduced by Linda Nicholson. London: Routledge, 17–34 and 107–25.

Benhabib, Seyla and Cornell, Drucilla (eds). 1987. *Feminism as Critique*. Minneapolis, MN: University of Minnesota Press; Cambridge: Polity Press in association with Blackwell.

Benveniste, Emile. 1971. 'Remarks on the Function of Language in Freudian Theory', in *Problems in General Linguistics*, trans. Mary E Meek. Coral Gables, FL: University of Miami Press, 65–75.

Berry, Philippa. 1992. 'Woman and Space according to Kristeva and Irigaray', in Philippa Berry and Andrew Wernick (eds), *Shadow of Spirit: Postmodernism and Religion*. London: Routledge, 250–64.

Berry, Philippa. 1994. 'The Burning Glass: Paradoxes of Feminist Revelation in *Speculum*', in Burke, Schor, and Whitford (eds), *Engaging with Irigaray*, 229–46.

Berry, Philippa. 1995. 'Kristeva's Feminist Refiguring of the Gift', *Paragraph* 18: 3, 223–40.

Blackburn, Simon. 1994. *The Oxford Dictionary of Philosophy*. Oxford: Oxford University Press.

Blumenberg, Hans. 1985. *Work on Myth*, trans. Robert M. Wallace. Cambridge, MA: MIT Press.

Bock, Gisela and James, Susan (eds). 1992. *Beyond Equality and Difference: Citizenship, Feminist Politics and Female Subjectivity*. London: Routledge.

Bordo, Susan. 1987. *The Flight to Objectivity: Essays on Cartesianism and Culture*. Albany, NY: State University of New York Press.

Braidotti, Rosi. 1989. 'The Politics of Ontological Difference', in Teresa Brennan (ed.), *Between Feminism and Psychoanalysis*. London: Routledge, 89–105.

Braidotti, Rosi. 1991. *Patterns of Dissonance: A Study of Women in Contemporary Philosophy*. Cambridge: Polity Press.

Braidotti, Rosi. 1993. 'Re-figuring the Subject', in Kunneman and Vries (eds), *Enlightenments*, 319–41.

Braidotti, Rosi. 1994a. *Nomadic Subjects: Embodiment and Sexual Difference in Contemporary Feminist Theory*. New York: Columbia University Press.

Braidotti, Rosi. 1994b. 'What's Wrong with Gender?', in Fokkelien van Dijk-Hemmers and Athalya Brenner (eds), *Reflections on Theology and Gender*. Kampen, The Netherlands: Kok Pharos Publishing House, 49–70.

Brooks, Geraldine. 1996. *Nine Parts of Desire: The Hidden World of Islamic Women*. Harmondsworth: Penguin.

Burke, Carolyn, Schor, Naomi, and Whitford, Margaret (eds). 1994. *Engaging with Irigaray: Feminist Philosophy and Modern European Thought*. New York: Columbia University Press.

Butler, Judith. 1987a. *Subjects of Desire: Hegelian Reflections in Twentieth-Century France*. Baltimore, MD: The Johns Hopkins University Press.

Butler, Judith. 1987b. 'Variations on Sex and Gender: Beauvoir, Wittig, Foucault', in Benhabib and Cornell (eds), *Feminism as Critique*, 128–42.

Butler, Judith. 1990. *Gender Trouble: Feminism and the Subversion of Identity*. London: Routledge.

Bynum, Caroline Walker, Harrell, Stevan, and Richman, Paula (eds). 1986. *Gender and Religion: On the Complexity of Symbols*. Boston, MA: Beacon Press.

Calasso, Roberto. 1994. *The Marriage of Cadmus and Harmony*. London: Vintage.

Canters, Hanneke. Forthcoming. 'A Different Way of Thinking and Writing: Looking Closely at Luce Irigaray and Toni Morrison'. Unpublished Ph.D. Thesis, University of Sunderland.

Carmody, Denise Lardner. 1989 (1979). *Women and World Religions*. Englewood Cliffs, NJ: Prentice Hall.

Cavarero, Adriana. 1995. *In Spite of Plato: A Feminist Rewriting of Ancient Philosophy*, trans. Serena Anderlini-D'Onofrio and Aine O'Healy. Cambridge: Polity Press.

Chanter, Tina. 1995. *Ethics of Eros: Irigaray's Rewriting of the Philosophers*. London: Routledge.

Chisholm, Dianne. 1994. 'Irigaray's Hysteria', in Burke, Schor, and Whitford (eds), *Engaging with Irigaray*, 263–84.

Chopp, Rebecca. 1993. 'From Patriarchy into Freedom: A Conversation Between American Feminist Theology and French Feminisms', in C. W. Maggie Kim, Susan M. St Ville, and Susan M. Simonaitis (eds), *Transfigurations: Theology and the French Feminists*. Minneapolis, MN: Augsburg Fortress Press, 31–48.

Christ, Carol P. and Plaskow, Judith (eds). 1989. *Weaving the Visions: New Patterns in Feminist Spirituality*. San Francisco, CA: HarperCollins.

Christ, Carol P. and Plaskow, Judith (eds). 1992 (1979). *Womanspirit Rising: A Feminist Reader in Religion*. San Francisco, CA: HarperCollins.

Cixous, Hélène. 1986. 'Sorties: Out and Out: Attacks/Ways Out/Forays', in *The Newly Born Woman*, trans. Betsy Wing. Minneapolis, MN: University of Minnesota Press.

Cixous, Hélène. 1993. 'We Who Are Free, Are We Free?', in Barbara Johnson (ed.), *Freedom and Interpretation: The Oxford Amnesty Lectures 1992*. New York: Basic Books, 17–44.

Clark, Kelly James. 1990. *Return to Reason*. Grand Rapids, MI: William B. Eerdmans.

Clemit, Pamela. 1993. *The Godwinian Novel: The Rational Fictions of Godwin, Brockden Brown, Mary Shelley*. Oxford: Clarendon Press.
Coakley, Sarah. 1996. 'Feminism', in Quinn and Taliaferro (eds), *A Companion to Philosophy of Religion*, 601–6.
Code, Lorraine. 1988. 'Experience, Knowledge and Responsibility', in Griffiths and Whitford (eds), *Feminist Perspectives in Philosophy*, 187–204.
Code, Lorraine. 1993a. 'Feminst Epistemology', in Jonathan Dancy and E. Sosa (eds), *A Companion to Epistemology*. Oxford: Blackwell, 138–42.
Code, Lorraine. 1993b. 'Taking Subjectivity into Account', in Alcoff and Potter (eds), *Feminist Epistemologies*, 15–48.
Code, Lorraine. 1995. *Rhetorical Spaces: Essays on Gendered Locations*. London: Routledge.
Collins (see Hill Collins).
Conze, Edward. 1959. *Buddism: Its Essence and Development*. Oxford: Oxford University Press.
Cornell, Drucilla. 1991. *Beyond Accommodation: Ethical Feminism, Deconstruction and the Law*. London: Routledge.
Cornell, Drucilla. 1993. *Transformations*. London: Routledge.
Cornell, Drucilla. 1995a. *The Imaginary Domain: Abortion, Pornography and Sexual Harassement*. London: Routledge.
Cornell, Drucilla. 1995b. 'What is Ethical Feminism?' and 'Rethinking the Time of Feminism', in *Feminist Contentions: A Philosophical Exchange*, introduced by Linda Nicholson. London: Routledge, 75–106 and 145–56.
Corner, Mark. 1991. *Does God Exist?* Bristol: Bristol Classical Press.
Craig, William Lane. 1989. '"No Other Name": A Middle Knowledge Perspective on the Exclusivity of Salvation through Christ', *Faith and Philosophy* 6, 172–88.
Daly, Mary. 1986 (1973). *Beyond God the Father: Towards a Philosophy of Women's Liberation*. London: The Women's Press.
Daly, Mary. 1987 (1978). *Gyn/Ecology: The MetaEthics of Radical Feminism*. Boston, MA: Beacon Press.
Daly, Mary. 1992a. *Outercourse: The Be-dazzling Voyage*. San Francisco, CA: HarperCollins.
Daly, Mary 1992b (1984). *Pure Lust: Elemental Feminist Philosophy*. San Francisco, CA: HarperCollins.
Davies, Brian. 1993 (1982). *An Introduction to the Philosophy of Religion*. Oxford: Oxford University Press.
Davis (see Franks Davis).
Delaney, C. F. (ed.). 1979. *Rationality and Religious Belief*. Notre Dame, IN: University of Notre Dame Press.

Derrida, Jacques. 1976. *Of Grammatology*, trans. Gayatri Chakravorty Spivak. Baltimore, MD: The Johns Hopkins University Press.

Descartes, René. 1986 (1641). *Meditations on First Philosophy*, trans. John Cottingham. Cambridge: Cambridge University Press.

Descombes, Vincent. 1980. *Modern French Philosophy*, trans. Lorna Scott-Fox and J. M. Harding. Cambridge: Cambridge University Press.

Dews, Peter. 1993. 'The Crisis of Oedipal Identity: Between Lacan and the Frankfurt School', in Kunneman and Vries (eds), *Enlightenments*, 357–77.

Dhanda, Meena. 1994. 'Openness, Identity and Acknowledgement of Persons', in Lennon and Whitford (eds), *Knowing the Difference*, 249–64.

Draper, Hal. 1977. *Karl Marx's Theory of Revolution: Part One. State and Bureaucracy*. New York: Monthly Review Press.

Elliott, Terri. 1994. 'Making Strange What Had Appeared Familiar', *The Monist: An International Journal of General Philosophical Inquiry* (General Topic – 'Feminist Epistemology: For and Against'), 77: 4 (October), 424–33.

Falk, Nancy Auer and Gross, Rita M. (eds). 1980. *Unspoken Worlds: Women's Religious Lives in Non-Western Cultures*. San Francisco, CA: Harper and Row.

Feuerbach, Ludwig. 1972. 'Preliminary Theses on the Reform of Philosophy', *Fiery Brook: Selected Writings of Ludwig Feuerbach*, trans. Zawar Hanfi. New York: Doubleday Press.

Feuerbach, Ludwig. 1989. *The Essence of Christianity*, trans. George Elliot. New York: Prometheus Books.

Fiorenza (see Schüssler Fiorenza).

Flax, Jane. 1983. 'Political Philosophy and the Patriarchal Unconscious: A Psychoanalytic Perspective on Epistemology and Metaphysics', in Harding and Hintikka (eds), *Discovering Reality*, 245–81.

Flax, Jane. 1990. *Thinking Fragments: Psychoanalysis, Feminism and Postmodernism in the Contemporary West*. Berkeley, CA: University of California Press.

Fodor, James. 1995. *Christian Hermeneutics: Paul Ricœur and the Refiguring of Theology*. Oxford: Clarendon Press

Frankenberry, Nancy. 1987. *Religion and Radical Empiricism*. Albany, NY: State University of New York.

Frankenberry, Nancy. 1994. 'Introduction: Prolegomenon to Future Feminist Philosophers of Religions', *Hypatia: A Journal of Feminist Philosophy*, (Special Issue: Feminist Philosophy of Religion), 9: 4 (Fall), 1–14.

Frankfort, Henri and Frankfort, Mrs Henri. 1949. 'Myth and Reality', *Before Philosophy*. Harmondsworth: Pelican Books, 11–36.

Franks Davis, Caroline. 1989. *The Evidential Force of Religious Experience.* Oxford: Clarendon Press.

Freud, Sigmund. 1951–73. *The Standard Edition of the Complete Psychological Works of Sigmund Freud*, 24 vols, trans. and ed. James Strachey, with Alix Strachey. London: The Hogarth Press.

Freud, Sigmund. 1971 (1923). 'The Ego and the Id', in Freud (1951–73), *The Standard Edition*, vol. 19, 1–66.

Freud, Sigmund. 1973 (1931). 'The Future of an Illusion' and 'Female Sexuality', in Freud (1951–73), *The Standard Edition*, vol. 21, 1–56 and 223–43.

Freud, Sigmund. 1961. 'The Uncanny', in Freud (1951–73), *The Standard Edition*, vol. 17.

Freud, Sigmund. 1991 (1915). 'Fixation to Traumas – The Unconscious', in *Introductory Lectures on Psychoanalysis*, vol. 1, The Penguin Freud Library, trans. James Strachey, ed. Angela Richards. Harmondsworth: Penguin.

Fricker, Miranda. 1994. 'Knowledge as Construct: Theorizing the Role of Gender in Knowledge', in Lennon and Whitford (eds), *Knowing the Difference*, 95–109.

Fricker, Miranda. 1996 (1995). 'Why "Female" Intuition?', *Women's Philosophy Review*, 5 (June), 36–44.

Furlong, Iris. 1992. 'The Mythology of the Ancient Near East', in Larrington (ed.), *The Feminist Companion to Mythology*, 3–22

Gale, Richard. 1991. *On the Nature and Existence of God.* Cambridge: Cambridge University Press.

Gandhi, Mahatma. 1926. 'Tough Questions', *Collected Works of Mahatma Gandhi*, vol. XXXI. New Delhi: Publications Division.

Gandhi, Mahatma. 1957 (1940). *An Autobiography: The Story of My Experiments with Truth.* Boston, MA: Beacon Press.

Gandhi, Mahatma. 1959. *What Jesus Means to Me*, comp. R. K. Prabhu. Ahmedabad, India: Navajiran Publishing House.

Garry, Ann and Pearsall, Marilyn (eds). 1996 (1992, 1989). *Women, Knowledge and Reality: Explorations in Feminist Philosophy*, second edition. New York and London: Routledge.

Gatens, Moira. 1991a. 'A Critique of the Sex/Gender Distinction', in Sneja Gunew (ed), *A Reader in Feminist Knowledge.* London: Routledge, 139–57.

Gatens, Moira. 1991b. *Feminism and Philosophy: Perspectives on Difference and Equality.* Cambridge: Polity Press.

Gatens, Moira. 1996. *Imaginary Bodies: Ethics, Power and Corporeality.* London: Routledge.

Goldenberg, Naomi. 1993. *Resurrecting the Body: Feminism, Religion and Psychoanalysis*. New York: Crossroads.

Goldenberg, Naomi. 1995a. Psychoanalysis and Religion: A Feminist Atheist's Perspective on Recent Work', in Joy and Neumaier-Dargyay (eds), *Gender, Genre and Religion*, 101–15.

Goldenberg, Naomi. 1995b. 'Return of the Goddess: Psychoanalytic Reflections on the Shift from Theology to Thealogy', in King (ed.), *Religion and Gender*, 145–64.

Goux, Jean-Joseph. 1994. *Oedipus, Philosopher*, trans. Catherine Porter. Stanford, CA: Stanford University Press.

Green, Karen. 1995. *The Woman of Reason: Feminism, Humanism and Political Thought*. Oxford: Polity Press.

Griffiths, Morwenna and Whitford, Margaret (eds). 1988. *Feminist Perspectives in Philosophy*. Bloomington, IN: Indiana University Press.

Grosz, Elizabeth. 1989. *Sexual Subversion: Three French Feminists*. London and Sydney: Allen and Unwin.

Grosz, Elizabeth. 1993a. 'Bodies and Knowledges: Feminism and the Crisis of Reason', in Alcoff and Potter (eds), *Feminist Epistemologies*, 187–215.

Grosz, Elizabeth. 1993b. 'Irigaray and the Divine', in C. W. Maggie Kim, Susan M. St Ville, and Susan M. Simonaitis (eds), *Transfigurations: Theology and the French Feminists*. Minneapolis, MN: Augsburg Fortress Press, 199–214.

Haack, Susan. 1994. *Evidence and Inquiry: Towards Reconstruction and Epistemology*. Oxford: Blackwell.

Hampson, Daphne. 1990. *Theology and Feminism*. Oxford: Blackwell.

Hampson, Daphne. 1996. *After Christianity*. London: SCM Press.

Hankinson Nelson, Lynn. 1990. *Who Knows: From Quine to a Feminist Empiricism*. Philadelphia, PA: Temple University Press.

Hankinson Nelson, Lynn. 1993. 'Epistemological Communities', in Alcoff and Potter (eds), *Feminist Epistemologies*, 121–59.

Hankinson Nelson, Lynn and Nelson, Jack. 1995. 'No Rush to Judgment', *The Monist: An International Quarterly Journal of General Philosophical Inquiry*, 77: 4 (October), 486–508.

Haraway, Donna. 1988. 'Situated Knowledges: The Science Question in Feminism and the Privilege of Partial Perspective', *Feminist Studies*, 14: 3 (Fall), 575–99.

Haraway, Donna. 1990 (1989). 'A Manifesto for Cyborgs: Science, Technology and Socialist Feminism in the 1980s', in Elizabeth Weedon (ed.), *Coming to Terms with Feminism, Theory, Politics*. New York: Routledge, 173–204. Reprinted 1990, in Linda Nicholson (ed.), *Feminism/Postmodernism*. London: Routledge, 190–233.

Harding, Sandra. 1976. 'Feminism: Reform or Revolution', in Carol Gould and Marx Wartofsky (eds), *Women and Philosophy: Toward a Theory of Liberation*. New York: Perigree Books, 271–84.

Harding, Sandra. 1983. 'Why Has the Sex/Gender System Become Visible Only Now?', in Harding and Hintikka (eds), *Discovering Reality*, 311–24.

Harding, Sandra. 1986. *The Science Question in Feminism*. Ithaca, NY: Cornell University Press; Buckingham, UK: Open University Press.

Harding, Sandra. 1987. 'The Instability of the Analytical Categories of Feminist Theory', in Sandra Harding and Jean F. O'Barr (eds), *Sex and Scientific Inquiry*. Chicago, IL: University of Chicago Press, 283–302.

Harding, Sandra. 1990. 'Feminism, Science and the Anti-Enlightenment Critiques', in Linda Nicholson (ed.), *Feminism/Postmodernism*. London: Routledge, 83–106.

Harding, Sandra. 1991. *Whose Science? Whose Knowledge? Thinking from Women's Lives*. Ithaca, NY: Cornell University Press; Buckingham, UK: Open University Press.

Harding, Sandra. 1993. 'Rethinking Standpoint Epistemology: What is "Strong Objectivity"?' in Alcoff and Potter (eds), *Feminist Epistemologies*, 49–82.

Harding, Sandra and Hintikka, Merrill (eds). 1983. *Discovering Reality: Feminist Perspectives on Epistemology, Metaphysics, Methodology and Philosophy of Science*. Dordrecht, Holland: Reidel.

Harrison, Jane Ellen. 1980 (1903). *Prolegomena to the Study of Greek Religion*. London: Merlin Press.

Hartsock, Nancy C. M. 1983. 'The Feminist Standpoint: Developing The Ground for a Specifically Feminist Historical Materialism', in Harding and Hintikka (eds), *Discovering Reality*, 283–310.

Hawley, John Stratton. 1986. 'Images of Gender in the Poetry of Krishna', in Bynum, Harrell, and Richman (eds), *Gender and Religion*, 231–56.

Hegel, Georg Wilhelm Friedrich. 1968. *Lectures on the History of Philosophy*, vol. 1, trans. Elizabeth Haldane. New York: Humanities Press.

Hegel, Georg Wilhelm Friedrich. 1977. *Phenomenology of Spirit*, trans. A. V. Miller. Oxford: Oxford University Press.

Hegel, Georg Wilhelm Friedrich. 1991. *Elements of a Philosophy of Right*, trans. H. B. Nisbet, introduced by Allen Wood. Cambridge: Cambridge University Press.

Hein, Hilde. 1996 (1992). 'Liberating Philosophy: An End to the Dichotomy of Spirit and Matter', in Garry and Pearsall (eds), *Women, Knowledge and Reality*, 437–53.

Hennessy, Rosemary. 1993. 'Women's Lives/Feminist Knowledge: Feminist Standpoint as Ideology Critique', *Hypatia: A Journal of Feminist Philosophy*, 8: 1 (Winter), 14–34.

Hester, Marcus (ed.). 1992. *Faith, Reason and Skepticism*. Philadelphia, PA: Temple University Press.

Hewitt, Marsha Aileen. 1995. *Critical Theory of Religion: A Feminist Analysis*. Minneapolis, MN: Augsburg Fortress Press.

Hick, John. 1978 (1963). *Evil and the God of Love*. New York: Harper and Row.

Hick, John. 1990. *A John Hick Reader*, ed. Paul Badham. London: Macmillan.

Hill Collins, Patricia. 1986. 'Learning from the Outsider Within: The Sociological Significance of Black Feminist Thought', *Social Problems* 33: 6, 14–32.

Hill Collins, Patricia. 1991. *Black Feminist Thought: Knowledge, Consciousness and the Politics of Empowerment*. London: Routledge.

Holtzer, Steven W. 1987. 'The Possibility of Incorporeal Agency', in Abraham and Holtzer (eds), 1987. *The Rationality of Religious Belief*, 189–209.

Homer. 1980. *The Odyssey*, World's Classics, trans. Walter Shewring, introduced by G. S. Kirk. Oxford: Oxford University Press.

hooks, bell. 1981. *Ain't I a Woman? Black Women and Feminism*. Boston, MA: South End Press.

hooks, bell. 1984. *Feminist Theory: From Margin to Center*. Boston, MA: South End Press.

hooks, bell. 1990. *Yearning: Race, Gender and Cultural Politics*. Boston, MA: South End Press.

hooks, bell and West, Cornell. 1991. *Breaking Bread: Insurgent Black Intellectual Life*. Boston, MA: South End Press.

Horkheimer, Max and Adorno, Theodor W. 1972. *Dialectic of Enlightenment*, trans. John Cumming. New York: Continuum, Seabury Press. Second edition, 1986. London: Verso.

Horowitz, Gad and Kaufman, Michael. 1987. 'Male Sexuality: Toward a Theory of Liberation', in Michael Kaufman (ed.), *Beyond Patriarchy*. Oxford: Oxford University Press, 81–102.

Irigaray, Luce. 1985a. *Speculum of the Other Woman*, trans. Gillian C. Gill. Ithaca, NY: Cornell University Press.

Irigaray, Luce. 1985b. *This Sex Which is Not One*, trans. Catherine Porter. Ithaca, NY: Cornell University Press.

Irigaray, Luce. 1989. 'Equal to Whom?', *Differences*, 1, 59–76.

Irigaray, Luce. 1991a. 'Love Between Us', in Eduardo Cadava, Peter

Connor, and Jean-Luc Nancy (eds), *Who Comes After the Subject?* London: Routledge, 167–77.

Irigaray, Luce. 1991b. *The Irigaray Reader*, ed. Margaret Whitford. Oxford: Blackwell.

Irigaray, Luce. 1991c. *Marine Lover of Friedrich Nietzsche*, trans. Gillian C. Gill. New York: Columbia University Press.

Irigaray, Luce. 1992. *Elemental Passions*, trans. Joanne Collie and Judith Still. London: The Athlone Press.

Irigaray, Luce. 1993a. *An Ethics of Sexual Difference*, trans. Carolyn Burke and Gillian Gill. Ithaca, NY: Cornell University Press; London: The Athlone Press.

Irigaray, Luce. 1993b. *Je, Tu, Nous: Toward a Culture of Difference*, trans. Alison Martin. New York and London: Routledge.

Irigaray, Luce. 1993c. *Sexes and Genealogies*, trans. Gillian C. Gill. New York: Columbia University Press.

Irigaray, Luce. 1994. *Thinking the Difference: Towards a Peaceful Revolution*, trans. Alison Montin. London: The Athlone Press.

Irigaray, Luce. 1995. 'Je – Luce Irigaray: A Meeting with Luce Irigaray', trans. Elizabeth Hirsch and Gaëton Brulotte, *Hypatia: A Journal of Feminist Philosophy*, 10: 2 (Spring), 96–114.

Irigaray, Luce. 1996. *I Love to You: Sketch of a Possible Felicity in History*, trans. Alison Martin. London: Routledge.

Jagentowicz Mills, Patricia. 1986. 'Hegel's *Antigone*', *The Owl of Minerva* (Spring), 131–52.

Jagentowicz Mills, Patricia. 1987. *Woman, Nature and Psyche*. London: Yale University Press.

Jaggar, Alison. 1983. *Feminist Politics and Human Nature*. Totowa, NJ: Rowman and Allanheld.

Jantzen, Grace. 1984. *God's World, God's Body*. Harlow, Essex: Longman.

Jantzen, Grace. 1987. 'Conspicuous Sanctity and Religious Belief', in Abraham and Holtzer (eds), *The Rationality of Religious Belief*, 121–40.

Jantzen, Grace. 1994. 'Feminists, Philosophers and Mystics', *Hypatia: A Journal of Feminist Philosophy* (Special Issue: Feminist Philosophy of Religion), 9: 4 (Fall), 186–206.

Jantzen, Grace. 1995. *Power, Gender and Christian Mysticism*. Cambridge: Cambridge University Press.

Jasper, Alison. 1996. 'The Shining Garment of the Text: Feminist Criticism and Interpretative Strategy for Readers of John 1:1–18'. Unpublished Ph.D. Thesis, Faculty of Divinity, University of Glasgow, Scotland.

Jay, Martin. 1993. *Downcast Eyes*. Berkeley, CA: University of California Press.

Johnson, Pauline. 1996. 'Nietzsche Reception Today', *Radical Philosophy: A Journal of Socialist and Feminist Philosophy* 80 (November/December), 24–33.

Joy, Morny. 1990. 'Equality or Divinity – A False Dichotomy?', *Journal of Feminist Studies in Religion*, 6: 1, 9–24.

Joy, Morny. Forthcoming. 'Passionate Involvements: Luce Irigaray and an Erotics of Ethics and Hermeneutics', in Gary Madison (ed.), *Ethics and Hermeneutics*. Evanston, IL: Northwestern University Press.

Joy, Morny and Neumaier-Dargyay, Eva K. (eds). 1995. *Gender, Genre and Religion: Feminist Reflections*. Waterloo, Ontario: Wilfrid Laurier University Press.

Kant, Immanuel. 1950 (1781, 1787). *Critique of Pure Reason*, trans. Norman Kemp Smith. London: Macmillan.

Kant, Immanuel. 1951 (1785). *Groundwork of the Metaphysics of Morals*, trans. H. J. Paton, *The Moral Law*. London: Hutchinson.

Kant, Immanuel. 1956 (1788). *Critique of Practical Reason*, trans. and introduced by Lewis White Beck. Indianapolis, IN: Bobbs-Merrill Educational Publishing.

Kant, Immanuel. 1960 (1793). *Religion within the Limits of Reason Alone*, trans. Theodore Greene and Hoyt Hudson. New York: Harper and Row.

Kates, Judith A. and Reimer, Gail Twersky (eds). 1994. *Reading Ruth: Contemporary Women Reclaim a Sacred Story*. New York: Ballantine Books.

Kearney, Richard. 1996. 'Narrative and Ethics', in *The Aristotelian Society, Supplementary Volume, LXX: The Symposia Read at the Joint Session of the Aristotelian Society and the Mind Association at University College, Dublin, July 1996*. Bristol: The Longdunn Press Ltd., 29–45.

Kearns, Emily. 1992. 'Indian Myth', in Larrington (ed.), *The Feminist Companion to Mythology*, 189–226.

King, Ursula (ed.). 1995. *Religion and Gender*. Oxford: Blackwell.

Knott, Kim. 1987. 'Men and Women, or Devotees? Krishna Consciousness and the Role of Women', in Ursula King (ed.), *Women in the World's Religions, Past and Present*. New York: Paragon Press, 111–28.

Kojève, Alexandre. 1980 (1947). *Introduction to the Reading of Hegel*, trans. James H. Nichols. Ithaca, NY: Cornell University Press.

Kolakowski, Leszek. 1989. *The Presence of Myth*, trans. Adam Czerniawski. Chicago, IL: University of Chicago Press.

Kollwitz, Käthe. 1989. *Die Tagebücher*, ed. Jutta Bohnke-Kollwitz. Berlin: Siedler.

Korsgaard, Christine M. 1995. 'A Note on the Value of Gender-Identification', in Nussbaum and Glover (eds), *Women, Culture and Development*, 401–4.

Korsgaard, Christine M. 1996. *Creating the Kingdom of Ends*. Cambridge: Cambridge University Press.

Kosman, Aryeh. 1992. 'Acting: Drama as the Mimesis of Praxis', in Amelie Oksenberg Rorty (ed.), *Essays on Aristotle's Poetics*. Princeton, NJ: Princeton University Press, 51–72.

Kretzmann, Norman. 1988. 'Warring Against the Law of My Mind: Aquinas on Romans 7', in Thomas V. Morris (ed.), *Philosophy and the Christian Faith*. Notre Dame, IN: University of Notre Dame Press, 172–95.

Kretzmann, Norman. 1997. *The Metaphysics of Theism: Aquinas' Natural Theology in Summa Contra Gentiles*, I. Oxford: Clarendon Press.

Kristeva, Julia. 1980 (1977). *Desire in Language: A Semiotic Approach to Literature and Art*, trans. Thomas Gora, Alice Jardine, and Leon S. Roudiez. New York: Columbia University Press.

Kristeva, Julia. 1982 (1980). *Powers of Horror: An Essay on Abjection*, trans. Leon S. Roudiez. New York: Columbia University Press.

Kristeva, Julia. 1984 (1974). *Revolution in Poetic Language*, trans. Margaret Waller, introduced by Leon S. Roudiez. New York: Columbia University Press.

Kristeva, Julia. 1986. *The Kristeva Reader*, ed. Toril Moi. Oxford: Blackwell.

Kristeva, Julia. 1987a (1985). *In the Beginning was Love: Faith and Psychoanalysis*, trans. Arthur Goldhammer, introduced by Otto F. Kernberg. New York: Columbia University Press.

Kristeva, Julia. 1987b (1983). *Tales of Love*, trans. Leon S. Roudiez. New York: Columbia University Press.

Kristeva, Julia. 1989 (1987). *Black Sun: Depression and Melancholia*, trans. Leon S. Roudiez. New York: Columbia University Press.

Kristeva, Julia. 1991. *Strangers to Ourselves*, trans. Leon S. Roudiez. New York: Columbia University Press.

Kristeva, Julia. 1992. *Talking Liberties*, ed. Derek Jones and Rod Stoneman. London: Channel 4 Television Broadcasting Support Services, 16–17.

Kristeva, Julia. 1993a. *Nations without Nationalism*, trans. Leon S. Roudiez. New York: Columbia University Press.

Kristeva, Julia. 1993b. 'The Speaking Subject is not Innocent', in Barbara Johnson (ed.), *Freedom and Interpretation: Oxford Amnesty Lectures*. New York: Basic Books, 156–60.

Kristeva, Julia. 1995. *New Maladies of the Soul*, trans. Ross Guberman. New York: Columbia University Press.

Kunneman, Harry and Vries, Hent de (eds). 1993. *Enlightenments: Encounters between Critical Theory and Contemporary French Thought*. Kampen, The Netherlands: Kok Pharos Publishing House.

Lacan, Jacques. 1977. *Ecrits: A Selection*, trans. Alan Sheridan. London: Tavistock.

Larrington, Carolyne (ed.). 1992. *The Feminist Companion to Mythology*. London: Pandora Press.

Lazreg, Marnia. 1990. 'Feminism and Difference: The Perils of Writing as a Woman on Women in Algeria', in Marianne Hirsch and Evelyn Fox Keller (eds), *Conflicts in Feminism*. London: Routledge, 326–48.

Lazreg, Marnia. 1994. 'Women's Experience and Feminist Epistemology: A Critical Neo-Rationalist Approach', in Lennon and Whitford (eds), *Knowing the Difference*, 45–62.

Lechte, John. 1990. *Julia Kristeva*. London: Routledge.

Lechte, John. 1994. *Fifty Key Contemporary Thinkers*. London: Routledge.

Le Doeuff, Michèle. 1989. *The Philosophical Imaginary*, trans. Colin Gordon. London: The Athlone Press.

Le Doeuff, Michèle. 1990. 'Women, Reason, Etc.', *Differences*, 2: 3, 1–13.

Le Doeuff, Michèle. 1991. *Hipparchia's Choice: An Essay Concerning Women, Philosophy, Etc.*, trans. Trista Selous. Oxford: Blackwell.

Lennon, Kathleen and Whitford, Margaret (eds). 1994. *Knowing the Difference: Feminist Perspectives in Epistemology*. London: Routledge.

Lerner, Gerda. 1993. *The Creation of Feminist Consciousness: From the Middle Ages to Eighteen-Seventy*. New York: Oxford University Press.

Levinas, Emmanuel. 1987. *Time and the Other*, trans. Richard A. Cohen. Pittsburgh, PA: Duquesne University Press.

Lloyd, Genevieve. 1993 (1984). *The Man of Reason: 'Male' and 'Female' in Western Philosophy*. London: Routledge.

Loades, Ann and Rue, Loyal D. (eds). 1991. *Contemporary Classics in Philosophy of Religion*. La Salle, IL: Open Court Publishing Company.

Locke, John. 1975. *An Essay Concerning Human Understanding*, ed. P. H. Niddith. Oxford: Clarendon Press.

Longino, Helen. 1990. *Science as Social Knowledge: Values and Objectivity in Scientific Inquiry*. Princeton, NJ: Princeton University Press.

Longino, Helen. 1994. 'In Search of Feminist Epistemology, *The Monist: An International Journal of General Philosophical Inquiry* (General Topic – 'Feminist Epistemology: For and Against'), 77: 4 (October), 472–85.

Lorde, Audre. 1983 (1981). 'An Open Letter to Mary Daly', in C. Moraga and G. Anzaldua (eds), *This Bridge Called My Back: Writings by Radical Women of Color*. New York: Kitchen Table, Women of Color Press, 94–7.

Lovibond, Sabina. 1989. 'Feminism and Postmodernism', *New Left Review*, 178 (November-December), 5–28.

Lovibond, Sabina. 1994a. 'Feminism and the "Crisis of Rationality"', *New Left Review*, 207 (September-October), 72–86.

Lovibond, Sabina. 1994b. 'The End of Morality?', in Lennon and Whitford (eds), *Knowing the Difference*, 63–78.

Mackie, J. L. 1955. 'Evil and Omnipotence', *Mind*, 64, 200–12.

Mackie, J. L. 1982. *The Miracle of Theism: Arguments For and Against the Existence of God*. Oxford: Clarendon Press.

Maeckelberghe, Els. 1994. *Desperately Seeking Mary: A Feminist Appropriation of a Traditional Religious Symbol*. Kampen, The Netherlands: Kok Pharos Publishing House.

Malcolm, Norman. 1977. 'The Groundlessness of Belief', in Stuart C. Brown (ed.), *Reason and Religion*. Ithaca, NY: Cornell University Press.

Mandela, Nelson. 1994. *Long Walk to Freedom*. London: Little, Brown and Company.

Martin, Michael. 1990. *Atheism: A Philosophical Justification*. Philadelphia, PA: Temple University Press.

Marx, Karl. 1992 (1974). 'On the Jewish Question (1843)', in Lucio Colletti (ed.), *Early Writings*, trans. Rodney Livingstone and Gregor Benton. Harmondsworth: Penguin, 243–57.

McCloskey, H. J. 1960. 'God and Evil', *The Philosophical Quarterly*, 10, 97–114.

McCord Adams, Marilyn. 1986. 'Redemptive Suffering: A Christian Solution to the Problem of Evil', in Audi and Wainwright (eds), *Rationality, Religious Belief and Moral Commitment*, 248–67.

McCord Adams, Marilyn. 1993. 'The Problem of Hell: A Problem of Evil for Christians', in Stump (ed.), *Reasoned Faith*, 301–27.

McCord Adams, Marilyn and Adams, Robert Merrihew (eds). 1990. *The Problem of Evil*. Oxford Readings in Philosophy. Oxford: Oxford University Press.

Merleau-Ponty, Maurice. 1964a. *Sense and Non-sense*, trans. Hubert and Patricia Dreyfus. Evanston, IL: Northwestern University Press.

Merleau-Ponty, Maurice. 1964b. *Signs*, trans. Richard C. McCleary. Evanston, IL: Northwestern University Press.

Mernissi, Fatima. 1993. *The Forgotten Queens of Islam*, trans. Mary Jo Lakeland. Cambridge: Polity Press.

Mernissi, Fatima. 1996. *Women's Rebellion and Islamic Memory*. London: Zed Books.

Meyers, Diana Tietjens. 1994. *Subjection and Subjectivity: Psychoanalytic Feminism and Moral Philosophy*. London: Routledge.

Midgley, Mary. 1984. *Wickedness*. London: Routledge and Kegan Paul.

Mitchell, Basil. 1973. *The Justification of Religious Belief*. London: Macmillan.

Moore, Adrian. 1997. *Points of View*. Oxford: Oxford University Press.

Morris, Thomas V. (ed.). 1994. *God and the Philosophers: The Reconciliation of Faith and Reason*. New York: Oxford University Press.

Mortley, Raoul. 1991. *French Philosophers in Conversation*. London: Routledge.

Moulton, Janice. 1992. 'A Paradigm of Philosophy: The Adversary Method' and 'The Myth of the Neutral "Man"', in Ann Garry and Marilyn Pearsall (eds), *Women, Knowledge and Reality: Explorations in Feminist Philosophy*, first edition. London: Routledge, 5–20 and 219–32.

Mukta, Parita. 1994. *Upholding the Common Life: The Community of Mirabai*. Delhi: Oxford University Press.

Mulhall, Stephen. 1994. *Faith and Reason*, Interpretation series, ed. Roy Harris. Trowbridge: Redwood Books.

Muraro, Luisa. 1994. 'Female Genealogies', in Burke, Schor, and Whitford (eds), *Engaging with Irigaray*, 327–31.

Murdoch, Iris. 1992. *Metaphysics as a Guide to Morals*. Harmondsworth: Penguin.

Nagel, Thomas. 1986. *The View from Nowhere*. New York: Oxford University Press.

Nagl-Docekal, Herta. 1993. 'Towards a Feminist Transformation of Philosophy', in Kunneman and Vries (eds), *Enlightenments*, 305–18.

Newman, Amy. 1994. 'Feminist Social Criticism and Marx's Theory of Religion', *Hypatia: A Journal of Feminist Philosophy* (Special Issue: Feminist Philosophy of Religion), 9:4 (Fall), 15–37.

Nicholson, Linda and Fraser, Nancy. 1990. 'Social Criticism without Philosophy', in Linda Nicholson (ed.), *Feminism/Postmodernism*. London: Routledge, 19–38.

Nietzsche, Friedrich. 1954. *The Portable Nietzsche*, ed. and trans. Walter Kaufman. Harmondsworth: Penguin.

Nietzsche, Friedrich. 1982. *Daybreak*, trans. R. J. Hollingdale. Cambridge: Cambridge University Press.

Nietzsche, Friedrich. 1989. *On the Genealogy of Morals*, trans. Walter Kaufman. New York: Vintage Books.

Noddings, Nel. 1984. *Caring: A Feminine Approach to Ethics and Moral Education*. Berkeley, CA: University of California Press.

Nussbaum, Martha. 1986. *Fragility of Goodness: Luck and Ethics in Greek Tragedy and Philosophy*. Cambridge: Cambridge University Press.

Nussbaum, Martha. 1992. 'Tragedy and Self-Sufficiency: Plato and Aristotle on Fear and Pity', in Amelie Oksenberg Rorty (ed.), *Essays on Aristotle's Poetics*. Princeton, NJ: Princeton University Press, 261–90.

Nussbaum, Martha. 1995. 'Emotions and Women's Capabilities', in Nussbaum and Glover (eds), *Women, Culture and Development*, 360–95.

Nussbaum, Martha and Glover, Jonathan (eds). 1995. *Women, Culture and Development: A Study of Human Capabilities*. Oxford: Clarendon Press.

Nussbaum, Martha and Sen, Amartya (eds). 1993. *The Quality of Life*. Oxford: Clarendon Press.

Nye, Andrea. 1992. 'Philosophy: A Woman's Thought or a Man's Discipline? The Letters of Abelard and Héloïse', *Hypatia: A Journal of Feminist Philosophy*, 7:3 (Summer), 1–22.

Nye, Andrea. 1994. *Philosophia: The Thought of Rosa Luxembourg, Simone Weil and Hannah Arendt*. London: Routledge.

O'Connor, June. 1991. 'Critical Response: Sin and Salvation from a Feminist Perspective', in Harold Hewitt, Jr (ed.), *Problems in the Philosophy of Religion: Critical Studies of the Work of John Hick*. London: Macmillan, 72–81.

O'Connor, June. 1995. 'The Epistemological Significance of Feminist Research in Religion', in King (ed.), *Religion and Gender*, 45–63.

Oliver, Kelly (ed.). 1993. *Ethics, Politics and Difference in Julia Kristeva's Writing*. London: Routledge.

O'Neill, Onora. 1989. *Constructions of Reason: Explorations of Kant's Practical Philosophy*. Cambridge: Cambridge University Press.

O'Neill, Onora. 1992. 'Vindicating Reason', in Paul Guyer (ed.), *A Companion to Kant*. Cambridge: Cambridge University Press, 280–308.

O'Neill, Onora. 1993. 'Justice, Gender and International Boundaries', in Nussbaum and Sen (eds), *The Quality of Life*, 303–23.

O'Neill, Onora. 1995. 'Justice, Capabilities and Vulnerabilities', in Nussbaum and Glover (eds), *Women, Culture and Development*, 140–52.

O'Neill, Onora. 1996. *Towards Justice and Virtue: A Constructive Account of Practical Reasoning*. Cambridge: Cambridge University Press.

Otto, Rudolf. 1923. *The Idea of the Holy: An Inquiry into the Non-rational factor in the Idea of the Divine and its Relation to the Rational*, trans. John W. Harvey. Oxford: Oxford University Press.

Ovid. 1955. *Metamorphoses*, trans. and introduced by Mary Innes. Harmondsworth: Penguin Classics.

Padgett, Alan G. (ed.). 1994. *Reason and the Christian Religion: Essays in Honour of Richard Swinburne*. Oxford: Clarendon Press.

Pastin, Mark. 1975. 'Modest Foundationalism and Self-Warrant', *American Philosophical Quarterly Monograph*, Series 9, 141–9.

Pateman, Carole. 1988. *The Sexual Contract*. Cambridge: Polity Press.

Phillips, D. Z. 1970. *Faith and Philosophical Enquiry*. London: Routledge and Kegan Paul.

Phillips, D. Z. 1986. *Belief, Change and Forms of Life*. London: Macmillan.

Phillips, D. Z. 1988. *Faith and Foundationalism*. London: Routledge and Kegan Paul.

Phillips, D. Z. 1993. *Wittgenstein and Religion*, Swansea Studies in Philosophy. London: Macmillan.

Pizan, Christine de. 1983 (1405). *The Book of the City of Ladies*, trans. Earl Jeffrey Richards. London: Picador.

Plantinga, Alvin. 1967. *God and Other Minds: A Study of the Rational Justification of Belief in God*. Ithaca, NY: Cornell University Press.

Plantinga, Alvin. 1979. 'The Probabilistic Argument from Evil', *Philosophical Studies*, 35, 1–53.

Plantinga, Alvin. 1981. 'Is Belief in God Properly Basic?', *Nous*, XV:1 (March), 41–51.

Plantinga, Alvin. 1983. 'Reason and Belief in God', in Plantinga and Wolterstorff (eds), *Faith and Rationality*, 16–93.

Plantinga, Alvin. 1992. 'Epistemology of Religious Belief', in Jonathan Dancy (ed.), *A Companion to Epistemology*. Oxford: Blackwell, 436–41.

Plantinga, Alvin. 1993. *Warrant and Proper Function*. New York: Oxford University Press.

Plantinga, Alvin and Wolterstorff, Nicholas (eds). 1983. *Faith and Rationality: Reason and Belief in God*. Notre Dame and London: University of Notre Dame Press.

Plato. 1977. *Timaeus and Critias*, trans. and introduced with an appendix by Desmond Lee. Harmondsworth: Penguin.

Prendergast, Christopher. 1986. 'The Order of Mimesis: Poison, Nausea, Health', 'The Economy of Mimesis' and 'Conclusion. Mimesis: A Matter for the Police?', *The Order of Mimesis: Balzac, Stendahl, Nerval, Flaubert*. Cambridge: Cambridge University Press, 1–24, 24–82 and 212–53.

Prevost, Robert. 1990. *Probability and Theistic Explanation*. Oxford: Oxford University Press.

Purkiss, Diane. 1992. 'Women's Rewriting of Myth', in Larrington (ed.), *The Feminist Companion to Mythology*, 441–57.

Quine, Willard van Orman. 1953. 'Two Dogmas of Empiricism' and 'Identity, Ostension and Hypostasis', *From a Logical Point of View: Logico-Philosophical Essays*. New York: Harper and Row, 20–46 and 65–79.

Quine, Willard van Orman. 1969. *Ontological Relativity and Other Essays*. New York: Columbia University Press.

Quinn, Philip. 1993. 'Abelard on Atonement: "Nothing Unintelligible, Arbitrary, Illogical or Immoral about It"', in Stump (ed.), *Reasoned Faith*, 281–300.

Quinn, Philip and Taliaferro, Charles (eds). 1996. *A Companion to Philosophy of Religion*. Oxford: Blackwell.

Radcliffe Richards, Janet. 1991 (1980) *The Sceptical Feminist: A Philosophical Enquiry*, second edition. Harmondsworth: Penguin.

Ranke-Heinemann, Uta. 1991. *Eunuchs for the Kingdom of Heaven: Women, Sexuality and the Church*. Harmondsworth: Penguin.

Rich, Adrienne. 1979. *On Lies, Secrets and Silence: Selected Prose 1966–78*. New York: Norton.

Rich, Adrienne. 1986. *Blood, Bread and Poetry: Selected Prose 1979–85*. New York: Norton.

Rich, Adrienne. 1995 (1986). *Of Woman Born: Motherhood as Experience and Institution*. New York: Norton.

Ricoeur, Paul. 1960. *Finitude et culpabilité, II. La symbolique du mal*. Paris: Aubier, Editions Montaigne.

Ricoeur, Paul. 1967. *The Symbolism of Evil*, trans. Emerson Buchanan. New York and London: Harper and Row.

Ricoeur, Paul. 1970. *Freud and Philosophy: An Essay on Interpretation*, trans. Denis Savage. New Haven, CT: Yale University Press.

Ricoeur, Paul. 1977. *The Rule of Metaphor*, trans. Robert Czerney. Toronto: University of Toronto Press.

Ricoeur, Paul. 1984–88. *Time and Narrative*, vols 1–3, trans. Kathleen (McLaughlin) Blamey and David Pellauer. Chicago, IL: University of Chicago Press.

Ricoeur, Paul. 1991. 'Life in Quest of Narrative', in David Wood (ed.), *On Paul Ricoeur: Narrative and Interpretation*. London: Routledge, 20–33.

Ricoeur, Paul. 1992. *Oneself as Another*, trans. Kathleen Blamey. Chicago, IL: University of Chicago Press.

Rooney, Phyllis. 1991. 'Gendered Reason: Sex Metaphor and Conceptions of Reason', *Hypatia: A Journal of Feminist Philosophy*, 6:2 (Summer), 77–103.

Rooney, Phyllis. 1993. 'Feminist–Pragmatist Revisionings of Reason, Knowledge and Philosophy', *Hypatia: A Journal of Feminist Philosophy*, 8:2 (Spring), 15–37.

Rossi, Philip J. and Wreen, Michael (eds). 1991. *Kant's Philosophy of Religion Reconsidered*. Bloomington, IN: Indiana University Press.

Roth, Michael. 1988. *Knowing and History: Appropriations of Hegel in Twentieth-Century France*. Ithaca, NY: Cornell University Press.

Rowe, William. 1979. 'The Problem of Evil and Some Varieties of Atheism', *American Philosophical Quarterly*, 16, 335–41.

Rowe, William. 1984. 'Evil and the Theistic Hypothesis: A Response to Wykstra', *International Journal for the Philosophy of Religion*, 16, 95–100.

Rowe, William. 1986. 'The Empirical Argument from Evil', in Audi and Wainwright (eds), *Rationality, Religious Belief and Moral Commitment*, 227–47.

Rowe, William. 1989 (1973). *Philosophy of Religion: Selected Readings*, second edition. New York and London: Harcourt Brace Jovanovich.

Saiving (Goldstein), Valerie. 1992 (1979, 1960). 'The Human Situation: A Feminine View', in Christ and Plaskow (eds), *Womanspirit Rising*, 25–42.

Saussure, Ferdinand de. 1974. *Course in General Linguistics*, trans. Wade Baskin. London: Fontana.

Schaberg, Jane. 1995. *The Illegitimacy of Jesus: A Feminist Theological Interpretation of the Infancy Narratives*. Sheffield: Sheffield Academic Press.

Scheman, Naomi. 1994. 'Feminist Epistemology', Abstract of Invited Paper, *APA Proceedings and Addresses*, 68:1, 78–80.

Schor, Naomi. 1994. 'Previous Engagements: The Receptions of Irigaray' and 'This Essentialism Which is not One: Coming to Grips with Irigaray', in Burke, Schor, and Whitford (eds), *Engaging with Irigaray*, 3–14 and 57–78.

Schüssler Fiorenza, Elisabeth. 1975. 'Feminist Theology as a Critical Theology of Liberation', *Theological Studies*, 36:4, 605–26.

Schüssler Fiorenza, Elisabeth. 1995. *Jesus, Miriam's Child, Sophia's Prophet: Critical Issues in Feminist Christology*. London: SCM Press.

Schwab, Gail M. 1994. 'Mother's Body, Father's Tongue: Mediation and the Symbolic Order', in Burke, Schor, and Whitford (eds), *Engaging with Irigaray*, 351–78.

Scruton, Roger. 1983. *Kant*, Past Masters series, ed. Keith Thomas. Oxford: Oxford University Press.

Scruton, Roger. 1996. *Modern Philosophy: An Introduction and Survey*. London: Mandarin.

Sells, Laura. 1993. 'Feminist Epistemology: Rethinking the Dualisms of Atomic Knowledge', Review Essay, *Hypatia: A Journal of Feminist Philosophy*, 8:3 (Summer), 202–10.

Senor, Thomas D. (ed.). 1995. *The Rationality of Belief and the Plurality of Faith*. Ithaca, NY: Cornell University Press.

Smith, Barbara. 1992. 'Greece', in Larrington (ed.), *The Feminist Companion to Mythology*, 65–101.

Sophocles. 1984. *The Three Theban Plays: Antigone, Oedipus the King, Oedipus at Colonus*, trans. Robert Fagles, introduced by Bernard Knox. Oxford: Penguin Classics.

Soskice, Janet Martin. 1985. *Metaphor and Religious Language*. Oxford: Clarendon Press.

Soskice, Janet Martin. 1994. 'Blood and Defilement', *European Theology Bulletin*, 2, 230–41.

Spelman, Elizabeth. 1990 (1988). *Inessential Woman: Problems of Exclusion in Feminist Thought.* Boston, MA: Beacon Press; London: The Women's Press.

Steiner, George. 1984. *Antigones: The Antigone Myth in Western Literature, Art, and Thought.* Oxford: Oxford University Press.

Stoller, Robert. 1968. *Gender and Sex*, 2 vols. New York: Jason Aronson.

Stump, Eleonore. 1988. 'Atonement According to Aquinas', in Thomas V. Morris (ed.), *Philosophy and the Christian Faith.* Notre Dame, IN: University of Notre Dame Press, 61–91.

Stump, Eleonore 1993. 'Aquinas on the Sufferings of Job', in Stump (ed.), *Reasoned Faith*, 328–57.

Stump, Eleonore (ed.). 1993. *Reasoned Faith: Essays in Philosophical Theology in Honor of Norman Kretzmann.* Ithaca, NY: Cornell University Press.

Stump, Eleonore and Kretzmann, Norman. 1981. 'Eternity', *Journal of Philosophy*, 78, 429–58.

Suchocki, Marjorie Hewitt. 1994. 'The Idea of God in Feminist Philosophy', *Hypatia: A Journal of Feminist Philosophy* (Special Issue: Feminist Philosophy of Religion), 9:4 (Fall), 57–68.

Sundara Rajan, R. 1987. *Towards a Critique of Cultural Reason.* Delhi: Oxford University Press.

Surin, Kenneth. 1986. *Theology and the Problem of Evil.* Oxford: Blackwell.

Swinburne, Richard. 1977. *The Existence of God.* Oxford: Clarendon Press.

Swinburne, Richard. 1981. *Faith and Reason.* Oxford: Clarendon Press.

Swinburne, Richard. 1986. *The Evolution of the Soul.* Oxford: Clarendon Press.

Swinburne, Richard. 1987. 'Knowledge from Experience, and the Problem of Evil', in Abraham and Holtzer (eds), *The Rationality of Religious Belief*, 141–67.

Swinburne, Richard. 1989. *Responsibility and Atonement.* Oxford: Clarendon Press.

Swinburne, Richard. 1991 (1979). *The Coherence of Theism.* Oxford: Clarendon Press.

Swinburne, Richard. 1996. *Is There a God?* Oxford: Oxford University Press.

Taliaferro, Charles. 1988. 'Revitalizing the Ideal Observer Theory', *Philosophy and Phenomenological Research*, 49, 123–38.

Taliaferro, Charles. 1997. *Contemporary Philosophy of Religion: An Introduction.* Oxford: Blackwell.

Tilghman, B. R. 1993. *An Introduction to Philosophy of Religion*. Oxford: Blackwell.

Todd, Janet (ed.). 1983. *Women Writers Talking*. New York: Holmes and Meier.

Tomberlin, James E. and Van Inwagen, Peter (eds). 1985. *Alvin Plantinga, Profiles*, vol. 5. An International Series on Contemporary Philosophers and Logicians. Dordrecht, The Netherlands: D. Reidel Publishing Co.

Trible, Phyllis. 1978. *God and the Rhetoric of Sexuality*. Philadelphia, PA: Fortress Press.

Trible, Phyllis. 1992 (1973). 'Eve and Adam: Genesis 2–3 Reread', in Christ and Plaskow (eds), *Womanspirit Rising*, 74–83.

Trigg, Roger. 1992. 'Reason and Faith, II', in Martin Warner (ed.), *Religion and Philosophy: Royal Institute of Philosophy Supplement*, 31. Cambridge: Cambridge University Press.

Trigg, Roger. 1993. *Rationality and Science*. Oxford: Blackwell.

Underhill, Evelyn. 1930 (1911). *Mysticism: A Study in the Nature and Development of Man's Spiritual Consciousness*. London: Methuen.

Violi, Patrizia. 1992. 'Gender, Subjectivity and Language', in Bock and James (eds), *Beyond Equality and Difference*, 164–76.

Ward, Graham (ed.). 1997. *The Postmodern God: A Theological Reader*. Oxford: Blackwell.

Warner, Marina. 1976. *Alone of All Her Sex: The Myth and the Cult of the Virgin Mary*. London: Weidenfeld and Nicholson.

Warner, Marina. 1995. *Six Myths of Our Time: Little Angels, Little Monsters, Beautiful Beasts and More*. New York: Vintage Books.

Weil, Simone. 1956. *The Notebooks of Simone Weil 1940–42*, trans. Arthur Wills. London: Routledge and Kegan Paul.

Weil, Simone. 1987. *The Need for Roots*, trans. Arthur Wills. New York and London: Ark Paperbooks.

Weir, Allison. 1993. 'Identification with the Divided Mother', in Oliver (ed.), *Ethics, Politics and Difference*, 79–91.

Weir, Allison. 1995. 'Toward a Model of Self-Identity: Habermas and Kristeva', in Johanna Meehan (ed.), *Feminists Read Habermas: Gendering the Subject of Discourse*. London: Routledge, 263–82.

Weir Allison. 1996. *Sacrificial Logics: Feminist Theory and the Critique of Identity*. London: Routledge.

White, Erin. 1995. 'Religion and the Hermeneutics of Gender: An Examination of the Work of Paul Ricoeur', in King (ed.), *Religion and Gender*, 77–101.

Whitford, Margaret. 1991a. 'Irigaray's Body Symbolic', *Hypatia: A Journal of Feminist Philosophy* (Special Issue: 'Feminism and the Body', edited Elizabeth Grosz), 6:3 (Fall), 97–112.

Whitford, Margaret. 1991b. *Luce Irigaray: Philosophy in the Feminine.* London: Routledge.

Whitford, Margaret. 1992. 'The Feminist Philosopher: A Contradiction in Terms?', *Women: A Cultural Review*, 3:2, 111–20.

Whitford, Margaret. 1994. 'Irigaray, Utopia, and the Death Drive', in Burke, Schor, and Whitford (eds), *Engaging with Irigaray*, 379–400.

Williams, Bernard. 1978. *Descartes: The Project of Pure Enquiry*. Harmondsworth, Penguin.

Wolterstorff, Nicholas. 1983. 'Introduction' and 'Can Belief in God Be Rational if It Has No Foundations?', in Plantinga and Wolterstorff (eds), *Faith and Rationality*, 5–7 and 136–40

Wolterstorff, Nicholas. 1986. 'The Migration of the Theistic Arguments: From Natural Theology to Evidentialist Apologetics', in Audi and Wainwright. (eds), *Rationality, Religious Belief and Moral Commitment*, 38–81.

Wolterstorff, Nicholas. 1996. *John Locke and the Ethics of Belief.* Cambridge: Cambridge University Press.

Wood, Allen. 1990. *Hegel's Ethical Thought*. Cambridge: Cambridge University Press.

Woolf, Virginia. 1981 (1929). *A Room of One's Own*. New York: Harcourt Brace Jovanovich.

Woolf, Virginia. 1991 (1938). *Three Guineas*. London: The Hogarth Press.

Wright, Elizabeth (ed.). 1992. *Feminism and Psychoanalysis: A Critical Dictionary*. Oxford: Blackwell.

Wykstra, Steven. 1984. 'The Humean Obstacle to Evidential Arguments from Suffering: Avoiding the Evils of "Appearance"', *International Journal for the Philosophy of Religion*, 16, 73–93.

Wyschogrod, Edith. 1990. *Saints and Postmodernism: Revisioning Moral Philosophy*. Chicago, IL: University of Chicago Press.

Young, Iris Marion. 1985. 'Humanism, Gynocentrism and Feminist Politics', *International Women's Studies Forum* 8:3, 173–83. Reprinted 1990, in *Hypatia Reborn*. Bloomington, IN: Indiana University Press, 231–48.

Young, Iris Marion. 1990a. *Justice and the Politics of Difference*. Princeton, NJ: Princeton University Press.

Young, Iris Marion. 1990b. 'The Ideal of Community and the Politics of Difference', in Linda Nicholson (ed.), *Feminism/Postmodernism*. London: Routledge, 300–23.

Young-Bruehl, Elisabeth. 1988. 'The Education of Women as Philosophers', *Mind and Body Politic*. London: Routledge, 155–69.

Zaehner, R. C. (ed.). 1973. *The Bhagavad-Gita*, with a commentary based on the original sources. Oxford: Oxford University Press.
Zagzebski, Linda (ed.). 1993. *Rational Faith*. Notre Dame, IN: University of Notre Dame Press.

Index